Wo

For Gabi

Words and Phrases

Corpus Studies of Lexical Semantics

Michael Stubbs

© 2002 by Michael Stubbs

BLACKWELL PUBLISHING
350 Main Street, Malden, MA 02148-5020, USA
9600 Garsington Road, Oxford OX4 2DQ, UK
550 Swanston Street, Carlton, Victoria 3053, Australia

The right of Michael Stubbs to be identified as the Author of this Work has been asserted in accordance with the UK Copyright, Designs, and Patents Act 1988.

All rights reserved. No part of this publication may be reproduced, stored in a retrieval system, or transmitted, in any form or by any means, electronic, mechanical, photocopying, recording or otherwise, except as permitted by the UK Copyright, Designs, and Patents Act 1988, without the prior permission of the publisher.

First published 2002 by Blackwell Publishing Ltd

4   2005

Library of Congress Cataloging-in-Publication Data

Stubbs, Michael, 1947–
  Words and phrases : corpus studies of lexical semantics / Michael Stubbs.
    p. cm.
  Includes bibliographical references and index.
  ISBN 0-631-20832-1 (hbk. : alk. paper)—ISBN 0-631-20833-X (pbk. : alk. paper)
  1. Semantics—Data processing. I. Title.
  P325.5.D38 S78 2001
  401'.43'0285—dc21   2001018462

ISBN-13: 978-0-631-20832-7 (hbk. : alk. paper)—ISBN-13: 978-0-631-20833-4 (pbk. : alk. paper)

A catalogue record for this title is available from the British Library.

Set in 10 on 12.5pt Galliard
by Kolam Information Services Pvt Ltd, Pondicherry, India

The publisher's policy is to use permanent paper from mills that operate a sustainable forestry policy, and which has been manufactured from pulp processed using acid-free and elementary chlorine-free practices. Furthermore, the publisher ensures that the text paper and cover board used have met acceptable environmental accreditation standards.

For further information on
Blackwell Publishing, visit our website:
www.blackwellpublishing.com

Contents

Figures, Concordances and Tables   xi
Acknowledgements   xii
Data Conventions and Terminology   xiv
Notes on Corpus Data and Software   xvi

PART I   Introduction   1

1   Words in Use: Introductory Examples   3
    1.1   Text and Discourse: Some Distinctions   5
    1.2   Language, Action, Knowledge and Situation   6
    1.3   Words and Expectations   7
    1.4   Language, Logic and Truth   8
    1.5   Common-sense Knowledge   9
    1.6   Linguistic Conventions   11
    1.7   Possible and Actual   13
        1.7.1   *Example 1: the ambiguity of* SURGERY   13
        1.7.2   *Example 2: the (non-)ambiguity of* BANK   14
        1.7.3   *Example 3: the days of the week*   16
        1.7.4   *Example 4: lonely hearts ads*   17
    1.8   Summary and Implications   19
    1.9   Background and Further Reading   21
    1.10   Topics for Further Study   22

2   Words, Phrases and Meanings: Basic Concepts   24
    2.1   Terminology   24
    2.2   Words: Word-forms and Lemmas   25
        2.2.1   *Example: the lemmas* CONSUME *and* SEEK   27
    2.3   Collocation   29
    2.4   Words and Units of Meaning   30

	2.5	Delexicalization	32
	2.6	Denotation and Connotation	34
	2.7	Relational Lexical Semantics	35
		2.7.1 Semantic fields	35
		2.7.2 Synonyms, antonyms and hyponyms	36
	2.8	Frequent and Less Frequent Words	39
		2.8.1 Content and function words: lexical density	39
		2.8.2 Core vocabulary	41
	2.9	Two Examples	43
		2.9.1 Example 1: Bloomfield's analysis of SALT	43
		2.9.2 Example 2: CAUSE problems *and* CAUSE amusement	45
	2.10	Summary and Implications	49
	2.11	Background and Further Reading	50
	2.12	Topics for Further Study	51

PART II   Case Studies   55

3 **Words in Phrases 1: Concepts, Data and Methods**   57

3.1	Background	57
3.2	Communicative Competence	60
3.3	Corpus Methods: Observing Patterns	61
3.4	Terminology	62
3.5	Corpus, Concordance, Data-base	66
3.6	The Cobuild Collocations Data-base on CD-ROM	67
	3.6.1 The corpus	67
	3.6.2 The data-base	69
	3.6.3 Precision and recall	70
3.7	Data for Semantics and Pragmatics	71
3.8	Summary and Implications	72
3.9	Appendix 1: Measures of Statistical Significance	73
3.10	Appendix 2: Further Notes on the Data-base	75
3.11	Background and Further Reading	77
3.12	Topics for Further Study	78

4 **Words in Phrases 2: A Case Study of the Phraseology of English**   80

4.1	Frequency of Phraseological Units	80
4.2	Strength of Attraction: Word-forms, Lemmas and Lexical Sets	81

4.3	Lexical Profiles: Comprehensive Coverage of Data	84
	4.3.1 *Example 1: lexical profile for* resemblance	85
	4.3.2 *Example 2: lexical profile for* reckless	85
	4.3.3 *Example 3: lexical profile for* backdrop	86
	4.3.4 *Example 4: lexical profile for* doses	86
4.4	A Model of Extended Lexical Units	87
	4.4.1 *Example 5: lexical profile for* UNDERGO	89
	4.4.2 *Example 6: lexical profile for* chopped	95
4.5	Summary and Implications	96
4.6	Background and Further Reading	97
4.7	Topics for Further Study	97

5 Words in Texts 1: Words, Phrases and Text Cohesion   100

5.1	Words and Co-text	100
5.2	Routine and Creativity	101
5.3	Variable Phrases and Textual Cohesion	102
5.4	Antonyms and Synonyms	103
5.5	Discourse Prosodies	105
5.6	Lexical Cohesion: Textual Examples	108
	5.6.1 *Example 1:* just large enough to see with the naked eye	108
	5.6.2 *Example 2:* causing untold damage	112
	5.6.3 *Example 3:* causing growing pains *and* undergoing a transition	115
	5.6.4 *Example 4:* undergoing rapid star formation	115
5.7	Collocations and Coherence	117
5.8	Summary and Implications	120
5.9	Background and Further Reading	121
5.10	Topics for Further Study	122

6 Words in Texts 2: A Case Study of a Short Story   123

6.1	Public Data and Replicable Experiments	123
6.2	Lexis and Text Structure	124
6.3	Analysis 1: Frequency Statistics (Descending Frequency Order)	126
	6.3.1 *Frequency of function words: statistics*	126
	6.3.2 *Interpretation*	127
	6.3.3 *Frequency of content words: statistics*	127
	6.3.4 *Interpretation*	128
6.4	Analysis 2: Frequency Statistics (Keywords)	129

	6.5	Analysis 3: Frequency Statistics (Order of Occurrence)	130
		6.5.1 Statistics	130
		6.5.2 Interpretation	132
	6.6	Analysis 4: A Vocabulary-management Profile	133
		6.6.1 Types and tokens, vocabulary and text	133
		6.6.2 Youmans's method	134
		6.6.3 'Eveline'	135
	6.7	A Further Note on Replication	140
	6.8	Limitations on the Analyses	141
	6.9	Summary and Implications	142
	6.10	Background and Further Reading	144
	6.11	Topics for Further Study	144

7 Words in Culture 1: Case Studies of Cultural Keywords — 145

7.1	Data and Citation Conventions	146
7.2	Text and Discourse	147
7.3	Case Study 1: ETHNIC, RACIAL and TRIBAL	147
7.4	Case Study 2: HERITAGE and CARE	149
	7.4.1 Keyword: HERITAGE	150
	7.4.2 Keyword: CARE	151
	7.4.3 Keyword: COMMUNITY	154
7.5	Case Study 3: PROPER STANDARDS	154
	7.5.1 Keyword: STANDARD	155
	7.5.2 Keyword: PROPER	156
	7.5.3 Keyword: TRENDY	160
7.6	Case Study 4: *Little Red Riding Hood*	161
7.7	Discursive Formations	164
7.8	Summary and Implications	166
7.9	Background and Further Reading	168
7.10	Topics for Further Study	168

8 Words in Culture 2: Case Studies of Loan Words in English — 170

8.1	Data	170
8.2	The Etymological Fallacy	171
8.3	Language Change	173
8.4	Terminology	174
8.5	Words, Politics and National Stereotypes	175

	8.6	Fields of Knowledge and Text-Types	177
	8.7	A Case Study of German Loan Words in English	178
	8.8	Frequency in the Vocabulary versus Frequency in Texts	184
	8.9	False Friends: *Flak*, *Blitz* and *Angst*	185
	8.10	The *OED* and Cultural Keywords	188
	8.11	A Further Note on Vocabulary and Text	190
	8.12	Summary and Implications	192
	8.13	Background and Further Reading	192
	8.14	Topics for Further Study	193

PART III   Implications   195

9 Words, Phrases and Connotations: On Lexico-grammar and Evaluative Language   197

9.1	Connotations	197
9.2	Verbs, Discourse Prosodies and Point of View	198
	9.2.1 *Example 1:* I was accosted in the street by a stranger	199
	9.2.2 *Example 2:* fears lurking just below the surface	201
	9.2.3 *Example 3:* LOITER *and other verbs*	202
	9.2.4 *Inter-collocations: the example of* STREET	203
9.3	A Lexico-syntactic Example: *MAKE one's way somewhere*	206
9.4	A Note on Syntax	210
9.5	A Cognitive View	210
9.6	A Syntactic Example: *BE*-passives and *GET*-passives	211
9.7	Summary and Implications	215
9.8	Background and Further Reading	216
9.9	Topics for Further Study	218

10 Data and Dualisms: On Corpus Methods and Pluralist Models   220

10.1	Principles	220
10.2	Problems?	221
10.3	Dualisms and Monisms	226
	10.3.1 *Cartesian dualism*	226
	10.3.2 *Monism: version 1*	229
	10.3.3 *Monism: version 2*	229
	10.3.4 *The Saussurian paradox*	231

10.4	Pluralist Positions	232
10.5	Brute and Institutional Facts	232
10.6	Physical, Psychological and Social	234
10.7	Worlds 1, 2 and 3	236
10.8	A Pluralist Model	238
10.9	Performance Data, Corpora and Routine Behaviour	239
10.10	Summary and Implications	242
10.11	Background and Further Reading	244

References	245
Name Index	259
Subject Index	263

Figures, Concordances and Tables

Figures

4.1	The prototypical uses of *undergo*	92
6.1	'Eveline', span 35	136
6.2	'Eveline', span 151	137
10.1	Process and product, potential and actual	238

Concordances

2.1	Fifty random examples of CAUSE (verb)	46
4.1	Sample concordance lines for *undergo*	92
8.1	Sample concordance lines for *angst-ridden* and *teen(age) angst*	189
9.1	Fifty examples of GET-passives	213
9.2	Fifty examples of BE-passives	214

Tables

3.1	Aspects of communicative competence	60
4.1	Positional frequency table for *undergo*, span 3:3	94
7.1	Positional frequency table for *proper*, span 3:1	159
9.1	BE-passives and GET-passives: occurrences per million words	215

Acknowledgements

Work in corpus linguistics is always based on previous work by many people who have designed and made available corpora and software. For access to the Bank of English corpus, I am very grateful to colleagues at Cobuild in Birmingham. For permission to use other corpus materials, I am most grateful to the Norwegian Computing Centre for the Humanities, Longmans Group UK Ltd, Christian Mair at the University of Freiburg, and the Institut für Deutsche Sprache in Mannheim. Textual and corpus data are from these sources unless otherwise stated.

For help with data-collection and programming, I am very grateful to student research assistants at the University of Trier. Volker Dellwo, Kirsten Günther and Christine Spies helped to extract data from different corpora and data-bases. Brigitte Grote, Oliver Hardt and Oliver Mason helped with corpus preparation and wrote concordance programs and other collocations software. Peter Dingley wrote the main programs for chapter 6. (And Timothy Grundy, in a seminar at the University of Basel, pointed out to me the linguistic interest of James Joyce's short story 'Eveline', which I discuss in chapter 6.)

For helpful critical comments on a draft of the complete book I am very grateful to Susan Hunston and also to two anonymous readers. For comments on draft chapters, and individual examples, I am most grateful to Horst Breuer, Wolfram Bublitz, Joanna Channell, Andrea Gerbig, Naomi Hallan, Tony Howatt, Gabi Keck, Brian Paltridge, Alison Sealey, John Sinclair, Christine Spies, Henry Widdowson and Gilbert Youmans; and to seminar audiences at universities in Germany (Bonn), Italy (Bologna and Parma), Luxembourg, Scotland (Edinburgh and Stirling), Sweden (Stockholm and Uppsala), and Switzerland (Fribourg). The term 'corpus semantics' (see pp. 4, 19–20, 50) is used by Teubert (1999a), and his papers (1999a, 1999b) show clearly why the study of meaning has to be at the centre of corpus linguistics.

Some chapters include data and discussion which have appeared previously in other articles of mine, but in all cases the analyses have been considerably developed. A brief account of some of the material in chapters 3 and 4 appeared in *Studia Anglica Posnaniensia* (1998). A briefer analysis of the 'causing untold damage' text in chapter 5 appears in my article in D. Schiffrin et al. (eds), *The Handbook of Discourse Analysis* (Blackwell, 2001). A discussion of some of the German loan-word data in chapter 8 appeared in my article in W. Mackiewicz and D. Wolff (eds), *British Studies in Germany* (Wissenschaftlicher Verlag Trier, 1997); and in my article "German loanwords and cultural stereotypes" in *English Today,* **14**, 1 (Cambridge University Press, 1998). The concordances of passives in chapter 9 appear in my article in *Applied Linguistics* (2001).

The author and publishers apologize for any errors or omissions in the above list of acknowledgements, and would be grateful to be notified of any corrections that should be incorporated in the next edition or reprint of this book.

Data Conventions and Terminology

1   An important feature of the book is that all data which are analysed in detail are attested in naturally occurring language use. Where necessary, the status of examples is indicated as follows:

[A]   *attested, actual, authentic* data: data which have occurred naturally in a real social context without the intervention of the analyst;
[M]   *modified* data: examples which are based on attested data, but which have been modified (e.g. abbreviated) to exclude features which are assumed to be irrelevant to the current analysis;
[I]   *intuitive, introspective, invented* data: data invented purely to illustrate a point in a linguistic argument.

Individual examples are not always marked in this way if their status is clear from the surrounding discussion.

2   Other conventions are as follows:
2.1   Single quotation marks (' ') for technical terms and for quotes from other authors.
2.2   Double quotation marks (" ") for meanings of linguistic expressions.
2.3   *Italics* for short forms cited within the text, e.g. the German sentence *Sie soll sehr klug sein* means "She is said to be very clever".
2.4   CAPITAL LETTERS for lemmas. Alternative terms for lemma include dictionary head-word and lexeme. A lemma is a set of morphological variants. Conventionally the base form of verbs and the singular of nouns are used to represent lemmas (see chapter 2). For example, *do*, *does*, *doing*, *did* and *done* are the forms of the lemma DO.
2.5   Asterisk (*) for ill-formed sequences, such as ungrammatical or semantically anomalous sentences, e.g. *She must can come; *He is a vegetarian and eats meat.
2.6   A question mark (?) before a form denotes a string of doubtful or marginal acceptability, e.g. ?he mayn't come.

By definition, asterisked and questioned items cannot be attested, and intuitive judgements on ill-formedness should be treated with care. Corpus data sometimes reveal that forms which are thought not to occur, do occur and are used systematically.

2.7 Diamond brackets (<...>) enclose attested collocates of a node word. The position of the collocates relative to the node can also be given. See chapter 2.

- node <N+1:... list of collocates>
- CAUSE <N + 1: problems, trouble, damage>

That is, the lemma CAUSE is often immediately followed, one word to the right, by the word-forms *problems*, *trouble* and *damage*.

Notes on Corpus Data and Software

The first widely used computer-readable corpora were set up in the 1960s and 1970s. The Brown Corpus is so named because it was prepared at Brown University in the USA by W. Nelson Francis. It consists of one million words of written American English, published in 1961, and sampled as text fragments of 2,000 words each. Such corpora may now seem rather small and dated, but they are carefully designed and can still provide useful samples of language in use. Many other corpora are now available. In preparing this book, I have used the following.

LOB (Lancaster–Oslo–Bergen) Corpus

The LOB corpus was designed as the British equivalent of the Brown corpus: one million words of written British English, also published in 1961, and sampled as text fragments of 2,000 words each, from informative texts, such as newspapers, learned and scientific writing, and imaginative fiction. For a list of textual categories, see *ICAME News*, 5, 1981, p. 4 (= *International Computer Archive of Modern English*, Bergen), and Biber (1988: 66ff).

FLOB and FROWN

These are the Freiburg versions of LOB and Brown, designed on the same lines as these earlier corpora, as samples of British and American English from thirty years later: material published in 1991. I am grateful to Christian Mair, University of Freiburg, for providing me with the sections of newspaper language.

London–Lund Corpus

This corpus was constructed at University College London and the University of Lund. The corpus is about 435,000 words of spoken British English, and contains 5,000-word samples of the usage of adult, educated, professional people, including face-to-face and telephone conversations, lectures, discussions and radio commentaries. For further details, see Svartvik and Quirk (1980), Svartvik et al. (1982) and Biber (1988: 66ff).

Longman–Lancaster Corpus

This corpus was constructed in collaboration between Longman Publishers and the University of Lancaster. It consists of about 30 million words of published English, including fiction and non-fiction: samples from well-known literary works and also works randomly sampled from books in print; and non-fiction texts from the natural and social sciences, world affairs, commerce and finance, the arts, leisure, and so on. For some purposes in this book, I have taken 2,000-word samples from 500 files, in order to construct a mixed sub-corpus of one million words. Otherwise I have taken examples from an 8-million-word sample of British English. Summers (1993) discusses the corpus design.

The Bank of English

Many individual examples in this book are drawn from the Bank of English corpus created by COBUILD at the University of Birmingham. COBUILD stands for Collins Birmingham University International Language Database. This corpus has been used in the design of major dictionaries and grammars (including Cobuild 1987, 1990, 1995a; Francis et al. 1996, 1998). By the late 1990s, the corpus totalled some 330 million words, including fiction and non-fiction books, newspapers, and samples of spoken English. The corpus is available in different forms: primarily the Bank of English itself, and a 50-million-word sub-corpus which is available over the internet as CobuildDirect. I have also used a data-base on CD-ROM (Cobuild 1995b), which was constructed from a 200-million-word sub-corpus. (This is described in detail in chapter 3.) Renouf (1987) and Sinclair (1991: 13–26) describe the early corpus development, and Baker et al. (1993) include several articles based on the corpus.

The British National Corpus

This is a 100-million-word corpus of British English, 10 million words of spoken English, and 90 million words of written English. It has been used in the design of major dictionaries: OALD (1995) and LDOCE (1995). For further details, see Aston and Burnard (1998). Simple searches can be done free over the internet.

Newspapers on CD-ROM

The CD-ROM versions of several newspapers can be a convenient source for some kinds of analysis. The text-types are obviously restricted, but perhaps less so than might appear at first sight, given the range of articles which appear in different sections of a major newspaper: not just news and political commentary, but also sports, and, especially in Sunday editions, cultural topics. As a subsidiary source of a few short examples, I have used *The Times* and the *Sunday Times* for 1995.

Institut für Deutsche Sprache (Mannheim Corpora)

The Institute for German Language in Mannheim holds large German-language corpora of literary and non-literary texts. I have used these for the small comparative study reported in chapter 8.

There are many other corpora available and any attempt to give a comprehensive list would be quickly out of date. In any case, if one is attempting to make statements about general English, it is best to sample data from different, independent corpora, since all corpora have their biases. Given the data which it is convenient and more difficult to collect, corpora have often tended to over-represent mass media language, and to under-represent spoken language. Readers can consult corpus linguistics web-sites for information on what is currently available.

Similarly, there are now many concordance programs and related suites of text processing software available, and a list of these would also be quickly out of date. Such programs allow texts to be searched for words, phrases and patterns, which can be displayed, in a convenient form, in contexts of varying size. In addition, they allow frequency lists of various kinds to be prepared, and they may allow texts or corpora to be compared with each other in different ways.

If the main need is for simple word-frequency statistics and a concordance program, it often hardly matters which specific software is used. Some older software may be restricted in whether it recognizes non-English alphabets, or in the length of texts which can be analysed. As with computer software more generally, what is used is often a question of personal preference, availability and convenience. The large publicly available corpora, such as the Bank of English and the British National corpus, have their own powerful access software. I have used these, as well as both commercially available software (Longman MiniConcordancer, MicroConcord and WordSmith Tools: see Scott 1997a) and other batch software, written by my students in Trier. Again, consulting corpus linguistics web-sites will provide information on what is currently available.

As starting points for information in the world-wide web on corpora and software, use a search engine to look for 'Corpus Linguistics', 'ICAME' (= International Computer Archive of Modern English), 'Oxford Text Archive', 'Cobuild', and 'British National Corpus'. Links will take you to other relevant sites.

Indeed, for some simple investigation of phraseology, the world-wide web can itself be used as a vast text collection. Some search engines can find exact phrases in texts on the web, return the frequency of these phrases, and allow you to study how they are used in their original full contexts. Try, for example, searching for the phrases *ripe old age*, *good old age* and *grand old age*, and check which is the most frequent variant. Or find out how frequently these phrases occur in longer phrases such as *LIVE to a ripe old age* or *REACH a grand old age*.

Part I

Introduction

1

Words in Use: Introductory Examples

The topic of this book is words and phrases: how they are used, what they mean, and what evidence and methods can be used to study their meanings.

Here is an initial example of the kind of question the book deals with. The individual word *round* can mean "circular", and the individual word *table* can mean "a piece of furniture with a flat top, which people can sit at, so that they can eat, write, and so on". The phrase *round table* has one meaning which is simply due to the combination of these individual meanings: something which is both "round" and a "table". However, it is also used in longer phrases such as *round table talks*. This means that a group of people, with interests and expertise in some topic, are meeting as equals to discuss some problem. This meaning relies on additional cultural knowledge: we would not fully understand the phrase unless we also knew that it is often used of discussions between political groups who are trying to reach agreement after some conflict.

In other phrases, *round* and *table* mean quite different things (*a round number, a table wine, a timetable*). Most everyday words have different uses and different meanings. Indeed, in isolation, some words seem to have so many potential meanings that it is difficult to see how we understand running text at all. However, words do not usually occur in isolation, but in longer phrases, and in the following examples it is quite clear which meaning of *round* is relevant:

- they sat *round* the table; they ran *round* the table; they came *round* to my house; they came *round* to my way of thinking; a *round* dozen; a *round* of applause; a *round* of drinks; a *round* of golf; the doctor is on her *round*

So, our knowledge of a language is not only a knowledge of individual words, but of their predictable combinations, and of the cultural knowledge which these combinations often encapsulate:

- Knights of the Round Table; table manners; drink someone under the table; payments made under the table

Major questions throughout the book will therefore be: What do words mean? In particular, what do they mean when they are used in short phrases and in longer connected text? How do the meanings of words depend on their different uses?

Chapter 1 starts to provide answers to these questions, and to show the close relations between how words are used and what they mean, and chapter 2 discusses some concepts which are required for a systematic study of these relations. Many of these concepts (such as denotation and connotation, lexical field, and sense relations) are widely used within traditional semantics. Here I show how attested data collected in large corpora can be used to illustrate and develop these concepts. The book will probably be of most interest to students who have already done at least an introductory course in linguistics, although all such concepts are explained with detailed examples.

Chapters 3 to 8 then provide case studies of: (1) words in phrases: how words are used in predictable combinations, which often have characteristic evaluative meanings; (2) words in texts: how recurrent words and phrases contribute to the textual organization; and (3) words in culture: how some words, especially in frequent phrases, acquire layers of meaning, and become cultural 'keywords'. Chapters 9 and 10 discuss some implications for linguistic theory. Much of the book consists of case studies, which are sometimes quite complex and take up whole chapters, but I also suggest smaller studies and projects which students can carry out. Corpus data are increasingly available, either for use on individual desk-top computers or over the internet, and this means that students can carry out their own genuine descriptive studies.

For hundreds of years, dictionaries of English have recorded and defined the meanings of words, though they often differ considerably in which phrases they include. As evidence, dictionary makers have used both their own intuitions and also attested uses of words, often in the form of thousands of quotations from printed books. However, it is only since the mid-1980s that computer-assisted methods have been able to provide evidence about word meaning by searching across large text collections. So, I will also discuss questions of method and evidence: How do we know what words mean? What evidence do we have? Is this evidence observable and objective? How can large text collections (corpora) be used to study what words mean? A shorthand description of this approach is corpus semantics: using corpus evidence to study meaning (Teubert 1999a).

1.1 Text and Discourse: Some Distinctions

Corpus semantics studies how words are used in text and discourse and uses observations of use as evidence of meaning.

The terms 'text' and 'discourse' are both used in different ways. I will use the terms to refer to naturally occurring, connected, spoken or written language, which has occurred in some real context, independently of the linguist. Usually, the terms mean stretches of language in use, such as conversations, lectures and stories: that is, units of language which are larger than single sentences. And text analysis is often seen as the study of how language is organized above the sentence or above the clause. It studies units such as (spoken) lectures or (written) short stories. For example, one could study the overall structure of a whole lecture, and note predictable differences in the language of different sections (introduction, main body of the argument, and conclusion), and how the lecturer marks divisions between sections, by saying things such as

- OK so let's look at the next main point now

However, there is a distinction between whole texts and long texts. Some whole texts may be very short, as in public notices, such as:

- Exit
- Private
- Wet paint
- Closed for lunch

It is therefore more accurate to say that text and discourse analysis study language in context: how words and phrases fit into both longer texts, and also social contexts of use (Widdowson 1995). This implies that language in use is an integral part of social action, and that we must study relations between language and culture. So, major themes in this book include: phrases and texts (the linguistic co-texts of language in use); socially recognized text-types (such as an advertisement or a short story); the social and cultural meanings conveyed by language; and the range of different functions which language serves (such as informing and evaluating).

These cultural meanings are constantly changing, and new text-types are constantly appearing. For example, one new type of public language is the written and spoken messages which it is impossible to escape in many towns. Written messages have long been common: everything from road signs, to messages on gravestones, and advertising, outside shops, on posters or neon signs. Such language usually has no identifiable author, and is not addressed to anyone in particular. From time to time, old text-types appear in new places: for example, in the 1980s poems appeared in London underground trains, in the slots previously reserved for advertising. (This idea has now spread to buses in Stockholm.) To some extent you can avoid reading such written messages, refuse to accept leaflets pushed into your hand as you walk through town, and throw away the unsolicited mail that arrives at your house, but it is more difficult to escape the wide range of spoken messages in public places. Their early ancestors were produced by the town crier, and announcements in railway stations and airports have long been common, but many stores, as well as trains themselves, now have a constant stream of messages to staff, advertising jingles and music, which customers can escape by going to a different shop, but which the staff cannot escape at all (Glück and Sauer 1990: 131–2).

1.2 Language, Action, Knowledge and Situation

Substantial arguments have been put forward that language, social action and knowledge are inseparable (section 1.9 gives references). The formulation which has had most influence on linguistics was put forward by J. L. Austin. As he put it (Austin 1962), people do things with words. Some actions can be performed only verbally (for example, apologizing or complaining), whilst others can be performed either verbally or non-verbally (for example, threatening). Austin pointed out that social relations – for example, being appointed to a job or getting married – can be created by people saying the proper words in their proper place. In addition, studies of how language is used in natural social settings show that communication is impossible without shared knowledge and assumptions between speakers and hearers, and show that communicative competence and cultural competence are inseparable. So, a study of how words are used can reveal relations between language and culture: not only relations between language and the world, but also between language and speakers with their beliefs, expectations and evaluations. A major finding of corpus semantics is that words and phrases convey evaluations more frequently than is recorded in many dictionaries.

Austin's argument means also that language and situation are inseparable. In some games and rituals, the relation may be deterministic: actual words and phrases may be laid down as part of the proceedings (for example, in religious ceremonies). Most everyday uses of language are much more flexible, although we are rarely, if ever, entirely free in what it is appropriate to say. Words occur in expected sequences in phrases and texts.

1.3 Words and Expectations

Occasionally, a single word or phrase may be enough to identify the text-type: if you hear the word *furlong*, you are probably listening to a horse-racing commentary, and if you hear the phrase *warm front*, it is probably a weather forecast. Any choice of words creates a mini-world or universe of discourse, and makes it likely that other words will be co-selected in the same context. So, much of this book concerns such expectations and the mechanisms of co-selection.

Sometimes, individual words can trigger assumptions and frames of reference, and words can acquire implications if they are repeatedly co-selected with other words. For example, in a large collection of texts, I found that the word GOSSIP frequently occurred in phrases with very negative connotations such as:

- baseless gossip; gossip-mongering; idle gossip; juicy gossip; name-calling and malicious gossip; scandal and gossip; sleazy gossip; titillating gossip; her affairs became common gossip

Even if everyone does it, and even if it can have positive functions of maintaining group solidarity, it is evident from such phrases that gossip is often talked of as an activity to be disapproved of.

Does the word GOSSIP imply to you a woman speaker, or can men also gossip? To what extent do such words for speech acts carry (in this case sexist) implications about speakers? In the text collection, I found that the word also occurred frequently in phrases such as

- the mothers stood gossiping in the alleys
- the women gossiped and the men smoked
- a gossiping old woman

Men certainly also gossip (though they may call it something different, such as *male bonding*!), but if the word is habitually used in such phrases, then this is likely to contribute to a stereotype that gossiping is something which mainly women do. As Cameron (1997: 455) puts it: 'both sexes engage in gossip, ... but its cultural meaning ... is undeniably "feminine".'

There are many terms in everyday English for different kinds of language behaviour, and by studying how these terms are used, it is possible to study the logical relations between them, and whether they have positive or negative connotations. TALK is a general word. CHAT is a sub-category of TALK: friendly talk. GOSSIP is a different sub-category: talk in which secrets are revealed and/or details of other people's lives are discussed, with the implication that the topics are trivial. CHATTER is rapid talk. PRATTLE is foolish talk. BABBLE is incoherent talk. CHAT and GOSSIP need more than one person, but babies can BABBLE on their own. GOSSIP, CHATTER and PRATTLE are disapproving terms. PRATTLE is definitely insulting. (See chapter 2.7.2 on superordinate terms and hyponyms.)

Evidence of such meanings comes from the typical phrases in which the words occur. Attested phrases containing the words above include:

- a friendly chat; they sat around chatting amiably; chat show
- chatterbox; chattering classes; scatter-brained chatter; he chattered without stopping; chattering all day long; a constant stream of chatter; he chattered away about nothing; the chatter of voices; his teeth chattered; the chatter of monkeys; chattering wheels
- he prattled away incessantly; she prattled on
- voices babbled; babies babble; he babbled on; he babbled away; the babbling river; the stream babbling and gurgling

1.4 Language, Logic and Truth

The relations between language, action, knowledge and situation imply that meaning is not restricted to matters of information and logic. We are not dealing only with whether statements are true or false, and everyday conversation often contains utterances which are logically tautological or contradictory. For example, I was on my way with a colleague to his place of work at a weekend, when he discovered that he had forgotten the key to an office he shared with others. He decided not to go all the way back home for the key, and remarked:

- either it's open or it isn't [A]

([A] = attested data: see Data Conventions and Terminology.)

From a purely logical point of view, this utterance conveys no information whatsoever: an office must be either open or locked. But he was implying something like: "Well, it's not all that important; if I can get in, then fine, but if not, it doesn't really matter; I'm not going all the way back home." In everyday uses of language, there is more to meaning than logic, and what is ill-formed from a logical point of view, may be quite normal in conversation. Different factors interact to determine the appropriateness of utterances: not only their logical structure and truth value, but also their rhetorical functions. We need to know what speech act is being performed in what speech event.

Truth conditions involve more than a correspondence between a sentence and the state of the world. In fact, sentences generally do not have a truth value at all. It makes no sense to ask whether the sentence *She came yesterday* is true or false. It depends who she is, when yesterday was, and where she came to. Only some sentences which express propositions about general states of affairs, such as *Ice floats on water*, will be true on each occasion of use. So, we have to distinguish between sentences (linguistic forms) and utterances (the use of sentences on specific occasions), or between what are sometimes called eternal sentences and occasion sentences (Seuren 1998: 317). Using substantial corpus data, Channell (1994: 115, 119) also shows that many utterances contain vague language, such as

- this impossible task of handling umpteen jobs with very little in the way of training
- there was no kind of social contact, there was no coffee room or anything

It is not possible to say exactly how many the speaker meant by *umpteen*, or exactly what the speaker meant by *no coffee room or anything*, but hearers generally have no problem in supplying a reasonable interpretation, such as "a place where staff could meet informally during work-breaks". Such utterances cannot be judged simply true or false, but show the kinds of inferences on which language in use often depends.

Furthermore, the concept of truth is applicable only to a narrow range of sentence-types. Only statements can be true or false, but not questions, requests or orders, expletives, promises, counter-factuals, such as

- If you weren't a policeman, I wouldn't have let you in [A]

and other utterances which express probabilities, beliefs or intentions. Truth and falsity are also problematic with respect to evaluative utterances. If someone says *That's super!*, then this may tell us something about the speaker, but little about the world.

1.5 Common-sense Knowledge

One of the major problems in studying language in use is to disentangle linguistic knowledge from background cultural assumptions. What is said can be a long way from what is meant, and a very large amount of language in use is indirect or vague in different ways. For example, I heard the following exchange between a husband and wife:

- *He*: When will dinner be ready?
- *She*: It's a very small chicken.

The second utterance is not a direct answer to the question. In order to see its relevance, *He* had to assume that *She* was being cooperative, and make a series of inferences along the lines of: we're having chicken for dinner, it's a small chicken, I know how long chickens take to cook, I know when the chicken went into the oven, you can't predict exactly how long these things take, but dinner will be ready soon. An important distinction (Widdowson 1978) is between cohesion and coherence. There is a cohesive link between the two utterances, in so far as *dinner* and *chicken* are in the same semantic field, but much still depends on inferring the point of the utterance from common-sense knowledge.

Language in use sets up expectations, and whenever two utterances occur in sequence, hearers will attempt to relate them: to use the first as a frame for the second. In a useful article on the inferences we perform on language, Brown (1994: 17) gives this example from local radio:

- The Suffolk doctor whose wife has been reported missing stayed firmly in his house today. Police have been digging in the garden. [A]

The relations between these two sentences seem obvious and natural, though they are not stated explicitly. Why is the doctor not named? Who reported his wife missing? What is the relation between his wife going missing, his staying indoors, and police digging in his garden? Why do we assume they were digging in his garden?: that is, the garden around his house? These examples pose problems for semantics, and no general method has been found for automatically identifying the referent of definite noun phrases such as *the garden*. This frequently requires information which is not explicit in the co-text, and in this case the information depends on inferences about suspicious circumstances, crimes, and common police procedures. The example also illustrates a further key distinction between meaning and reference. We know what the phrase *the garden* means, but we do not necessarily know what an utterance of the phrase refers to. (See chapter 2.6 on denotation and reference.)

Such examples depend on schematic knowledge: sets of taken-for-granted knowledge about how the world works. We all have such schematic knowledge about schools, so that when a schools is mentioned in conversation, we automatically assume it to be populated with teachers and pupils, without need for them to be explicitly mentioned. Suppose I say:

- I used to teach in a school. The pupils were horrible. [I]

I do not expect the definite noun phrase to be questioned with *What pupils?*

People certainly say unexpected things in jokes and ironic remarks, but this is itself an indication that there are expectations to be broken. We often recognize the existence of norms only when they are broken. Each utterance sets up a frame with built-in default expectations; but these default values can be over-ridden. However, it might be that discourse has no clear-cut mandatory rules, but rather depends on maxims of cooperativeness or guiding principles (Grice 1975). One reason why discourse structure is likely to be less deterministic than phonological or syntactic structure is that discourse is the joint construction of at least two speakers. It is difficult to see how A could place absolute constraints on what B says.

It is plausible that languages are tightly patterned at the lower levels of phonology, morphology and syntax, and that discourse is more loosely constructed. Nevertheless, menus, stories and telephone conversations have beginnings, middles and ends, and that is already a structural claim. Jakobson (1971: 242–3) puts it like this:

> [I]n the organization of linguistic units there is an ascending scale of freedom. In the combination of distinctive features into phonemes, the freedom of the individual is zero.... Freedom to combine phonemes into words is... limited to the marginal situation of word coinage. In forming sentences with words the speaker is less constrained. And finally, in the combination of sentences into utterances,... the freedom of any individual speaker to create novel contexts increases substantially, although... the numerous stereotyped utterances are not to be overlooked.

Jakobson here mentions explicitly 'numerous stereotyped utterances', but perhaps did not appreciate their extent. In chapters 3 and 4, I will show that the freedom to combine words in text is much more restricted than often realized. I will also show that the lexical organization of text is distinctly different from the linguistic organization which has usually been described at lower levels.

1.6 Linguistic Conventions

We often rely on social knowledge in order to make inferences which are not expressed in the textual cohesion, and we must distinguish what can be inferred from the language itself, and what must be inferred from real-world knowledge. For example, a sentence such as *My sister is sick* has as one of its presuppositions "I have a sister". As Horn (1996, citing earlier work by Grice and others) points out, if this presupposition is not part of hearers' real-world knowledge, the communication does not break down simply because a felicity condition for such a sentence has been broken. The hearer infers the presupposition, and is more likely to say *Oh dear!* than *What sister?* The presupposition signals that the information is non-controversial rather than common knowledge.

Even in the case of utterances which are very indirect indeed, there may be a balance between inferences based on the particular situation of utterance and inferences based on predictable linguistic patterns. I heard the following utterance from a surgeon to a patient in a hospital:

- Right! a little tiny hole and a fishing expedition, is that it?

The intended meaning of this utterance would be completely irretrievable without knowledge of the specific situation of utterance. I assume that the surgeon intended to convey the information that "I am going to operate on you and remove your appendix", and, in addition, to convey reassurance by implying "but don't worry, I do this kind of thing every day, it's routine, I know what I'm doing, and I can even joke about it". How can I make such inferences? Parts of the original utterance can, as it were, be translated: *a hole and a fishing expedition* meant "a surgical incision and the removal of the appendix". There is obviously some relation in meaning between a fishing expedition and a surgical operation, but we would not expect this to be recorded in dictionaries. In individual utterances, it may be that idiosyncratic meanings will always depend partly on specific context-bound interpretations and will never be fully explicable.

However, other parts of the surgeon's utterance have conventional meanings. The combination *little tiny* has connotations of the language used to children. Evidence for these connotations comes in turn from the frequent use of *little* in attested phrases such as

- beautiful little, charming little, cute little, lovely little, nice little

The connotations of *little* become even clearer if *little* is contrasted with *small*, which often occurs in rather formal phrases such as

- comparatively small, exceedingly small, relatively small

Typical phrases are *pretty little girl*, but *comparatively small quantity* (see chapter 7.6).

So, the surgeon's utterance is multifunctional. As well as indirectly expressing propositional meaning, he simultaneously expressed interpersonal meaning: the social relations between doctor and patient, and authority, reassurance, and joking. And although part of the meaning depends heavily on social context, part is also conveyed by linguistic convention. How connotations can be identified more formally is a major topic in chapters 7, 8 and 9.

1.7 Possible and Actual

A brief summary of the argument so far is the slogan 'meaning is use'. Words do not have fixed meanings which are recorded, once and for all, in dictionaries. They acquire, or change, meaning according to the social and linguistic contexts in which they are used. Understanding language in use depends on a balance between inference and convention. Here are more detailed examples which use textual data to show that our communicative competence relies on knowledge of what is expected or typical.

1.7.1 Example 1: the ambiguity of SURGERY

In isolation, many individual words are ambiguous or indeterminate in meaning, but this hardly ever troubles us in practice, because the phrases in which they occur are not ambiguous. For example, *surgery* can mean

1   a medical procedure involving cutting a patient's body open
2   the branch of medicine concerned with this procedure
3   the room or house where a doctor works
4   the time of day when a doctor sees patients

However, in different phrases, the ambiguity disappears. For example, senses (1) to (4) are conveyed unambiguously by these attested examples, respectively:

[1]   plastic surgery; he had to undergo surgery; patients who need surgery
[2]   progress in surgery has made heart transplants possible
[3]   she had her surgery in Cemetery Road; he had to be rushed to the surgery
[4]   she was taking evening surgery; his surgery ends at eleven

It is not difficult to find words in the immediately surrounding text which discriminate between these different senses with a high degree of probability. For example, sense (1) is signalled by co-occurring verbs such as *carry out*, *need*, *respond to* or *undergo*, or adjectives such as *cosmetic*, *extensive*, *major* or *successful.* (The phrase *undergo surgery* is analysed in chapter 4.4.1.) It is possible to invent examples where the verb *remove* could occur in sense (3): *we had to remove it through his surgery door* [I]. But the phrase *surgery to remove* signals sense (1): *surgery to remove two wisdom teeth.*

In other words, cases of apparent multiple ambiguity at word level are usually illusory: they dissolve in context. Combinations of words in phrases are therefore a good candidate for the basic semantic unit of language in use. Instead of regarding the meaning as being carried by the individual word, we could see things as follows. The word *surgery* conveys a rather general meaning: "something to do with medicine". It is the phrase which conveys the precise meaning. The following formulation might be a slight exaggeration, but it makes a useful point: it is not the words which tell you the meaning of the phrase, but the phrase which tells you the meaning of the individual words in it. I will return to this point later (chapter 9), since it questions the principle of compositionality, that is, the assumption that the meaning of larger units (such as phrases) is equal to the sum of the meanings of smaller units (such as words).

Translators obviously have to take such cases into account. It does not make sense to ask for a translation of *surgery* into German. The word would have four different translations for the four senses I have identified: (1) *Operation* or *operativer Eingriff*, (2) *Chirurgie*, (3) *Praxis* or *Sprechzimmer*, and (4) *Sprechstunde*. In turn, these individual German words would have different translations into English, according to context: *Praxis* can mean "doctor's practice", but also "practice" in the sense of "practice versus theory".

1.7.2 Example 2: the (non-)ambiguity of BANK

Here is a similar example of a semantic problem which is posed in many introductions to linguistics. In isolation, the word BANK is ambiguous, and dictionaries distinguish two main senses. Sense 1 is the "place where you keep money", either the institution thought of as the abstract organization, or as a particular building. Sense 2 is a little more difficult to define precisely, since there is a range of related meanings. It means an "area of sloping, raised ground" (*grassy bank*), often the raised ground around a stretch of water (*river bank*) or under shallow water (*sand bank*), or something of the same general shape (*bank of fog, bank of switches*). Let us call these the "money"-BANK and the "ground"-BANK senses. It is certainly possible to invent sentences, and to imagine circumstances, where the word is still ambiguous:

- the supermarket is opposite the bank   [I]

However, even such sentences are most unlikely to be ambiguous, in practice, in a larger context. Depending on what has been said previously, this could mean "opposite a bank of daffodils". However, a hearer is most likely to assume a parallel construction and to assume that the supermarket and the bank are both buildings.

So, in isolation the word is ambiguous, but this statement depends on a very artificial assumption, since the word never occurs in isolation. It either occurs in a physical context, for example, on a sign above a building (and probably also in a phrase such as *Bank of Scotland*), or it occurs in co-text, with other words around it. I studied all occurrences of *bank* ($n = 82$) and *banks* ($n = 28$) in their linguistic contexts in a corpus of one million words of written English (LOB: see Notes on Corpus Data and Software). In the vast majority of cases, any potential ambiguity was ruled out due to words within a short span to left or right. Many occurrences were in fixed phrases which signalled unambiguously the "money" or "ground" sense:

- bank account, bank balance, bank robbery, piggy bank
- canal bank, river bank
- the South Bank (= "an area along the Thames in London"), the Left Bank (in Paris), Dogger Bank, Rockall Bank, Icelandic Banks (= "fishing areas in the Atlantic")

In addition, the word usually co-occurred, within a few words to left or right, with other words which clearly signalled one or other semantic field:

- cashier, deposit, financial, money, overdraft, pay, steal
- cave, cod, fish, float, headland, sailing, sea, water

So, the two senses occurred in complementary distribution, either in one lexical context or the other, not both. Even in short phrases, only very few cases remained ambiguous, such as

- the Worthing bank murder case

(Worthing is a town in the south of England.) However, even here, everyday expectations probably tip the interpretation towards the sense which goes along with *bank raid*. Often, the sense was over-determined, and occurred both in a fixed phrase and alongside several disambiguating words in lexical strings such as

- money–deposits–Bank of England–paid–instalment
- shallows–sea–cod–Icelandic Banks–haddock

This simple case illustrates several principles which will be central to the whole book. (1) It is impossible to observe the meaning of a word: meaning is an invisible (arguably mental) phenomenon. However, it is quite possible to observe evidence from which meanings can be reliably inferred. A major type of evidence of the meaning of a word is the other words round about it, especially repeated patterns of co-occurrence. (2) The meaning of a word is not independent of the environment, including the co-text, in which it occurs. In fact, it is rather misleading to talk of a word occurring in an environment. A word predicts that other related words will occur round about it, and the co-text predicts the word, or one very like it. (3) Invented and decontextualized examples may exaggerate difficulties of interpretation. A theory of semantics should deal primarily with normal cases: what does typically occur, not what might occur under strange circumstances. (4) Findings such as those above, from one small corpus, are predictions which can be checked on other corpora. Readers can check my findings about BANK on data from other corpora. (These principles were first discussed thoroughly with reference to corpus study in Sinclair (1987) and Sinclair (1991). See also chapter 6 on replicability.)

So, one of the main topics of this book is how large corpora can be searched for observable patterns which provide evidence of what words mean.

1.7.3 Example 3: the days of the week

The BANK example illustrates the difference between what speakers can say and what they usually do say, but we have to deal with both: it would be misleading to base a description only on frequency of actual occurrence. Frequency becomes interesting when it can be interpreted as typicality, and speakers' communicative competence includes tacit knowledge of behavioural norms.

In corpora of 150 million words, I found that the words for different days of the week differed considerably in frequency. Rounded to the nearest 50, occurrences were:

Sunday	17,350
Saturday	14,600
Friday	10,650
Monday	9,500
Wednesday	8,150
Thursday	6,900
Tuesday	6,750

It would be absurd to base a description of English merely on frequencies, and to argue that *Sunday* is over twice as common as *Tuesday*, and should therefore be twice as prominent in our description. However, the category days-of-the-week is culturally structured, and there are cultural reasons why people talk most often about the weekend, less often about the beginning and end of the working week, and less often again about the days in the middle of the week.

The seven words also tend to occur in different phrases, such as

- Friday night; Saturday night; Sunday afternoon; Monday morning; that Monday morning feeling; Monday morning blues

Of course, it is formally possible (i.e. grammatical) to say *Sunday night*, but *Saturday night* is more frequent, and this is a fact with cultural significance. Words have a tendency to co-occur with certain other words, and culturally and communicatively competent native speakers of English are aware of such probabilities and of the cultural frames which they trigger.

The words for the days of the week are not the names of things which exist independently in the external world. Suppose you are shipwrecked and washed ashore on a desert island, where you lie in a coma for some time. You wake up, but do not know how long you have been unconscious. There is no way to observe what day of the week it is, and no way to find out. The week is a cultural reality, whose conventions are maintained by talk (and other social activities). This does not mean that the days of the week are not real: they are real, and they have a real effect on our behaviour. However it means that they are mental and social constructs which are maintained by language and its use. They do not refer directly to the external world, but only indirectly, via cognitive representations, to a reality which they have helped to create.

1.7.4   Example 4: lonely hearts ads

The next example illustrates that many things are possible, but that what actually occurs is often very predictable. Lonely hearts ads are an example of a text-type which is highly conventionalized and restricted in its forms and meanings. A page of ads can be read in any order, but readers can predict the semantic structure of any individual ad, the speech acts it expresses, and much of its vocabulary and grammar: each ad is a standard solution to a standard problem. Here are two attested examples:

- MUCH-TRAVELLED engineer/manager/lecturer, now retired into writing and sociobiological research, seeks female friend/lover, similarly

fit and active, to share and exchange ideas, interests and ambitions. Box... etc.
- ATTRACTIVE PROFESSIONAL, degree educated woman, 43, divorced one child, Bristol area, would like to meet similar man, 45–55 for caring relationship. Box... etc.

It would be possible to write ads in different forms, but in practice their form is very restricted, due largely to constraints on space (and the amount of money one is willing to spend). Some of the main patterns are as follows. The propositional content varies very little. There is an obligatory proposition: "X is looking for Y", with a small amount of variation then possible: "with a view to friendship, marriage, sex, etc." And there is a request: "please get in touch", traditionally via a box number, and more recently via recorded telephone messages. The most frequent syntactic structure is also simple:

NP1 seeks NP2 for X

This corresponds to the content: "person 1 seeks person 2 for friendship, etc." The most frequent verbs are *seeks* and *would like to meet* (sometimes abbreviated to *wltm*).

The NPs (noun phrases) have a head noun denoting a person, which is always marked as male or female, though this may require some inferences. Optional, but frequent (especially for the sender), is their profession. There is a description of the addressor, and a description of the hoped-for addressee (often in less detail: after all, the writer knows what s/he is like, but being too specific about the addressee might cut out too many potential responses). The NPs are often long and complex, mainly due to the occurrence of relative clauses, and (very frequently) strings of adjectives which usually denote personality and appearance. Other frequent linguistic features include: elliptical sentence structure, and lexical abbreviations, which may not always be interpretable to readers unfamiliar with the genre (e.g. *gsoh* = good sense of humour; *ns* = non-smoker: *tlc* = tender loving care). These statements certainly do not account for all examples which occur, but for the most frequent patterns. Deviations from the basic schema (such as using humour or self-deprecation) can be interpreted only with reference to the prototype.

By looking at large corpora, it is also possible to state the most frequent vocabulary which occurs. In a corpus of 200 million words (Cobuild 1995b), the word *seeks* occurred 7,847 times. It does not occur only in lonely hearts ads, but it often does, as can be seen from the ten words which most frequently co-occur with it (within four words to left and right):

- female 1,113, black 972, male 785, attractive 619, similar 568, guy 499, lady 493, man 425, caring 401, professional 389

In turn, the word *caring* occurred 4,814 times. Its ten most frequently co-occurring words (within four words to left and right) were

- seeks 401, loving 353, honest 336, sincere 194, make 159, very 155, more 149, people 149, children 128, kind 128

This starts to show the typical phrasings used in such texts. For example, the following phrases all include both *seeks* and *caring*:

- *seeks* a sincere, *caring* single lady
- *caring*, Christian-minded, romantic, *seeks* attractive, reliable female
- Black male, 31, *seeks caring* lady
- various interests, own flat and car, *seeks caring*, ambitious lady
- kind, honest, reliable, boyish, 35, *seeks caring*, genuine female, for lasting relationship
- male, 35, quiet, honest, *caring*, *seeks* down-to-earth female, 25–34, for lasting friendship

In this example I have deliberately taken a text-type which is much more restricted in its forms than much language use. However, all language use is restricted to some extent, and a main topic of this book will be to show just how strong the co-occurrence relations between words often are.

1.8 Summary and Implications

In this chapter I have introduced some of the topics which arise in the study of language in use. The meaning of words depends on how they are combined into phrases, and on how they are used in social situations. It follows that their meaning depends on both linguistic conventions and also on inferences from real-world knowledge. These linguistic and social expectations mean that, although we are in principle free to say whatever we want, in practice what we say is constrained in many ways. The main evidence for these constraints comes from observations of what is frequently said, and this can be observed, with computational help, in large text collections.

Two shorthand ways of referring to the approach I take in this book are (1) 'meaning is use', and (2) 'corpus semantics'.

1 *'Meaning is use'* is a convenient phrase, but is merely a shorthand way of referring to a complex set of ideas. The meaning of words and phrases differs according to their use in different linguistic and social contexts.
2 *'Corpus semantics'* refers to an approach to studying language in which observational data from large text collections are used as the main evidence for the uses and meanings of words and phrases.

A corpus is a large sample of how people have used language. Meanings are invisible and cannot be observed directly, but if we put (1) and (2) together, then we have empirical observational methods which can be used in semantics, since words acquire meanings from their frequent co-occurrence with other words. I have also introduced the following supporting concepts:

3 *Expectations.* Our interpretation of what other people say or write depends partly on our expectations of what is likely to occur. Our communicative competence involves knowledge (often unconscious) of what is probable, frequent and typical.
4 *Real-world inferences.* Sometimes our interpretations depend on non-linguistic knowledge: that is, our background, encyclopedic knowledge of the everyday world (such as why policemen might be digging in a garden). Meanings are not always explicit, but implicit. Speakers can mean more than they say.
5 *Linguistic conventions.* However, our (unconscious) knowledge of what is probable also involves expectations of language patterns. Our knowledge of a language involves not only knowing individual words, but knowing very large numbers of phrases (such as *river bank, sand bank, bank clerk, piggy bank*), and also knowing what words are likely to co-occur in a cohesive text (*bank, water, fish,* or *bank, money, robbery*).
6 *Text-types.* Different text-types have different patterns of expectation. For example, most lonely hearts ads use a restricted set of verbs which have typical subjects and objects. The semantic pattern is very simple, and much of the vocabulary and grammar is predictable, but there is scope for considerable lexical variation.

So, the central programme of corpus linguistics is to develop a theory of meaning (Teubert 1999a, 1999b). When people hear or read a text, they are usually interested in its meaning, not in its wording or grammar, and they generally remember its content, not how the content was phrased. Yet, as Pawley (2000) puts it, recent linguistic theories have often not recognized that anything is being said at all. In following chapters, I will discuss more detailed examples of the predictable co-occurrence of words and other linguistic patterns, and methods for studying patterns of co-occurrence and of probability.

1.9 Background and Further Reading

An important line of thought on language in use has its origins in problems with concepts of truth and falsity, which were realized in philosophy from the late nineteenth century onwards. Levinson (1983) and Seuren (1998: 377, 384) discuss the formal semantic background to such work.

A second important line of thought, which relates language and social action, has sources in twentieth-century linguistics, anthropology and philosophy. Malinowski (1923) talked of language as a 'mode of action' or 'behaviour', and related ideas of meaning as use were proposed by Firth (1957) and Wittgenstein (1953). The two classic books on speech act theory are Austin's discussion of *How to Do Things with Words*, based on lectures given in 1955 (published as Austin 1962), and Searle's discussion of *Speech Acts* (Searle 1969). Searle (1971) contains important papers by Austin, Searle and Strawson. Cole and Morgan (1975) edited a collection on *Speech Acts*, which contains important papers on indirect speech acts: Grice (1975), published there for the first time, but already widely circulated in manuscript form, Gordon and Lakoff (1975, originally published 1971), and Searle (1975). Searle (1976) is another important updating of the theory.

In this work, from the 1960s and 1970s, the term 'speech acts' became standard, although it is slightly unfortunate as a term, since such acts can be performed in both speech and writing. There are differences between the acts which are performed in spoken and written forms, and indeed some acts can only be performed in writing (such as a signature, a last will and testament). 'Language acts' would have been more accurate, but is scarcely used as a term.

There are useful textbook accounts available in many places. Again, Levinson (1983) and Seuren (1998) explain the impact of such ideas within linguistics, and give a wider account of their history. Seuren discusses ideas about language and logic from the Greeks and Romans onwards, and the problems recognized in truth-conditional semantics in the late nineteenth and early twentieth centuries, and gives an account – by someone actively involved – of attempts within Chomskyan linguistics to integrate semantics into syntactic theory. He argues however, that the Firthian approach to studying language in context 'proved largely sterile' (p. 170), and Halliday is not mentioned at all in his account. From my approach in this book (and in Stubbs 1996), it is clear that I disagree with this judgement.

Lyons (1977) and many articles in linguistic encyclopedias and reference books, such as Sadock (1988), provide more general discussion of different approaches to the study of language in use. See also Saville-Troike (1989), Mey (1993), Schiffrin (1994), and Van Dijk (1997a, 1997b). By the 1990s, these broad strands of work on language in use had led to constructivist theories of social organization (Searle 1995), and radical reinterpretations of Grice's theories (Levinson 2000).

Firthian work has also been radically developed by corpus methods: Sinclair (1987) and Sinclair (1991) were the first books to demonstrate the methods; Hunston and Francis (2000) give a detailed account; and Partington (1998) is a good introductory textbook. It is neo-Firthian work which is most immediately relevant to the methods I discuss in this book.

1.10 Topics for Further Study

(1) Collect your own data on the actual occurrence of words for related speech acts in phrases and texts:

GOSSIP, NAG, CARP, COMPLAIN, WHINGE
PROMISE, OATH, VOW, PLEDGE, GUARANTEE

Study the words they repeatedly co-occur with, and use this evidence to provide a description of their meanings, including whether they express the speaker's attitude to the language behaviour: approving, neutral or disapproving.

(2) In section 1.7.3, I discussed words for days of the week and some phrases in which they occur. Analyse other sets of words which form well-defined semantic sets: for example, months of the year, numbers, or girls' names and boys' names. Some sets are small and finite (months); others are larger and open-ended (professions); others have clear central members, but also other members about which there might be dispute (colours). Investigate why members of such sets differ in frequency, and consider what relations this shows between what is possible in the language system, what is frequent in language use, and how choices express cultural meanings. See Firth (1957: 12) for a classic proposal for such studies.

(3) In section 1.7.4, I described some central features of lonely hearts ads. Study further examples, and propose a more formal description of their

vocabulary and grammar. Useful references are: Mills (1995: 167–9); Yule (1996: 250–1), who gives American examples; Sandig and Selting (1997), who give German examples (translated into English); and Nair (1992), who gives examples of Indian matrimonial advertisements, which are different, but also highly conventionalized.

(4) Study other text-types which are highly restricted in form (vocabulary and grammar) and function, such as other kinds of classified ads, weather forecasts (newspapers or television; perhaps contrasting general-purpose or specialized shipping forecasts), horoscopes, and menus. In these cases too, the possible or expected vocabulary and grammar can be specified in detail.

2

Words, Phrases and Meanings: Basic Concepts

In chapter 1, I introduced some ideas about the ways in which language is used in different text-types, and gave some initial examples of the importance of phraseology in studying meaning. In this chapter, I will provide a more detailed discussion of the main concepts which are needed for studying phraseology. This involves discussing several concepts which are central to lexical semantics, and which are discussed in many student introductions, including: denotation and connotation; synonymy, antonymy and hyponymy; and lexical fields. However, I will try to show that corpus data can provide a new way of looking at these concepts. In particular, an approach from corpus semantics shows that we have to discuss the relation between words in the lexicon (words in the language system) and words in texts (words in use).

2.1 Terminology

First, we need some essential terms.

Phrase. The unit of meaning in connected language in use is usually not a single word in isolation, but a longer unit of at least a few words in length. Much of this book discusses the nature of these extended lexical units, but when I need a neutral term for a string of words, I will talk of a 'phrase'. For example, the phrases *provide help* and *provide shelter* illustrate frequent uses of the verb PROVIDE.

Collocation. This is a lexical relation between two or more words which have a tendency to co-occur within a few words of each other in running text. For example, PROVIDE frequently occurs with words which refer to valuable things which people need, such as *help* and *assistance, money, food* and *shelter*, and *information*. These are some of the frequent collocates of the verb.

Attested language. Almost all the examples which I cite are from real language in use, which was produced for some real communicative purpose.

That is, I did not invent the examples just to illustrate a point of argument. I will refer to such data as attested data.

Corpus. Almost all of these examples are taken from corpora (singular *corpus*, plural *corpora*). A corpus is a collection of texts. There are many text collections (such as newspapers published on CD-ROM), which can be useful for some purposes. However, the term 'corpus' is usually used for a text collection which has been designed for linguistic research, in order to represent some aspect of language. It could be a collection from a given text-type (such as casual conversation, scientific research articles or science fiction novels), or it could be designed to sample as wide a range of text-types as possible, including written and spoken, formal and informal, fiction and non-fiction, language produced by or for children and adults, and texts from different historical periods.

2.2 Words: Word-forms and Lemmas

The word 'word' is ambiguous. First, we have to distinguish between 'lemmas' and 'word-forms' as follows. (An alternative term for 'lemma' is 'lexeme'.) I will use upper-case for lemmas and lower-case italics for word-forms. For example, verbs occur in different inflectional forms: the lemma TAKE is realized in text by the word-forms *take, takes, took, taking* and *taken*. Similarly, the lemma of the noun RABBIT is realized by the word-forms *rabbit, rabbits, rabbit's* and *rabbits'*; and the lemma of the adjective BIG is realized by *big, bigger* and *biggest*. Dictionaries of English conventionally use the base form of a verb to represent the lemma (for example, *want* represents WANT), and the singular of a noun (*table* represents TABLE).

Generally, dictionaries group only words from one part of speech under a single lemma, but they are not always consistent on how the grouping is done. For example, CONFUSE would typically include *confuse* and *confused*, but *confusing* might be included under this lemma as part of the verb, or listed separately as an adjective, and the noun *confusion* would typically be listed separately. Lemmatization looks simple, but in fact involves many decisions.

We need to distinguish between word-forms and lemmas, because we need to distinguish between units of texts and units of the vocabulary of a language. Usually the length of an individual text or the size of a corpus is given in statements such as

[1]   This novel is 50,000 words long.
[2]   This corpus consists of 50 million words.

These statements refer to a sequence of word-forms one after the other. Word-forms are the only lexical units which are directly observable. They are the units which occur in actual texts, and, in a written text, they are strings of letters separated by spaces or punctuation marks. In fact, they provide us with a definition of a text, which consists of a linear string of word-forms. In a written text, they occur one after the other in space; in a spoken text, one after another in time.

In a text or corpus, as in statements [1] and [2], it is likely that the word-form *the* occurs frequently: if it occurs 3,500 times, then I count it 3,500 times. If the forms *want*, *wants*, *wanting* and *wanted* all occur, then I count each occurrence separately. We can count words in a text by counting word-forms, but this is quite different from counting words in the vocabulary of a language. A statement such as

[3] This learner of English has learned 2,000 words

does not refer to the length of a text which someone has produced, but to the size of the vocabulary which they can draw on to produce texts. It means 2,000 different lemmas. The vocabulary of a language can be recorded in a dictionary, either of general English or of a sub-variety (e.g. a dictionary of technical and scientific terms). So we also have statements such as

[4] This dictionary contains 50,000 words.

In a dictionary, I would expect *the* to occur just once as a head-word. Traditionally, dictionaries list the head-word WANT just once, with a note that it occurs in different forms (*want*, *wants*, etc.).

In summary: Word-forms are directly observable units; a text consists of a sequence of word-forms. The sequence is crucial: if we change the sequence, we have changed the text. Lemmas are not directly observable, but abstract classes of word-forms; a vocabulary is usually represented as a list of lemmas. It may be convenient to present the list alphabetically, but this order has nothing to do with the organization of the vocabulary; in fact, it hides many kinds of semantic relations between words. Lemmas could, for example, be grouped according to different semantic areas (this type of book is called a thesaurus).

It is useful to think initially in terms of the correspondences

    text   word-forms
    vocabulary lemmas

However, this is a provisional correspondence only. First, we will later need a further distinction between word-tokens and word-types (see chapter 6.6.1). Second, lemmas are not the only lexical units in the vocabulary. The assumption that single lemmas are the main unit of meaning has underlain the construction of English-language dictionaries for hundreds of years. However, corpus work provides a lot of evidence that units of meaning are both smaller and larger than the lemma.

2.2.1 Example: the lemmas CONSUME and SEEK

The following example shows the importance of the distinction between word-form and lemma. The word-form *consuming* occurs in the phrases *consuming passion* and *time-consuming*. Several other words, such as *costly*, *difficult* and *expensive*, co-occur with this second phrase, in longer phrases, such as

- very expensive and time-consuming; often difficult and time-consuming

The word-forms *consume* and *consumed* do not occur in such phrases at all. However, all three forms share the collocates

- more, quantities, calories, energy, oil

That is, all three forms are used in a literal sense of "consume an amount of fuel", but *consuming* occurs in additional, quite specific phrases. These differences would be missed if the lemma CONSUME was analysed as a whole.

Here is a more complex example. In chapter 1.7.4, I showed that in lonely hearts ads the word-form *seeks* is frequent, as in

- female 31, single, *seeks* well-educated gentleman

In this text-type, it frequently co-occurs with words such as

- attractive, black, caring, female, guy, lady, male, man, professional, similar

However, the word-forms *seek*, *seeking* and *sought* all co-occur with a very different set of words, including

- advice, asylum, help, support

If we looked only at the lemma SEEK, we would miss this striking difference.

In a corpus of 200 million words, I studied the 20 most frequent collocates of the different forms of SEEK: that is, the word-forms which co-occured most frequently with the different forms of the lemma. (The data-base which I used was Cobuild 1995b: this is described in chapter 3.6.) The collocates shared by the word-forms were as follows.

- *seek*, *seeking* and *sought* have 6 shared collocates: <asylum, court, government, help, political, support>
- *seek* and *seeking* have 10 shared collocates: <advice, also, asylum, court, government, help, new, people, political, support>
- *seek* and *sought* have 9 shared collocates: <advice, also, asylum, court, government, help, political, refuge, support>
- *seeking* and *sought* have 7 shared collocates: <also, asylum, court, government, help, political, support>
- *seeks* and *seek* have only one shared collocate: <professional>
- *seeks* and *sought* have no shared collocates
- *seeks* and *seeking* have no shared collocates

The overlap in their collocates gives us one measure of the semantic distance between the word-forms. We have three word-forms which form a tight cluster, with several overlapping collocates, largely from political and legal contexts, in the semantic field of "help and support", but the word-form *seeks* is only distantly attached to this cluster. (Tuldava, 1998: 142, proposes a simple way of calculating the overlap between two sets of items.)

These findings are not a statement about the whole language, but about the text-types sampled in the corpus which I studied. Obviously, if the corpus had contained no magazines with lonely hearts ads, then I would have found no such examples of *seeks*. Equally obviously, the corpus must have contained enough examples to make collocations such as *seeks–caring* more frequent than other collocations. I therefore checked a separate independent 100-million-word corpus for uses of *seeks* (the British National Corpus). This corpus contained examples from other personal adverts and from newspaper headlines, but it also contained other uses:

- guitarist seeks working band
- Microsoft seeks partners
- where a buyer seeks to reject goods supplied under a sale contract
- in his Symphonic Etudes, he consciously seeks an orchestral sonority

Adverts and headlines share the need to use short words. Other uses tend to be from formal, frequently legal, texts.

This example illustrates important principles. First, an exclusive concentration on only the most frequent collocations may hide variation in the language. Second, collocations may differ quite sharply in different text-types. Many text-types are specialized in their uses of language, and no corpus can fairly represent every one of them.

2.3 Collocation

The CONSUME and SEEK examples introduce the concept of collocation: the co-occurrence of words. We can talk of a node-word co-occurring with collocates in a span of words to left and right:

collocates ... node ... collocates
———————— span ————————

A 'node' is the word-form or lemma being investigated. A 'collocate' is a word-form or lemma which co-occurs with a node in a corpus. Usually it is frequent co-occurrences which are of interest, and corpus linguistics is based on the assumption that events which are frequent are significant. My definition is therefore a statistical one: 'collocation' is frequent co-occurrence.

What is node and what is collocate depends on the focus of study, and relations are rarely symmetrical. In a phrase such as *bonsai tree*, there is a much stronger prediction from left to right than from right to left, and such asymmetry is much more general. For example, the word *cushy* is quite rare. When it occurs, there is a high probability (about one chance in seven) that it will occur in the phrase *cushy job*. Other recurring collocates of *cushy* include *up-bringing*, and general nouns such as *number* and *situation*. However, the word *job* is much more frequent, co-occurs with a wide range of other words, and has only a low probability (about one in 5,000) of co-occurring with *cushy*.

One further term allows us to state collocations succinctly. A 'span' is the number of word-forms, before and/or after the node (e.g. 4:4, 0:3), within which collocates are studied. Position in the span can be given as $N-1$ (one word to the left of the node), $N+3$ (three words to the right), and so on. There is some consensus, but no total agreement, that significant collocates are usually found within a span of 4:4 (Jones and Sinclair 1974). There is a problem here, to which there is currently no solution. Lexical units may consist of collocations, and be larger than individual word-forms. Yet I am using word-forms – whose orthographic representation is often arbitrary: e.g. *already* but *all right* – to measure span (Mason 1999).

We now have a convenient notation for presenting information on collocations. A statement such as

- node < ... list of collocates ... >

says that the collocates listed are those that typically co-occur within a given span of the node, usually 3:3 or 4:4. Here is a real example:

- seeking 11,735 <asylum, help, advice, support, information>9%

This says: in a corpus, the word-form *seeking* occurred 11,735 times; in 9 per cent of cases it occurred with one of these five collocates. (The data here are from Cobuild (1995b), which uses evidence from a 200-million-word corpus to calculate the most frequent collocates of word-forms in a span of 4:4. In chapters 3 and 4, I use this data-base for an extended case study.)

Collocation is a relation between words in a linear string: a node predicts that a preceding or following word also occurs. Linear co-occurrence is traditionally referred to as a 'syntagmatic' relation. The prediction will only rarely be 100 per cent: there is usually choice, and *seeking* can obviously co-occur with different words. The term for this relationship of choice is 'paradigmatic'. However, this choice is not entirely free either, and often it is surprisingly restricted. With *seeking* there is almost a one-in-ten chance that it co-occurs with one of only five semantically related words.

These syntagmatic co-occurrence relations often cross-cut the way in which dictionaries have traditionally represented head-words. Sometimes different forms of a lemma behave differently (the SEEK example), but sometimes forms which are usually regarded as separate lemmas behave similarly. One such case is the collocational relation between the lemmas ARGUE and HEAT. One finds

- argue heatedly; heated argument; in the heat of the argument

These phrases cross-cut the traditional parts of speech, since the collocations are, respectively, between verb (ARGUE) and adverb (HEAT), adjective (HEAT) and noun (ARGUE), and noun (HEAT) and noun (ARGUE). In this case, the collocation is between semantic units, irrespective of grammatical category; but there is still a restriction on word-form, since the form *heat* has to occur: *heated argument*, but not **hot argument*.

2.4 Words and Units of Meaning

Dictionaries are mainly organized around individual words (lemmas), which are listed alphabetically with their meanings, but they do also usually list other longer phrases, where the meaning may not be predictable from the individual word-forms. The term 'lexical item' is therefore used to cover a range of individual words and phrases such as

- near, near-sighted, Near East
- nurse, nursery, nursery rhyme, nursery school
- nuclear family, nuclear winter

However, dictionaries differ greatly on how many such larger units are identified (these examples are from Cobuild 1995a).

Such phrases are often seen as an exception to the usual word–meaning correspondence, however there is often a lack of correspondence between words and units of meaning. Sometimes this is evident in arbitrary word-divisions and spelling conventions. We write *already*, and *almighty*, but *all right* (though many people write *alright*). We write *another* as one word, but *of course* as two. We write both *maybe she'll go away* and *she may be going away*. And it is largely a matter of personal choice whether we write *match box*, *match-box* or *matchbox*. Forms such as *I'll* and *it's* are written as one word-form (at least without a space in the middle), but are easily interpretable as two: *I will* and *it is*. (Though many people confuse *it's* and *its*.) Sometimes the apostrophe-*s* represents a word (as in *she's*), but sometimes it represents the possessive-*s* (*the man's hat*). We would usually think of the apostrophe-*s* as being attached to individual words (*Susan's bicycle*), but in *the king of England's hat* and *the boy across the road's bicycle*, the possessive-*s* is attached to a larger unit (see Bloomfield 1933: 178–9):

- the [king of England]'s hat
- the [boy across the road]'s bicycle

There are also cases where conventional word boundaries (spaces in writing) cross-cut the semantic units. A *small farmer* is not a farmer who is only five feet tall, but a farmer with a *small farm* or *smallholding*. A *heavy smoker* is not a smoker who weighs twenty stone, but someone who smokes heavily. Palmer (1971: 45) gives several examples, such as:

- a [small farm] -er, a [heavy smok] -er, a [criminal law] -yer, an [artificial flor] -ist

Some words have no independent existence at all, but occur only in one combination, for example *dint*, *kith* and *spick*, as in *by dint of*, *kith and kin* and *spick and span*. And *span* here is arguably not the same word as in *a span of six years* or *attention span*. In a few such often-cited cases, given one word, a hearer can predict with almost 100 per cent certainty what the following one or two words will be. Words such as *kith* are certainly very restricted in their occurrence, though even apparently fixed phrases can be manipulated, as in the attested example:

- no more expensive to call your kith in Sydney than your kin in Southampton

Similarly, the word *amok* is almost always immediately preceded by RUN, but I have two examples of *an era gone amok* and *journalism gone amok*.

2.5 Delexicalization

The following examples also show that individual words are not always the unit of meaning. Some verbs, which are written as separate words, seem to carry little meaning. Quirk and Stein (1991) discuss examples of some common verbs in V–NP constructions:

- take a decision; take a look; take a shower; take a sip
- have a chat; have a drink; have a look; have a shower; have a swim; have a try
- give a scream; give a shout; give a speech
- make a mistake; make a note; make a suggestion

In these cases, almost all the meaning seems to be in the noun, and some of the phrases mean almost the same as corresponding verbs: for example, *to take a look* = *to look*, *to have a wash* = *to wash*. In such cases the verb is said to be delexicalized (although desemanticized would be a more logical term). By far the most frequent use of TAKE and MAKE is in phrases such as

- take place, take part, take care, make sure, make sense, make clear

I searched for the lemma pair *TAKE a* in a corpus of over two million words. There were over 400 examples, but in only about 10 per cent of these did TAKE have a literal meaning of "grasp with the hand" or "transport". The most common use by far is in combinations such as

- take a close look at; took an interest in; take a deep breath; takes a photograph; take a decision

where TAKE is delexicalized, and where almost all the meaning is carried by the noun.

The phenomenon of delexicalization is much more common than even these examples might suggest. Adjectives are usually thought of as narrowing the meaning of a noun. Thus *a red house* is more specific than *a house*, and the class of *dangerous dogs* is smaller than the class of *dogs*. Sinclair (1992) calls this use 'selective': the adjective selects a smaller set from the larger set. However, he distinguishes this from a 'focusing' use, and argues that:

> The meaning of words chosen together is different from their independent meanings. They are at least partly delexicalized. This is the necessary correlate of co-selection.... [T]here is a strong tendency to delexicalize in the normal phraseology of modern English.

He gives examples of adjective-noun pairs where the adjective is co-selected with the noun and shares part of the meaning. If the noun occurs on its own, little meaning would be lost:

- physical attack, physical damage, physical proximity
- scientific analysis, scientific experiment, scientific study
- general drift, general opinion, general public, general trend

Selective and focusing adjectives can be distinguished as follows.

selective	focusing
outward-looking	inward-looking
independent	dependent
separate choice	co-selected with noun
adds separate meaning	repeats part of meaning of noun
narrows meaning of noun	intensifies meaning of noun

Lorenz (1999) discusses similar examples of focusing adverbs:

- diametrically opposed, firmly entrenched, heavily loaded, instantly recognizable, irretrievably lost, readily available, ruthlessly exploited

In these cases, the adverb contributes little to the propositional meaning, but it emphasizes what the speaker regards as important. Similarly, *distinctly* is frequently used either in phrases where it adds little propositional meaning, or where it emphasizes the speaker's disapproval of something:

- distinctly different, distinctly audible, distinctly visible

- distinctly alarming, distinctly dated, distinctly inferior, distinctly nervous, distinctly odd, distinctly peculiar, distinctly queasy, distinctly uncomfortable, distinctly uneasy, distinctly unimpressed

Positive phrases do occur, but even phrases such as *distinctly better* imply that, up till now, things have been pretty bad.

We now have several cases where units of meaning do not coincide with individual words. Taken separately, they look like minor exceptions to the idea that individual words have individual meanings, but taken together, they start to throw considerable doubt on the status of words as the normal units of meaning.

2.6 Denotation and Connotation

So far, all my examples have been of relations between words and words (e.g. collocation), but words are used to talk about things in the world, and we therefore also need concepts to talk about relations between words and the world: reference and denotation.

Reference is the relation in a particular instance of use. If I say *Look at that huge dog over there*, then I have made an act of reference. It is not individual nouns which refer, but noun phrases: in this case *that huge dog*. Denotation means the appropriate range of reference of a word: for example, the word *dog* can appropriately be used to refer not only to small spaniels but also to large Saint Bernards. Reference and denotation are most obviously relevant to noun phrases and nouns, but they also apply to verbs and adjectives: for example, we might debate whether we could agree on the exact denotational boundaries between WALK, STROLL and HIKE, or between RED and PINK.

In summary: Reference is a speech act which picks out a referent in a concrete situation. Reference concerns language use. Denotation is a relation between a term in the language and a range of potential referents in the world. Denotation concerns the language system.

Different terms are used in this area. Denotation is also referred to as cognitive, conceptual, logical, ideational and propositional meaning. An everyday term is the 'literal meaning' of a word. This is often contrasted with connotation, which is also called affective, associative, attitudinal and emotive meaning.

Words can have the same denotation but different connotations. For example, *die* is a neutral word, but *pass away* attempts to express the speaker's sympathy, and *snuff it* expresses no sympathy at all. Such alternative words often exist in taboo areas, such as death: a *coffin* is neutral, but a *casket* sounds more dignified. Some words express little denotational meaning. I gave the example in chapter 1, that nothing is inherently *super*: the word expresses much about the opinion of the speaker, but little if anything factual about the world. Connotation is sometimes thought of as personal or emotional associations, conveying the attitude of an individual speaker, and if such meanings were purely personal and subjective, then they would be of limited interest. However, connotations are also widely shared within a speech community (see chapters 7, 8 and 9).

Denotation is usually taken to be a stylistically neutral and objective relation between a word and the world. It is often thought of as the most important part of the meaning: the basic or core meaning, which is not deniable. Connotations are often thought of as subjective, second-order or peripheral meanings, which depend on a relation between the word and the speaker/hearer. However, what is primary or secondary depends on one's point of view, and the expression of attitude may be the main function of the utterance. The distinction between denotation and connotation is usually clear, although the boundary can be hazy. It is often not easy to decide what is the primary denotation and what is the secondary connotation, and different dictionaries can differ considerably in what they present as part of the inalienable, undeniable denotational meaning, and what is merely implied or connoted.

2.7 Relational Lexical Semantics

The vocabulary of a language is not an unstructured list of words. In addition to the syntagmatic and paradigmatic relations between words, which I have started to illustrate, there are other relations which are repeated across many pairs and sets of words, and which make broad cuts across the vocabulary:

semantic fields
content and function words
core and non-core vocabulary

2.7.1 Semantic fields

The vocabulary of a language is internally structured by many clusters of words, which stand in different relations to each other, sometimes logical relations of sameness, difference and entailment, and sometimes vaguer relations within a topic area or semantic field. For example, there is an elaborate vocabulary for talking about horses in English. The following 'horsy' words all occurred as collocates (in a span of about 10:10) of 230 examples of *horse* in a 2-million-word corpus. They include words for types and colours of horse, movements that horses make, equipment used with horses, people who deal with horses, along with phrases and idioms which contain the word *horse*:

- bay, mare, pony, racehorse, roan, thoroughbred
- bolt, canter, gallop, rear, trot
- flank, hock, hooves
- mount, ride, on horseback
- harness, horseshoe, reins, saddle
- blacksmith, cowboy, jockey
- rocking-horse, runaway horse
- horse box, horse trough, stable
- don't look a gift horse in the mouth; don't get on your high horse; you can take a horse to water, but you can't make it drink; you're a dark horse; straight from the horse's mouth

Often words cluster because things in the world cluster; such as *horse*, *saddle* and *ride*, but there are always also conventional and recurrent ways of phrasing things.

2.7.2 *Synonyms, antonyms and hyponyms*

Semantic fields are not merely lists of words related by topic: they are also organized by relations amongst these words. Although words are inherently fuzzy in meaning, the vocabulary is structured. A *bush* is smaller than a *tree*, even if this is not a logical distinction and the boundary is unclear, and even if some large bushes are larger than some small trees. To *stroll* is to move more slowly than to *walk*, which is to move more slowly than to *run*: even if some people walk very fast.

Synonyms are words which mean the same. It is often said that it is difficult to find examples which are entirely convincing. After all, there would seem to be no reason why a language should have words which mean exactly the same. Certainly, it is rare to find words which are equivalent in both denotation and connotation. Candidates are *couch*, *settee* and *sofa*, which have the same denotation, though they occur in different collocations:

- casting couch, couch-potato, psychiatrist's couch, sofa-bed

Other candidates are pairs of words such as **glasses** and **spectacles**, where the second is stylistically more formal; and *car* and **automobile**, which are used in different national varieties. In some taboo areas of the vocabulary there are many synonyms which are close in both meaning and use. For example, there are many informal and pejorative words meaning "mad", such as

- bananas, barmy, bonkers, crackers, crazy, cuckoo, dotty, loony, loopy, nuts, potty, unhinged

Death is another taboo area where there are many approximate synonyms, such as the many words and phrases for "die":

- expire, give up the ghost, pass away, perish, shuffle off this mortal coil, snuff it

and many more. There are also several words and expressions for the dead human body, which illustrate relations between denotation, connotation and text-type. As usual all examples below are attested. *Body* is a neutral term, which is used in a wide range of contexts. *The deceased* denotes someone who has recently died, it connotes respect, and it is often used in legal contexts. A *corpse* connotes unpleasantness and often occurs in reports of a crime. A *stiff* is a slang term for a corpse, certainly disrespectful, possibly slightly old-fashioned, and possibly largely restricted to American detective fiction. A *cadaver* is a technical term, often used in medical contexts, especially with reference to study by medical students.

- Lenin's body lay in state
- a body was washed up on the beach
- determine the identities of the deceased
- the family of the deceased
- the corpse was barely recognizable
- the corpse was found floating in the river
- they found a stiff in the river
- anatomical investigations of a human cadaver

A *carcass* is used of larger animals, especially if they can be useful as meat, for either humans or animals. If it is used of humans, it is rude (*move your carcass over here*). *Carrion* is used of the decayed bodies of animals which are food for scavenging animals and birds.

- the carcass of a dead buffalo
- vultures picking at a lion's carcass
- meat left on the chicken carcass
- crows feeding on carrion

The approximate synonyms are distinguished partly by their denotations, but also by their connotations, and by the text-types they typically occur in. The contemporary variation in the lexis is due to historical changes in English. It was the influence of French and Latin after the Norman invasion of 1066 which contributed greatly to the expansion of the English vocabulary, via the semantic fields which were developed within social institutions such as the law and medicine and their associated bodies of knowledge and text-types. The core word is the Germanic *body*. Others are of Romance origin: *corpse* (compare French *corps*, Latin *corpus*), *cadaver* (compare French *cadavre*, Latin *cadaver*), *deceased* (compare French *décès*, Latin *decessus*).

Such sets of words also provide an insight into the way in which English categorizes a small part of the social world. There are several terms for dead humans. There are terms for dead animals, if they are useful as a food source. There are terms for large dead trees (*log*, *lumber*, *timber*), especially if they are useful and/or cultivated. But there are no terms for dead insects or smaller dead plants. The vocabulary embodies a hierarchy of importance and gives decreasing attention to humans, animals and plants.

Antonyms are words which are opposite in meaning. Speakers can often give immediate clang responses when asked for the opposite of a word (for example, *wet–dry*, *up–down*, *hot–cold*), but this provides another example of the limited relevance of asking for the meaning of isolated words. Does it really make sense to ask for the meaning of *dry*? Or to ask for its opposite? The word has a core-meaning and a prototypical antonym. If you ask for a clang response in isolation, people will probably say *wet*. However, this only works in some cases. Compare

dry socks	wet socks
dry season	wet season *or* rainy season
dry wine	sweet wine
dry skin	moist skin?
dry humour	unsubtle humour?
a dry area	an area which has pubs
a dry run	the real thing?
dry land	sea?
dry-cleaning	washing?

Dry means different things in these different phrases, not to mention *high and dry* and *there were few dry eyes in the house*. Conversely, several uses of *wet* do not have an obvious opposite at all: *wet blanket*, *wet nurse*, *feel like a wet rag*, *a Tory wet* (a British English term for a Conservative politician, especially in Margaret Thatcher's government, who holds moderate views).

There are many similar examples. A clang response to the opposite of *white* would probably be *black*, but compare:

white wine   red wine
white collar blue collar
white coffee black coffee

(and white coffee is, well, coffee-coloured, that is, light brown).

Antonymy has traditionally been regarded as a paradigmatic opposition permanently available in the lexicon of the language. However, it is better seen in addition as a syntagmatic relation, which is realized in co-text. For example, the commonest collocate of *bride* is its antonym *groom*: that is, the words often co-occur (usually in the phrase *bride and groom*), rather than being available in paradigmatic opposition to each other (and often they could *not* substitute for each other). Out of context, the antonym of *conventional* might be *modern*, but in a text about weapons, the antonym might be *chemical* or *nuclear*.

Hyponymy is the logical relation of class inclusion. A *buttercup* is a kind of *flower*, which is a kind of *plant*; a *spaniel* is a kind of *dog*, which is a kind of *animal*. There is a large number of approximate synonyms, and more and less specialized hyponyms, for groups of people: this is not surprising, since the different ways in which people can be grouped is of inherent social interest. *Group* is a neutral superordinate word for a collection of things, animals or people. One hyponym is *crowd*: a "very large group of people". In turn, a hyponym of *crowd* is *mob*: an "unruly crowd".

2.8 Frequent and Less Frequent Words

Words in texts are distributed very unevenly: a few words are very frequent, some are fairly frequent, and most are very rare. These facts are due to two distinctions which provide ways of talking about the vocabulary of a language and about the distribution of the vocabulary in texts: function and content words, and core and non-core words.

2.8.1 Content and function words: lexical density

In English and in many other languages, there is a distinction which divides the whole vocabulary into two major categories: content words tell us what a text is about, and function words relate content words to each other. The distinction is made in most grammars of English, but since many linguists make essentially the same distinction, there are several terms in use. Content words are also referred to as major, full and lexical words. They carry most of the lexical content, in the sense of being able to make reference outside language. Function words are also referred to as minor, empty, form, structural and grammatical words. They are essential to the grammatical structure of sentences. Their function is internal to the language, for example in making explicit the relation of lexical words to each other. The distinction is made by Henry Sweet in his famous grammar of 1891:

> In a sentence such as *The earth is round*, we have no difficulty in recognizing *earth* and *round* as ultimate independent sense-units.... Such words as *the* and *is*, on the other hand, though independent in form, are not independent in meaning: *the* and *is* by themselves do not convey any ideas, as *earth* and *round* do. We call such words as *the* and *is* form-words, because they are words in form only. When a form-word is entirely devoid of meaning, we may call it an empty word, as opposed to full words such as *earth* and *round*. (Sweet 1891: 22)

It is possible to conceive of a communicative system which has only content words, but not of a system which has only function words. For example, in a telegram one can omit function words and still have a comprehensible message:

- Please meet Harry airport six Saturday evening [1]

These two semantic categories divide the traditional parts of speech into two broad sets:

content words: noun, adjective, adverb, main verb
function words: auxiliary verb, modal verb, pronoun, preposition, determiner, conjunction

The boundary between the two word classes is not perfectly clear-cut. For example, modal verbs (*must, can, should*, etc.) express obligation, permission and ability, and therefore convey content; and pronouns can have extra-linguistic reference. However, as well as the rough semantic distinction, content and function words have strikingly different formal characteristics. Briefly: content classes have many members (there are tens of thousands of nouns, but only a couple of dozen pronouns), and are open to new words (for example, new nouns and verbs are being constantly invented; it is very rare for new pronouns to enter the language). And only content words take inflections (such as plural inflections on nouns, person endings on verbs).

This distinction between two classes in the vocabulary is relevant to text structure, because different types of texts have predictably different proportions of content and function words. Certain restricted text-types, mainly lists of different kinds, consist entirely of content words. However, usually the difference between text-types is one of proportion. On average, written texts have a higher proportion of content words than spoken texts, because written texts can be more tightly packed with information.

The lexical density of a text is the proportion of lexical words expressed as a percentage. If N is the number of running word-forms in text, and L is the number of lexical word-forms, then

$$\text{lexical density} = 100 \times L/N$$

Ure (1971) studied corpora of 42,000 words of spoken and written texts, and showed a strong tendency for written texts to have a lexical density of over 40 per cent (range 36 to 57) and for spoken texts to be under 40 per cent (range 24 to 43). There are functional interpretations for these findings. On average, a written text is shorter and has fewer repetitions than a comparable spoken text. It is permanent, highly edited and redrafted, rather than being unplanned and spontaneous, as casual conversation is. A written text is relatively context-free, though never entirely so, whereas a spoken text can rely to a large extent on the immediate physical context. We would therefore expect the information load to be higher in a written text: since it is permanent, readers can reread obscure sections. Spoken texts must, on the other hand, be understood while they are being produced: they must be more predictable.

So, on average, written texts are less predictable, and spoken texts are more predictable. In turn, content words are less predictable: there are thousands of them. Function words are more predictable: there are small numbers of them. For example, there are only half a dozen frequent conjunctions. We would expect, therefore, that written texts have a higher proportion of unpredictable content words, and that spoken texts have a higher proportion of more predictable function words. More recent studies with larger corpora confirm Ure's findings (Stubbs 1996: 71–6).

2.8.2 Core vocabulary

Another way of comparing texts is to calculate what percentage of words from the core vocabulary they contain. By definition, the core vocabulary is known to all native speakers of the language. It is that portion of the vocabulary which speakers could simply not do without.

Suppose we have sets of words which are related by approximate synonymy and hyponymy:

- break, burst, chip, crack, shatter, smash, snap

- gaze, glance, glimpse, look, peer, watch
- quake, quiver, shake, shudder, tremble
- display, exhibit, expose, flaunt, show
- drudgery, labour, toil, work
- dirty, filthy, grimy, grubby, soiled, unclean

I think there would be widespread agreement that one word in each list is somehow more basic than the others:

- break, look, shake, show, work, dirty

Such intuitions are partly based on frequency, but also on functional criteria, such as which words would be most easily understood by children or non-native speakers, or which words it would be most useful to introduce in the early stages of teaching English as a foreign language.

The core vocabulary will certainly contain the most frequent words in the language. The 100 most frequent word-forms from a large general corpus will be mainly function words such as

- the, of, and, to

plus a few content words such as

- think, know, time, people, two, see, way, first, new, say, man, little, good

And the 2,000 or 3,000 most frequent word-forms will include words which are indispensable for discussion of a wide range of topics. However, beyond the top few hundred words in different general corpora, word frequency varies greatly, and merely reflects the content of the texts in the corpora. Therefore raw frequency lists often have odd gaps, because, for example, the word *Sunday* is twice as frequent as *Tuesday* (see chapter 1.7.3). However, the vocabulary is a structured whole, not an unordered list of words. Therefore, the core vocabulary contains common closed sets of words, such as days of the week, months and seasons, numbers, and sets with a few frequent members such as colours, major family members, parts of the body, and common professions.

The main defining criterion of core vocabulary is that of maximum usefulness. This criterion can be operationalized in two main ways. We can discover which words are widely and relatively evenly distributed in texts of different kinds, and we can discover which words can be used for defining other words:

1 *Distribution in texts*. The core vocabulary includes words which occur not only frequently, but with a relatively even distribution across a wide variety of texts and text-types. For example, *doctor* will occur in texts of many kinds, both everyday and specialist, whereas *paediatrician* may be common in a few texts, but only on restricted specialist subjects. Core vocabulary is not restricted to specialist fields or genres: for example *children* (versus *offspring* or *progeny*), *brothers* and *sisters* (versus *siblings*), and *stomach* (versus *abdomen*). And core vocabulary is neutral stylistically, neither markedly casual nor formal: for example, *child* (versus *kid* or *kiddy*), *drunk* (versus *pissed* or *inebriated*), and *give* (versus *award* or *donate*).
2 *Semantic usefulness*. Core words are often useful for defining other words: that is, they are not hyponyms with a narrow denotation. For example, the core words *laugh* and *softly* can be used to define non-core *chuckle*. Similarly, *clumsy* and *walk* can be used to define *waddle*.

Sometimes, the two criteria coincide: for example, *paediatrician* is a hyponym of *doctor*, and *award* and *donate* are hyponyms of *give*.

2.9 Two Examples

Here are two small case studies which use corpus data to document the main principle of this chapter: that observable corpus data can provide evidence of both denotational and connotational meaning.

2.9.1 Example 1: Bloomfield's analysis of SALT

In what was for many years the main student textbook in American structuralist linguistics, semantics was regarded as 'the weak point in language study', since a study of meaning would require human knowledge to advance 'very far beyond its present state' (Bloomfield 1933: 140). Bloomfield put forward a general argument that meanings were simply too complex to analyse systematically:

> The situations which prompt people to utter speech, include every object and happening in their universe. In order to give a scientifically accurate definition for every form of a language, we should have to have a scientifically accurate knowledge of everything in the speaker's world. (p. 139)

He concluded that meanings 'could be analysed or systematically listed only by a well-nigh omniscient observer' (p. 162). In addition, he attributed a special status to a particular form of 'scientifically accurate knowledge':

> We can define the names of minerals, for example, in terms of chemistry and mineralogy, as when we say that the ordinary meaning of the English word *salt* is "sodium chloride (NaCl)"... but we have no way of defining words like *love* or *hate*, which concern situations that have not been accurately classified – and these latter are in the great majority. (p. 139)

Both of these arguments are usually regarded today as faulty. First, 'everything in the speaker's world' is not an unorganized flux, but categorized by social cognition into lexical fields. Second, it is odd to argue that the 'ordinary meaning' of *salt* is NaCl. It is not necessary to know this meaning at all in order to use the word appropriately in most everyday situations. Most native speakers of English probably do not know the chemical formula for table salt, and the "NaCl" meaning is often quite irrelevant to the use of the word.

Third, some of Bloomfield's arguments seem very strange indeed:

> We have defined the *meaning* of a linguistic form as the situation in which the speaker utters it and the response which it calls forth. (p. 139)

This statement is understandable in view of Bloomfield's behaviourist assumptions: situations provide stimuli which evoke responses in speakers. It is nevertheless odd to say that the meaning *is* the situation. More reasonable might be an argument which runs: meanings are essentially mental or psychological events, they take place inside people's brains or minds, and we have no idea how this works. The process is unobservable and we may as well give up trying to study it. Bloomfield was driven to this position (which he stated very clearly, even if he did not always follow it himself) because of his view of scientific methodology that linguistics must be based on observable facts.

An answer to Bloomfield's pessimistic view is to look at some data on usage. We can then agree with Bloomfield's own argument about the necessity for observable facts, but use it against his position. There are many observable patterns, and some aspects of meaning are observable: meaning is use. So, to answer the question 'what does *salt* mean?', we will observe how it is used in attested data. In a corpus of over two million words, the most frequent combinations were *salt and pepper* and *salt water*. The first of these occurs frequently in recipes, often in longer phrases such as

- season with salt and pepper; a good sprinkling of salt and pepper; salt, pepper and mustard

In cooking contexts, the antonym pairs are *salt–sugar*, or *salty–sweet*, but the antonym of *salt water* is *fresh water*. However, in German, fresh water is *Süsswasser* (= "sweet water"). In other words, these are linguistic facts, not facts which relate directly to the world. The plural *salts* occurs with quite different collocates:

- copper salts, iron salts, mineral salts, vegetable salts

In these cases *salt* does not mean "NaCl". We see here again the principle that different forms of a lemma may not have the same meaning. In addition, there are several idioms where the "NaCl" meaning may be remote to modern speakers:

- rubbed salt into the wounds; has to be taken with a pinch of salt; the salt of the earth; if he is worth his salt

The literal denotation of "NaCl" can explain the history of the phrases (for example, salt used to be a very valuable commodity, used for preserving food), but now this is largely lost in extended metaphorical meanings, which may rely in turn on intertextual Biblical allusions.

In conclusion: (1) The lemma SALT does not always mean "NaCl". (2) Admittedly, we cannot directly observe the meanings of SALT, but corpus data provide much evidence for these meanings. (3) These meanings depend on relations with other words in the co-text, or with other words in other texts.

2.9.2 *Example 2:* CAUSE problems *and* CAUSE amusement

Here is a second small case study which further illustrates three principles. (1) Words should be studied, not in isolation, but in collocations. (2) Findings from one corpus should be checked against an independent corpus. (3) Potential counter-examples should be carefully checked.

The lemma CAUSE almost always co-occurs with unpleasant collocates. Evidence of this can be seen in concordance 2.1, which presents some raw data on the verb lemma from a spoken corpus. A concordance is the main tool of corpus linguistics. The computer is programmed to search for all examples of a node word in a corpus and to print them out in the centre of the page or screen within a given context, of a few words to left and right.

In a detailed study (Stubbs 1995a), I looked at the 38,000 occurrences of the lemma CAUSE (verb and noun) in a corpus of 120 million words of general English. Amongst its 50 most frequent collocates, within a span of 3:3, there were only words (most frequently abstract nouns) with unpleasant connotations. The most frequent were

1. ody's land as long as you don't cause a criminal offence then you've g
2. erm bankrupt some firms and so cause a lot of social disruption
3. t you get a pay rise that would cause a public outcry?" And the Guardi
4. at to say the wrong thing would cause a row er Joanna said er don't
5. here. Erm originally it used to cause problems between the children an
6. But it's not the sutures that cause the wound to heal [FOX] it's
7. t make weapons of war you would cause unemployment but there's no reas
8. ly go and do anything they want cause whatever misery they want cause
9. blizzards for fifty years have caused a state of emergency in souther
10. that's another area that that's caused antagonism between us is the fa
11. erm has MX's behaviours ever caused argument or conflict between yo
12. illiam Hague in the by-election caused by the erm er move er [ZF1] of
13. on are are of are generated and caused by the Holy Spirit Himself. You
14. nine per cent of all illness is caused directly or indirectly by a bas
15. now it sort of [pause] If I say caused problems I don't mean it full-
16. ay it was total negligence that caused this and I don't feel that thes
17. events that were happening that caused us to go downhill effectively e
18. nd the harm if you like that is caused you if you can't have children.
19. any issues which have caud you caused you particular stress or distre
20. ed to any school so that always causes a bit of erm er er er confusion
21. t so many kilograms per hectare causes a loss of something or [F01] Mm
22. ir own crowd so to speak and it causes a major disruption not so much
23. [M02] right. Oh uh the air u causes a vacuum and that's why it stic
24. d a bit of a smokescreen. If he causes chaos in class then the teacher
25. and that the sheer trauma of it causes him a heart attack? [M01] Mm.
26. Y the lack of air on the inside causes it to stay down. [M02] Pulls it
27. r than to look what cau at what causes it which would mean you'd have
28. there are many theories on what causes its stages. Too much dairy in t
29. ies away from home. This always causes pressures doesn't it. [F02] I t
30. rea is a horrific disease which causes severe dementia in middle age.
31. so that the depression is what causes the spending. It's not like the
32. asked them that there that it causes this many problems with that ma
33. here's more than one thing that causes warming and cooling you know.
34. No. [M01] Would you say that it causes you inconvenience [F01] Mm. [M0
35. how much extra work it [pause] causes. [M0X] Well what they've done i
36. ll see people getting drunk and causing a fuss and running amok. [M21]
37. hree years [M01] Yeah [F01] Erm causing a great deal of furore in the
38. to erm to that behaviour that's causing a problem for us we can call
39. break off at speed and that is causing City all sorts of problems.
40. round on the street of er kids causing criminal damage to property
41. n remember [laughs] practically causing G B H on my best friend [laugh
42. ildren by going out to work and causing infant mortality because a chi
43. it was extra-terrestrial beings causing it or maybe some kind of pract
44. esday afternoons. This last was causing some concern to students becau
45. minister to those whose past is causing the future to look very bleak
46. tion you cause an ice age or by causing the ice age you shut down the
47. st to find out what is actually causing the problem [F02] Mhm [F01] An
48. if there's a if a group's been causing trouble we'll try and get them
49. ery much. [F01] Okay. [FOX] I'm causing you problems aren't I? [F01] N
50. what er the the thing that was causing you the upset was it the becau

Concordance 2.1 Fifty random examples of CAUSE (verb)

Notes: The data are from the spoken language sub-corpus of the Bank of English.
[FOX] etc. are speaker identification codes.

- CAUSE <problem(s) 1806, damage 1519, death(s) 1109, disease 591, concern 598, cancer 572, pain 514, trouble 471>

The lemma often occurs in longer combinations of verb plus adjective plus noun, such as

- cause considerable damage; cause great problems; cause major disruption; cause severe pain

Not all widely used dictionaries explicitly draw attention to these negative uses. Some do, but others give a neutral definition such as "a cause is something which produces an effect". However, the examples in corpus-based dictionaries (such as CIDE 1995; Cobuild 1995a; LDOCE 1995; OALD 1995) include:

- heavy traffic is causing long delays; the cold weather caused the plants to die; it was a genuine mistake but it did cause me some worry; the cause of the fire was carelessness; causes of war; cause for anxiety; cause of the accident; cause of the crime problem; her rudeness was a cause for complaint

A minority of examples in these dictionaries are neutral or positive, such as *every cause for confidence*, though there is no indication of how much less likely positive examples are.

Corpus data allow collocates to be extensively documented. In my data, collocates which occurred as subject or object of the verb CAUSE or as prepositional object of the noun CAUSE include:

- abandonment, accident, alarm, anger, annoyance, antagonism, anxiety, apathy, apprehension, breakage, burning, catastrophe, chaos, clash, commotion, complaint, concern, confusion, consternation, corrosion, crisis, crowding, damage, danger, death, deficiency, delay, despondency, destruction, deterioration, difficulty, disaster, disease, disorganization, disruption, disturbance, disunity, doubt, errors, frustration, harm, hostility, hurt, inconvenience, interference, injury, interruption, mistake, nuisance, pain, pandemonium, quarrel, rejection, ruckus, rupture, sorrows, split, suffering, suspicion, trouble, uneasiness, upset

I give quite a long list because it shows very clearly that there is a very simple semantic pattern ("bad things get caused"), which is realized by considerable lexical variation.

(A much less frequent sense of CAUSE as "aim or principle" is signalled by different collocations, including: *devoted service to this cause*; *conviction that your cause is right*; *plead a cause*; *take up causes*. Causes in this sense are *good*, *glorious*, *just* and *worthy*, but also *lost* and *foolish*.)

If different samples of data gave different results, then these unpleasant associations might be a feature of the corpora, not a collocational property of the word. I had no reason to suspect that my corpus was biased by containing lots of texts about gloomy things, but I carried out the same analysis on other independent corpora. For example, a corpus of 425,000 words, comprising texts about environmental issues, contained three or more examples of the collocates

- blindness, cancer, concern, damage, depletion, harm, loss, ozone, problems, radiation, warming

These collocates reflect the environmental topics (in phrases such as *cause global warming*), but the same simple semantic pattern holds. (See Gerbig 1996 for a detailed analysis.)

However, the question now arises as to whether there are counter-examples to the generalization. A possible collocate of the verb CAUSE is *amusement* as in *to cause someone amusement*. Are such occurrences genuine counter-examples to the expected negative uses of CAUSE? First, I studied the 100 occurrences of the word-form *amusement* itself in over six million words of running text. I ignored a few phrases such as *amusement arcade* and *amusement park*. In some cases, negative connotations are signalled by an adjective at N−1; many of the remaining examples implied a degree of *schadenfreude* towards the butt of the amusement, and thereby disapproval of those who are amused:

- derived malicious amusement; with wicked amusement; for his own twisted amusement; with a little sardonic amusement; silly boyish amusement; a look of contemptuous amusement
- she was listening with more amusement than respect
- suppressed amusement at his outrageous manners
- vulgar aspects seem to have been a source of some amusement
- landing flat on my back, much to the amusement of the lads

(The last example is from Cobuild 1995a.) Certainly, not all examples are disapproving, though even more positive cases may imply a condescending, patronizing attitude:

- Lovat listened with affectionate amusement

- Victor stood watching her in fond amusement

However, the crucial question is whether collocations of CAUSE-*amusement* are disapproving. I found eight examples in nearly 60 million words of data. In six of these cases it is evident, even from a small context, that disapproval is being expressed of the person who is amused, or the amusement is at someone's expense:

- it caused a certain amount of amusement in the lab
- the affair with Kim caused her a great deal of amusement
- the veiled hints caused us plenty of amusement
- the amusement caused by my looking so hot
- the unexpected reference caused titters of amusement
- are also cause for sardonic amusement

In summary: The collocation CAUSE-*amusement* does not provide counter-examples to the generalization that CAUSE has overwhelmingly unpleasant connotations.

2.10 Summary and Implications

In this chapter I have introduced the main terms and concepts which I need in the subsequent chapters:

word-form and lemma
collocation (node, span and collocates)
denotation and connotation
semantic (or lexical) fields
content and function words
core and non-core vocabulary
I have used two main arguments:

1   Individual words often do not correspond to units of meaning. Individual forms of a lemma may have quite different uses, and often the unit of meaning is a longer phrase or collocation.
2   There are many structural relations within the vocabulary of a language, including logical relations between words, such as synonymy, antonymy and hyponymy. These relations hold between words in the vocabulary, but also between word-forms in texts where they contribute to text cohesion (see chapters 5 and 6). In addition, words can be divided into broad classes, such as content and function words, core and non-core

vocabulary. These distinctions also concern how words are used in texts: for example, the density of information in a text, or how specialized the text-type is.

Two brief case studies showed that corpus data can provide evidence of both denotation (the SALT example) and connotation (the CAUSE example). The principle 'meaning is use' leads to observational methods of corpus semantics. The main tool of corpus semantics is the concordance, which allows words and their characteristic collocates to be studied in detail.

I have also now given initial examples of the main empirical methods which underlie corpus semantics. The primary data are texts. Linguistics studies human language: but this is not directly observable. Even individual languages (such as English, German or Swahili) are highly abstract objects, and also not directly observable. However, languages are realized in texts, and these texts are observable. They exist independently of the observer, and provide publicly accessible, objective data. The patterns in large collections of texts are also not directly accessible to the individual human observer, but if texts are stored as a corpus, in computer-readable form, then computer-assisted methods can be used to discover their structure and regularities.

The interpretation of such data involves constant subjective decisions. However, these decisions are testable and can be checked by independent observers. Data and methods therefore make possible the replicable and empirical analysis of meaning. Chapter 3 will describe in more detail how patterns can be discovered in corpus data.

2.11 Background and Further Reading

Amongst the most influential early discussions of the main concepts of lexical semantics (including semantic fields, synonymy, antonymy and hyponymy, and semantic features) were two textbooks by Lyons (1968, 1977). These discussions are, however, not based on textual or corpus data: indeed, in the two volumes and over 800 pages of Lyons (1977), there is not a single example of a naturally occurring text. Cruse (1986) provides a widely used textbook on lexical semantics, and Aitchison (1987) provides a very readable student introduction to many aspects of meaning and to the organization of the 'mental lexicon'. These are only four books out of very many, and lexical semantics is discussed in most introductions to linguistics.

For more detailed discussions of core vocabulary and lexical density, see Stubbs (1986) and Stubbs (1996: 71ff), respectively, and further references there. There are many further references to work on collocations and phraseology in general in chapter 3.11, below.

2.12 Topics for Further Study

(1) Use corpus data to state the collocates of BOGGLE. (Does it always collocate with *mind*?) And *blithering*. (Are there any other forms of a lemma BLITHER?) And GRUFF. (The phrase *gruff voice* is common, but there are also other collocates. Do the collocates share a semantic feature?)

(2) Some words and phrases usually occur in the negative (Buyssens 1959; Laduslaw 1996: 328; Sinclair 1998):

- not bad-looking; wouldn't budge; didn't cut much ice; didn't drink a drop; wouldn't lift a finger to help me; not so much as a red cent; I've never set eyes on her

Are these phrases always negative? Or are there exceptions?

(3) Study examples of adverb–adjective phrases such as

- absolutely certain, potentially dangerous, singularly stupid, specially designed, totally different, understandably reluctant, virtually impossible

Is it possible to make generalizations about the adjectives which typically follow these adverbs? A useful article is by Louw (1993), who analyses the negative implications of *utterly*, as in *utterly confused* and *utterly ridiculous*.

(4) Study the sets of words which make up semantic fields, such as cooking and furniture. Some examples include

- boil, cook, fry, grill, roast, sauté
- garlic, herbs, parsley, spices
- bookcase, chair, cupboard, desk, furniture, table
- chair, chaise longue, couch, sofa, stool

State the semantic relations which hold between the words in such sets, such as hyponymy and approximate synonymy. And list some of the conventional phrases in which the words occur.

(5) Compare two or three different dictionaries to see whether they agree on the central and more peripheral meanings of the following words:

- acquisitive, affectation, aloof, antiquated, avaricious

- gaggle, garish, gimmicky, glamorize, glib, grandiose, grovel

For example, the word *gaggle* denotes a kind of "group", but also expresses criticism or disapproval. Is the denotation more basic? Or are denotation and connotation equally central in a phrase such as *a gaggle of teenagers*? Consider whether the words express disapproval as an inherent part of their denotation, or whether the disapproval is a deniable connotation.

(6) There are many hyponyms for *group*, and denotations and connotations differ in different phrases. There are specialized words for groups of animals which collocate only with certain animal names, and therefore have a more restricted denotation than the superordinate:

- flock, gaggle, herd, pride, shoal

Some of these words can be used for people, often, though not always, with pejorative connotations:

- following the herd, a clergyman's flock

Use corpus data to study the collocates and meanings of these words, and others such as

- band, bunch, clan, crew, crowd, gang, horde, mob, rabble, team, tribe

Why should there be so many different words for talking about groups of people?

(7) Study the concordance lines for the verb CAUSE in section 2.9.2, and identify all the object noun phrases. What are the most frequent collocates? Are there any counter-examples to the generalization that what is caused is something bad? If yes, what explains the counter-examples?

(8) Set up a list of core vocabulary for English or some other language, as the basis for vocabulary teaching in the initial stages of learning a foreign language. This would involve quite a substantial project, rather than just a study question: perhaps a project for a final-year undergraduate dissertation. The project would involve at least the following steps.

Use frequency lists (from a large raw corpus or from a corpus-based dictionary) to establish a starting list. For English, the Cobuild Dictionary (1995a) gives lemmas in frequency bands up to 30,000, and the Cobuild Collocations Dictionary on CD-ROM (1995b) gives the 10,000 most frequent word-forms (see chapter 3, below). Extract the top 2,000 or 3,000 lemmas. Develop this list by completing sets of words which are incompletely represented. Test the list in various ways. Check that the candidate words are evenly distributed across many texts and not clustered in just one or two texts. Check that the list does not include hyponyms which are too specialized. Check what text coverage the list provides: a reasonable aim might be 95 per cent in texts from a general corpus. Compare the list against well-known published lists (such as those at the end of LDOCE, 1995, or OALD, 1995).

Any list is only as good as the corpus or data-base on which it is based. The original corpus must at least contain a wide selection of text-types: spoken and written, formal and informal, fiction and non-fiction, intended for children and adults, and must sample widely used genres.

Part II
Case Studies

3

Words in Phrases 1: Concepts, Data and Methods

In chapters 1 and 2 I showed that it is not individual words which are the basic units of meaning, but longer phrases and collocations, and it is these longer units which contribute to what speakers recognize as idiomatic language. In chapters 3 and 4, I will present a more detailed model of these lexico-semantic units. The two chapters really have to be read together, since chapter 3 discusses concepts, data and methods, and chapter 4 presents findings.

The analysis is based on the most frequent collocates of a sample of 1,000 English word-forms. I have taken these from a data-base, Cobuild Collocations on CD-ROM (Cobuild 1995b), which gives the top 20 collocates, with examples, for each of the 10,000 most frequent word-forms in a 200-million-word corpus.

These data show that all the most frequent words in the language occur in lexico-semantic units, with often surprisingly high strengths of attraction between collocates. Such a model has implications for a theory of language production which shows the idiomatic nature of much language use, a theory of language comprehension which shows how collocational units contribute to textual cohesion, and a theory of language structure which shows the variable and probabilistic nature of language units.

3.1 Background

It has often been claimed that semi-fixed phrases or routine formulae are a peripheral phenomenon of only limited interest. First, collocation is often thought of as an area where no generalizations are possible: 'simply an idiosyncratic property of individual words' (Leech 1981: 17). Examples often cited include verbs which have a narrow collocational range, especially in V–NP structures, such as

- to curry favour; to foot the bill; to levy a tax; to quash an appeal; to shrug one's shoulders; to strike a balance

Sometimes the lack of correspondence between form and meaning is emphasized. For example, *rancid, rotten* and *sour* are often said to have the same denotational meaning, but to occur in different collocations: *rancid butter, rotten eggs* and *sour milk*. Similarly, *grill* and *toast* mean the same, yet we *grill meat* but *toast bread*. Sometimes a general verb is required: *make headway* but not *achieve headway (Trask 1993: 49, 239). But sometimes a general verb (such as *make* or *do*) is impossible (*tell a story, tell/crack a joke*), or different verbs are possible to express similar meanings (*do/take/sit an exam, perform a dance*). The list of restrictions or preferences seems endless. A related argument in favour of idiosyncracy and uniqueness is that collocations differ across languages: in English one *brushes* one's teeth, but in French one *washes* them (*se laver les dents*), and in German one *cleans* them (*die Zähne putzen*).

Admittedly the collocational behaviour of every word is different, in its fine details, from that of every other word. However, it does not follow that there are no general patterns or principles to be discovered. If, instead of talking of collocational restrictions, we talk of preferences, then strong probabilistic relations become apparent (Hanks 1987: 121).

Second, it has often been implied that there are relatively few fixed phrases, which can be listed, and may be useful to foreign language learners, as in these examples from English and German:

- I don't believe a word of it.   Ich glaub dir kein Wort.
- It's very nice to meet you.   Erfreut, Sie kennenzulernen.
- Have you heard the news?   Hast du schon gehört?
- Can I take a message?   Soll ich was ausrichten?
- [On a town map] You are here.   Standort.

However, corpus research shows that words are typically used in routine phrases, and that even the most frequent words have typical collocates and typical uses. A few observations on these English and German examples will emphasize some important concepts:

1 It is implausible that such phrases and sentences are created individually on each occasion of use. They are conventional ways of saying conventional things, and often of expressing speech acts, such as frequent questions, complaints or greetings.
2 Many other perfectly grammatical ways of saying the same things are conceivable: but people just don't say them. It would be perfectly grammatical in German to put on a town plan a red dot and the sentence *Sie sind hier* (= "You are here"), but that is just not the way it is said.

3   Every native speaker has thousands upon thousands of multi-word units stored in memory. It is difficult to see how people could speak fluently, or understand other fluent speakers, if they could not rely on familiar chunks of language behaviour.
4   The examples are all transparent in meaning: that is, they are idiomatic, but they are not idioms. More accurately, they pose no problem for *de*coding: even if you have never heard these combinations before, you will understand them, as long as you understand the individual words. But they do pose a problem for *en*coding: you just have to know that these are the conventional ways of saying these things. Fillmore et al. (1988: 504–5, following Makkai 1972) distinguish in this sense between idioms of decoding and encoding.

So here is one of the central puzzles around the concept of linguistic competence. What is meant by idiomatic language? Why is it that some language sounds natural, whereas other language, which is fully grammatical, 'doesn't sound quite right'? Speakers have strong intuitions about such characteristics of language use, but the basis for these feelings – about what is natural, native-like, authentic, typical and representative – is not well understood.

Recognition of the importance of phraseology has grown fast. Searle (1975: 68ff) discusses 'standard' or 'conventional' uses of certain linguistic forms to perform directives, and argues (pp. 77–8) that there is a conversational maxim: 'Speak idiomatically unless there is some special reason not to.' He argues that 'in order to be a plausible candidate for use as an indirect speech act, a sentence has to be idiomatic', and that 'within the class of idiomatic sentences, some forms tend to become entrenched as conventional devices for indirect speech acts'. For Searle, this is a side argument, which he does not fully develop. However, since the mid-1980s, a growing amount of work, especially in corpus-based lexicography and in language teaching, has emphasized the pervasive occurrence of phrase-like units of idiomatic language use. In a now frequently cited article, Pawley and Syder (1983) claimed – plausibly, though not based on empirical data – that native speakers know 'hundreds of thousands' of multi-word units.

Work in phraseology (see section 3.11) has revealed many frequently recurring collocations and phrase-like units. The term '(semi-) fixed phrases' is often used, but is misleading. The units are rarely invariant, and often not even continuous. They are idiomatic, but only rarely idioms; they have typical components, but are highly variable, with probabilistic relations between the components; they are typically realized by a sequence of several word-forms, but their boundaries do not correspond systematically to syntactic units; and indeed they do not fit into traditional concepts of either lexis or syntax. There is no standard term for these variable phrasal units. Fillmore et al. (1988) propose that the traditional term 'constructions' is appropriate. Sinclair (1996) talks of 'extended units of meaning', but proposes also (1998) that another traditional term 'lexical items' could be used.

So, the occurrence of extended lexical units is now well documented, and it is increasingly argued that collocation is a fundamental organizing principle of language in use. Some general characteristics of such units have been described, but we still lack a systematic account of how they can be identified and modelled. I will show, from a sample of English vocabulary, that all the most frequent words have strong phraseological tendencies. That is, they have a strong tendency to collocate with restricted sets of words. I will present evidence on both the strength of attraction between words and on the nature of such lexical relations.

3.2 Communicative Competence

Phrasal units play an important role in speaking fluently and idiomatically, and Hymes's (1972) concept of communicative competence shows how they can be located within a general model of language use. Hymes (1972, and see also 1992) proposes a way of avoiding the over-simplified polarization made by Chomsky (1965) between competence and performance. He discusses not only whether (1) a sentence is formally possible (= grammatical), but distinguishes further whether an utterance is (2) psycholinguistically feasible or (3) sociolinguistically appropriate. In addition, not all possibilities are actually realized, and Hymes proposes a further distinction between the possible and the actual: (4) what actually, in reality, with high probability, is said or written. This four-way distinction is shown in table 3.1.

Chomsky (1986) has reformulated the competence–performance distinction in terms of I-language (internal) and E-language (external), and

Table 3.1 Aspects of communicative competence (based on discussion in Hymes 1972)

I-language, language as knowledge:
  what can be said, the creative possibilities of the system

1 formally possible (grammatical)
2 psycholinguistically realizable (feasible)

E-language, language as social behaviour:
  what is frequently said, the routine realization of the system

3 sociolinguistically appropriate (appropriate)
4 actually said or written (performed)

Widdowson (1991) points out implications of these distinctions for corpus linguistics. I-language is concerned with two of Hymes's characteristics of linguistic competence: what is possible and/or psycholinguistically feasible. This is a first-person, participant perspective: I-language is knowledge, and a matter of individual psychology. E-language is concerned with the other and/or actually performed, and therefore with the realization of the system in social interaction. This is a third-person, observer perspective: E-language is behaviour, a matter of social actions and events. And whilst a corpus can be a collection of the linguistic behaviour of an individual (such as the works of Shakespeare), it is usually a sample of the linguistic behaviour of a community of speakers.

Partington (1998: 18) notes that the 'formally possible' dimension refers to context-free aspects of language, whereas the other three dimensions are context-bound: that is, constrained by other knowledge systems. He also proposes that the four dimensions can be interpreted as increasingly powerful refining mechanisms on what is actually said or written. The grammar specifies what could potentially occur, but this is constrained by what is psychologically feasible, sociolinguistically appropriate, and actually frequent in the discourse community.

Whereas much (Chomskyan) linguistics has been concerned with what speakers can say, corpus linguistics is also necessarily concerned with what speakers do say. But note the *also*. It is misleading to see only frequency of actual occurrence (see chapter 1.7.3). Frequency becomes interesting when it is interpreted as typicality, and speakers' communicative competence includes tacit knowledge of behavioural norms. In an article which updates his 1972 work, Hymes (1992: 52) emphasizes the importance of Pawley and Syder's (1983) work.

3.3 Corpus Methods: Observing Patterns

Possibilities for lexical studies have developed very rapidly since the late 1980s, as a result of the availability of large computer-readable corpora: collections of texts comprising samples of many different text-types. Computer-assisted methods for storing and processing corpora of hundreds of millions of running words have led to a 'flourishing renaissance of empiricism' in linguistics (Church and Mercer 1994), and work with corpora has led to major advances in the practice of lexicography and in the theory of lexico-grammar.

The basic tool is the concordance (or KWIC index: Key Word in Context). This is a simple use of technology: search, find, display. The computer can rapidly search large amounts of data for a word, and print out all occurrences in the centre of the screen or page within a limited span, which is usually either an arbitrary number of characters or words in a single line, or within sentence or paragraph boundaries. The evidence is then in a convenient form to be inspected for patterns of co-occurrence. In the simplest case, this provides many naturally occurring examples, which are often inaccessible to introspection. Concordances are not an invention of computational linguistics, and, for culturally important books – traditionally, the Bible and Shakespeare – they have existed for hundreds of years, and have been used as a way of studying words or phrases in context. They have long given a concrete interpretation to the slogan that meaning is use in context (more accurately co-text). (See chapter 1, above.)

Large corpora, which contain a wide range of texts and text-types, can provide empirical evidence on the frequency of collocations. Yet, even with concordances, unaided human observation may still be of limited use in seeing significant linguistic patterns. Further computer assistance is necessary to allow the human linguist to see the wood for the trees. Therefore, a concordance is often just the first stage in an analysis. The computer can manipulate the concordance lines themselves in many ways: sorting them alphabetically to left or right often makes it much easier for the human being to spot other patterns. With only a few hundred concordance lines, patterns can then often be identified by eye, but with common words, a large corpus might produce tens of thousand of concordance lines. So, these lines become the input to further programs, which search for the most frequent co-occurrences in a given span.

In other words, progress in corpus linguistics comes not directly from the huge raw corpora which are available, but because corpora can be pre-processed, and turned from raw data into a data-base (such as Cobuild 1995b). In the remainder of this chapter and in the next, I will discuss: some findings which are possible with such a data-base; further details of the raw data and of the data-base; the structure of extended lexical units, including the strength and nature of the relations within such units; a more formal model of the units; and some implications for linguistic description.

3.4 Terminology

It is an odd failing of linguistics that it has no convincing descriptive theory of units of meaning. It has, for example, no widely accepted methods of segmenting spoken or written discourse into semantic units. Advances in a theory of units of meaning have come largely from practical activities (such as dictionary making and language teaching) rather than from theoretical linguistics. The descriptive and theoretical questions have been sharpened by

Sinclair (1996), who argues for 'extended units of meaning'. He puts forward the hypothesis that units of meaning are 'largely phrasal', that only a few words are selected independently of other words, and that 'the idea of a word carrying meaning on its own [can] be relegated to the margins of linguistic interest, in the enumeration of flora and fauna for example' (p. 82).

There are two closely related key ideas. First, meaning is typically dispersed over several word-forms which habitually co-occur in text. Second, these co-occurring word-forms 'share' semantic features. There is unfortunately no standard terminology, and different writers have talked of semantic-feature 'sharing', 'copying', 'bleaching' and 'elimination'. Alternatively, words are said to be 'co-selected', such that words in the collocation are 'delexicalized' (Sinclair 1991: 113; Bublitz 1996). For example, in a phrase such as *physical assault*, the adjective adds little to the meaning of the noun, but merely emphasizes or focuses on an expected feature: the default interpretation of an *assault* is that it is *physical*. (In a phrase such as *intellectual assault*, the adjective would have its own independent meaning.) The same phenomenon (see chapter 2.5 above) can be seen in common collocations such as

- added bonus, advance warning, completely forgot, full circle, general consensus, heavy load

In chapter 2, I discussed this idea and introduced other concepts, which I can briefly summarize here. Given the ambiguity of the term 'word', we need to distinguish between word-form and lemma (shown in upper case). I will talk of collocates (word-form or lemma) which co-occur with a node word within a span (e.g. of 4 : 4, four words to left and right of the node). These terms (see also Sinclair 1991: 169ff) provide the concepts we need for identifying and describing extended lexical units of meaning. I will use 'phrase' as a neutral, non-technical term, to mean just a string of words, of indeterminate length. The typical collocates of a node can be given as sets of items in diamond brackets, with position relative to node marked if relevant, for example:

- CONFORM <standard(s), pressure(s), rules...>
- seeking <asylum, help, advice, support...>

Although sets of collocates are usually open-ended, and the relations probabilistic, it is nevertheless possible to discover the typical collocates of a node. Different statistical measures of typicality can be combined to filter out idiosyncratic collocates (Stubbs 1995a). We can therefore use the following notation to indicate raw frequencies of occurrence of node and collocates, or the percentage of occurrences of the node in which a given collocate co-occurs. For example, the lemma COMMIT has a strong tendency to co-occur with one of a small set of semantically related words, such as

- adultery, atrocities, hara-kiri, offence, sin

Out of over 3,000 occurrences of the word-form *commit* in the 200-million-word corpus, 15 per cent co-occur with the single word *suicide*, and nearly 30 per cent co-occur with one of only three lemmas. We can show this as:

- commit 3,179 <suicide 15%, crime(s) 10%, murder 4%> 29%

There are similar patterns with other forms of the lemma COMMIT. One type of collocational pattern, then, is a strong probabilistic syntagmatic relation between a word and a small set of words, which themselves share a semantic feature. With COMMIT, the unit is the combination of the lemma, plus a noun phrase containing an abstract noun, which can in turn be characterized by a semantic descriptor such as "crimes and/or behaviour which is socially disapproved of".

I will often give raw figures for sample lexical items, since it is important to keep in mind just how many attested collocations (typically dozens or hundreds) the analysis is based on, and also to give readers enough data to allow them to re-interpret examples if necessary. I will list collocates in descending order of frequency. However, absolute (and even relative) frequencies may depend on the text selection in the corpus (see below), and no great weight should be attached to small percentage differences. Frequency figures are only part of the surface evidence for deeper patterns of tendency and typicality.

Sinclair (1991: 111–12; 1996) proposes four types of co-occurrence relations in extended lexico-semantic units.

(1) A collocation is a node–collocate pair: this is a purely lexical relation, non-directional and probabilistic, which ignores any syntactic relation between the words. For example:

- applause 2,207 <loud, thunderous, rapturous, spontaneous, polite, warm, enthusiastic> 13%

These node–collocate pairs occur as both *ADJ–N* (*thunderous applause*) and *the N–BE–ADJ* (*the applause had been thunderous*). The term *collocation* makes no claims about syntax. However, an important principle of corpus linguistics is that descriptions are sensitive to frequency of occurrence. Typically, a more delicate description will reveal lexico-syntactic relations: in this case, the *ADJ–N* pattern is much more frequent. In other words, there is often a blend of collocation and colligation.

(2) Colligation is the relation between a pair of grammatical categories or, in a slightly wider sense, a pairing of lexis and grammar. For example, the word-form *cases* frequently co-occurs with the grammatical category of quantifier, in phrases such as *in some cases, in many cases*.

- cases <some, many, most, more, both, several>

(See G. Francis 1993: 141, for an excellent discussion of the characteristic blend of collocation and colligation in phraseological units.)

(3) Semantic preference is the relation, not between individual words, but between a lemma or word-form and a set of semantically related words, and often it is not difficult to find a semantic label for the set: see COMMIT above. Another example is the word-form *large*, which often co-occurs with words for "quantities and sizes":

- large 56,145 <N+1: number(s), scale, part, amounts, quantities, area(s)> 20%

In the 200-million-word corpus, at least 25 per cent of the 56,000 occurrences of *large* collocated with words for quantities and sizes: this is the typical, central use of the word. It would be possible to provide an (almost?) definitive list of the words in this lexical field in English: certainly, the most frequent 20 or so would account for most cases:

(4) A discourse prosody is a feature which extends over more than one unit in a linear string. For example, the lemma CAUSE occurs overwhelmingly often with words for unpleasant events (see chapter 2.9.2), whereas PROVIDE occurs with words denoting things which are desirable or necessary. Data on the top few collocates from 200 million words are:

- cause 25,407 <problems, death, damage, concern, trouble, cancer, disease> 16%
- provide 28,278 <information, service(s), support, help, money, protection, food, care> 16%

Discourse prosodies express speaker attitude. If you say that something is *provided*, then this implies that you approve of it. Since they are evaluative, prosodies often express the speaker's reason for making the utterance, and therefore identify functional discourse units.

Studies which use corpus data to investigate this phenomenon have been published only since the early 1990s, and terminology is still variable. Several studies use the term 'semantic prosodies' (Louw 1993; Sinclair 1996). 'Pragmatic prosodies' might be a better term, since this would maintain a standard distinction between aspects of meaning which are independent of speakers (semantics) and aspects which concern speaker attitude (pragmatics). I will here prefer the term 'discourse prosodies', both in order to maintain the relation to speakers and hearers, but also to emphasize their function in creating discourse coherence: see chapter 5. (Tognini-Bonelli 1996: 193, 209, also uses the term 'discourse prosody' for these reasons.)

The distinction between semantic preference and discourse prosody is not entirely clear-cut. It is partly a question of how open-ended the list of collocates is: it might be possible to list all words in English for quantities and sizes, but not for "unpleasant things". It is also partly a question of semantics versus pragmatics. In addition, the preference–prosody distinction may depend on how delicate the analysis is. For example, Klotz (1997) confirms the negative discourse prosody on CAUSE as a verb, but points out further restrictions. In a single-object construction, the noun can be an illness: *smoking causes cancer*. But in a double-object construction, an illness is not possible **smoking caused him cancer*. In two-place predicates, frequent exponents are nouns for feelings: *would have caused you agony, causes them inconvenience*. In other words, the lemma CAUSE has a strong negative prosody, but if we take syntax into account, then there are relations of semantic preference between the verb CAUSE and sets of abstract nouns, such as "illnesses" and "personal feelings".

These four relations will be developed in chapter 4 into a model of the structure of extended lexical units.

3.5 Corpus, Concordance, Data-base

Different kinds of raw and processed data can be used in such studies. A raw corpus is often input to a concordance program, whose output – the concordance lines – then becomes the input to a statistical analysis, which lists typical collocations.

A corpus is the first-order data. Since a raw corpus of any realistic size is far too large for the human analyst to be able to observe and remember significant patterns, it is usually the input to programs which can produce concordance lines and calculate word frequencies. These are second-order data, and can be a great practical help in seeing patterns. However, beyond a few hundred concordance lines at most, the amount of data is again beyond the capacity of unaided observation and memory. So these data can be input to further programs, which can help in identifying significant patterns, by using statistical methods or different displays (such as positional frequency tables: see chapter 4). These programs produce third-order data. Ideally, these data are further organized into systematic sets of statistics which give comprehensive coverage of a well-defined subset of the language in a convenient form, such as the most typical collocates for the most frequent word-forms in English, plus associated sample concordance lines.

3.6 The Cobuild Collocations Data-base on CD-ROM

3.6.1 *The corpus*

The raw first-order data for the Cobuild (1995b) collocations CD-ROM consisted of a corpus of 200 million running words of general English: about 70 per cent British, 25 per cent American, and 5 per cent other native varieties. About 65 per cent of the text samples are from the mass media, written and spoken: newspapers and magazines, but also radio (especially BBC World Service). About 7 per cent is transcribed spoken language: over half of this is spontaneous conversation, the rest is from scripted radio broadcasts. The corpus did not contain highly technical and scientific books and articles, though there is a lot of specialized vocabulary in relatively popular academic books and the like.

Possible bias errors due to the composition of any corpus should be borne in mind. For example, the frequent collocates of *commit* <*suicide, crime(s), murder*> may be partly due to the frequency of crime reporting in the mass media. The influence of topics in the (partly British) national press is seen in the frequency of head-words and of their top collocates, such as the following head-words beginning with *c*, here shown with the absolute frequency of the head-word and the phrase as a percentage of this frequency:

- ethnic *cleansing* (2,071, 45 %); *cluster* bombs (1,614, 7 %); issued a *communique* (1,060, 15 %); *composite* trading (1,893, 45 %); *contempt* of court (2,118, 13 %); National *Curriculum* (4,116, 35 %)

Such collocations can provide limited information on key phrases and topics of interest to the press, but they do also indicate a topical bias in the corpus. This bias is unlikely to affect the general principles discussed below, but it certainly affects the absolute frequency of occurrence of individual words and of their most frequent collocates.

Firth (1957: 12–13) pointed out long ago that different collocations are found in different text-types, and Biber (1993a, 1993b) argues that much work still underestimates the extent of register differences in collocational behaviour. An extreme example occurs in a study of an 8-million-word corpus of Associated Press news-wire stories, mainly about the stock market. The word *food* was high in frequency, but *eat* was not among its collocates, since 'food is not eaten at Wall Street but rather traded, sold, offered, bought, etc.' (Smadja 1993: 169).

Occasionally, a single word-form, such as *seeks*, is highly frequent in a restricted text-type (chapters 1.7.4 and 2.2.1, above). Other examples are *chopped* and *grated*, which are very frequent in recipes (see chapter 4.4.2, below), but some influences of text-type on vocabulary are less obvious. For example, the data-base gives as the top 20 collocates of *certain*, mainly collocates with the "not very much" meaning (*a certain amount, to a certain extent*), or with the "indefinite reference" meaning (*certain people, in certain areas*). Only two of the collocates have the "certainly true" meaning (*seems certain, know for certain*). Biber (1993a, 1993b) shows that these distinct uses occur with quite different percentages in different genres. The use of a large undifferentiated corpus has in this case averaged away these differences, and made it look as though one meaning of *certain* is much more prevalent than the other. Biber (1993a:186) claims that

> for many words, there is no general pattern of use that holds across the whole language; rather, different word senses and collocational patterns are strongly preferred in different registers.

It is frequently argued that generalizations may conceal systematic patterns, because they average away differences. However, that is the whole point of averages. It depends how delicate you want the description to be. In addition, just how many words are involved in sharply different collocations in different text-types is not known.

In any case, language in the mass-media is itself highly influential, newspapers are the most widely read long texts, and collocations from this source are therefore important. A striking example was provided by the British prime minister Tony Blair on the day after the death of Princess Diana in 1997. He used, on television, the phrase *The People's Princess*, which fits into the same pattern as other phrases such as *People's Palace*, and which was immediately known around the world and endlessly repeated. However, there is no well-developed theory of corpus construction which takes into account the potential impact of the language used. W. N. Francis (1979) proposed the term 'reception index' for the number of times an utterance is heard or read: perhaps only 'one' for an utterance elicited by a linguist from an informant, but '50 million' for a commentary at a major sports event. A measure of influence might, in principle, be based on library lending statistics, best-seller lists, or exam lists (of the classics which are read year after year for English literature exams round the world), though it is difficult to see how such measures could be made more than rough and ready.

3.6.2 The data-base

It is worth emphasizing just how large the Cobuild (1995b) data-base is. For 10,000 head-words, it lists the up-to-20 most frequent collocates, within a span of 4 : 4. For each collocate, it gives a random sample of 20 concordance lines of 80 characters (usually 6 or 7 words to left and right), plus a slightly expanded context, of 15 words or so to left and right, with a broad indication of genre, e.g. 'British newspapers'. This is a total of 10,000 times 20 times 20 (= 4 million) concordance lines.

(Calculated slightly differently: the four million concordance lines amount to $4 \times 30 = 120$ million words of co-text, which is sampled around the 10,000 head words in their most frequent uses. Not all nodes have 20 collocates, since a collocation must occur at least 15 times in the corpus to be recorded. Concordance lines are selected at random, which leads to some repetition, though even if these figures are reduced by something over 10 per cent, the data-base still amounts to 100 million words.)

The 10,000 head-words are unlemmatized word-forms. This is essential, not only because different forms of a lemma may have quite different collocates, but also because they usually also have very different frequencies of occurrence. For example, in the 200-million-word corpus, forms of EDUCATE occur as follows: *education* (33,052) occurs about 1,000 times more frequently than *educates*, about 50 times more frequently than *educating*, and about 25 times more frequently than *educate*. This means, however, that, for many lemmas, only some word-forms are frequent enough to appear in the list of head-words: the data-base has findings for *education* 33, 052, and *educated* 3, 981, but forms of the verb in *-e*, *-es*, *-ing* were not frequent enough to be listed. (This places some restrictions on calculations possible with the data-base: see appendix 2 to this chapter, section 3.10.)

The absolute frequency of word-forms in the head-words list varies from a few words around 700 (e.g. *allergies, deficiencies, handkerchief, garnish*), up to relatively few words over 50,000 (e.g. *believe, car, change, fact*), and a few words over 100,000 (e.g. *before, end, home*). That is, the least frequent words in the data-base occur around four times per million running words. The vast majority of words occur between 1,000 and 10,000 times in the corpus. These figures correspond to data cited by Hayes (1988), who studied the 10,000 most frequent word-forms in a reference corpus of American English. The least frequent words amongst the 10,000 occurred three times or more per million running words.

The 10,000 word-forms probably represent around 5,000 lemmas. Some lemmas have only one form (e.g. *amid*); sometimes both singular and plural of nouns occur in the head-word list (e.g. *eye*, *eyes*), but sometimes only the singular is frequent enough to occur (e.g. *abbey*); and similarly for parts of verbs (as with EDUCATE above). So a rough estimate is that the head-word list contains twice as many word-forms as lemmas. Lists of core vocabulary usually contain 2,000 to 3,000 lemmas (Stubbs 1986), so the list of headwords certainly contains those word-forms which are the most frequent in the core vocabulary of English. The data-base gives information on the central core of the vocabulary, and, as I will show, all the words in this core show strong phraseological tendencies.

Appendix 2 to this chapter (section 3.10) contains further notes on some limitations of the data-base.

3.6.3 Precision and recall

Precision and recall are two measures conventionally used in the information retrieval literature (Ball 1994; Clear 1996). The precision is high if a large percentage of what is retrieved is relevant. Precision is easy to check, at least roughly, since irrelevant cases are observable, and the Cobuild data-base scores high on this measure.

The recall is high if a high percentage of relevant cases is found. This is much more difficult to check, since you cannot observe what has not been found. It may be that the data-base omits collocations which are common, but only in text-types unrepresented in the corpus (due to its topical bias). In other words, the success of recall is dependent on the representativeness of the corpus. Alternatively, a purely formal analysis may miss semantic patterns. For example, the top 20 collocates of *somewhat* show that the word is used in comparisons, often in concessive contexts:

- somewhat 8,015 <more, different, less, also, though, still, although, seems, similar, since, better, seemed, become, feel, higher, view, seem, later, however, perhaps>

However, the concordance lines show a different pattern. They contain phrases such as:

- somewhat cruelly; somewhat more awkward and conspicuous; somewhat negatively; somewhat on the defensive

On its own, the collocates list contains no evidence of a discourse prosody, since a shared semantic feature, especially a very general one such as "unpleasant", can be lexicalized in many ways (De Beaugrande 1996: 516). This will not be picked up in a list of the most frequent word-forms, but the concordance lines make the pattern obvious to a human analyst. The important principle is that semantic and pragmatic relations do not always show up as simple formal relations, and third-order data must constantly be checked against second- and first-order data.

3.7 Data for Semantics and Pragmatics

In this book I mainly emphasize the value of corpus data for the study of meaning. I should therefore stress that I do not entirely reject introspective data, and I frequently appeal to native-speaker intuition. In many areas of semantics and pragmatics, intuitions are strong and stable, across all native speakers, whether linguistically naive or trained, and must be given the status of data (Seuren 1998: 386). Katz (1981: 121) puts it like this:

> [I]t is easy to produce cases in semantics that are as clear as the clearest in syntax. For example, it is clear that *crowd* and *mob* are semantically similar in having senses that express a group action, that both are antonymous with *solo* in this respect, that **naked nude** is redundant, and that *Jones murdered Smith* analytically entails *Jones killed Smith*.

Katz gives examples of synonymy, antonymy and logical entailment (hyponymy). Thus, any native speaker knows that a *nightmare* is a frightening dream. We could check this in a dictionary, which records the intuitions of highly trained lexicographers (and other data), but it is unnecessary to demand corpus evidence of all lexical relations.

However, there are many cases in the literature where the intuitions of native speakers are less certain, or where intuitions are demonstrably unreliable or just missing altogether. A famous case (Chomsky 1957: 100–1) where native speakers have problems, but may be persuaded to agree, after some training, is this:

[1]   Everyone in the room knows at least two languages.
[2]   At least two languages are known by everyone in the room.

The consensus is usually that both sentences are ambiguous, but that the preferred interpretation for [1] is that "everyone speaks two languages but not necessarily the same two", whereas the 'normal interpretation' (Chomsky 1957: 101) for [2] is that "there are two languages (say French and German) which are spoken by everyone, though individuals may also speak other languages". However, it is difficult to arrive at a clear consensus in such cases.

In other areas again, native-speaker judgements are unreliable or restricted. Native speakers have strong and reliable intuitions that some words are more frequent than others: there is not much doubt that *luck* is more frequent than *lute*. But native speakers are unreliable in judging the most frequent uses of frequent words, for example that TAKE is most frequent in its delexicalized uses in phrases such as *take place* and *take a photograph*. Similarly, many judgements about connotations are perfectly reliable (e.g. neutral *crowd* versus pejorative *mob*). However, my intuitions tell me that *friends* is neutral, whereas *cronies* is distinctly pejorative and insulting. Yet, this is confirmed by the entries only in some dictionaries (e.g. OALD 1995), whereas other dictionaries (e.g. Cobuild 1995a) record it as informal but not as pejorative.

It may also be that intuitions about the core meaning of a word are reliable, but that intuitions about its potential use in different situations are not. Lyons (1987: 169–70) gives the example of BACHELOR. Speakers of English will agree on the denotation (a bachelor is an "unmarried man"), but they disagree (I have tested this in elicitation experiments) about whether the word can appropriately be used to refer to cases such as: a monk; a sixteen-year-old male; a widower; a man of ninety years who has never married.

The major advantage of using large corpora for the study of meaning is that they contain a vast amount of data of a kind which was previously not available. However, there is no point in being purist about data. On the contrary, it is essential to compare findings from different independent corpora (since all corpora have gaps and biases), and to cross-check corpus findings with data from different sources.

3.8 Summary and Implications

I have now presented the concepts which are needed for the case study in the next chapter:

word-form and lemma
corpus and concordance
node, collocate and span
collocation and colligation
semantic preference and discourse prosody
extended lexical unit and delexicalization

first-, second- and third-order data

Corpus studies show that what typically occurs in language use is only a small percentage of what seems possible within the language system. A large amount of language use consists of words occurring in conventional combinations. Such collocations are not an idiosyncratic and peripheral phenomenon, but a central characteristic of language in use. Native speakers' unconscious knowledge of collocations is an essential component of their idiomatic and fluent language use and an important part of their communicative competence.

3.9 Appendix 1: Measures of Statistical Significance

For two main reasons, I present no figures on the statistical significance of the strength of node–collocate attraction.

First, the classic statistical tests assume populations in which variables are randomly distributed: but this assumption does not hold for natural language texts. If we toss a coin, then we will sometimes get a sequence of several heads in a row, but, on average and approximately, it will come down heads in 50 per cent of cases, and tails in 50 per cent. A typical text in English will contain many instances of the word *the*, spread throughout the text, and followed in almost all cases by nouns. We will never find a sequence of several in a row, and there is no chance at all that they will all be clustered together at the beginning of the text.

Second, for most of the cases which I discuss, the levels of co-occurrence are so far above what one might expect by chance, that citing a probability level is rather pointless. Take this illustrative case, with simplified, but realistic figures. Suppose the absolute frequencies of node and top collocate in the 200-million-word corpus are each 2,000, and that they co-occur 200 times:

- node 2,000 <collocate 10 %>

The node and collocate each occur 2,000 times in 200 million running words: at a random point in the corpus, the chance of either one being the next word is one in 100,000 (= 200 million/2,000).

So, the chance of the collocate being the word immediately after the node is one in 100,000. In the span of 4 : 4 around the node, the chance is 8 in 100,000. The node occurs 2,000 times, therefore the collocate could be *expected* to occur 0.16 (= 2,000 × 8/100,000) times in its environment. That is, there is less than one chance in five of seeing the collocation at all in a corpus of 200 million words. But the collocate is *observed* to occur 200 times in the span around the node. This is 1,250 (= 200/0.16) times more frequently than expected by chance.

Alternatively we calculate things as follows. The chance of both node and collocate occurring together at some random point is the product of their individual probabilities of occurrence (1/100,000 × 1/100,000): one in 10,000 million. Across the whole corpus, they could be expected to co-occur 0.02 times (= 200 million × 1/100,000 million). This assumes adjacent co-occurrence. If we calculate co-occurrence in a span of 4 : 4, then they could be expected to co-occur 0.16 times (= 8 × 0.02). But they are observed to co-occur 200 times: this is 1,250 times more frequently than expected by chance.

If node and collocate co-occur in only 1 per cent of cases, this rate of co-occurrence is still 125 times more frequent than expected by chance. A calculation with figures such as *node* 2,000 <collocate 10 %>, where the absolute frequency of the collocate is 20,000, also gives a rate of 125 times more frequent than expected by chance.

A real example of a node–collocate pair with comparable figures to this last case is:

- heated 2,470, debate 17,441; heated <debate 10 %>

Given the non-random distribution of ADJ–N pairs in running text, their co-occurrence becomes more likely than one in 125. But out of 40 random examples of the collocation, most (over 75 per cent) were in the phrase *heated debate*, a few (20 %) were in a longer phrase such as *a very heated, extremely emotional debate*, and only one had the sequence N–BE–ADJ (*the debate has been heated*): the central pattern is clear. There is no doubt that *heated debate* is a phrasal unit. Other collocates of *heated* indicate related phrases such as *heated discussion*, *heated argument* and *heated exchange*. Although there are obviously other phrases such as *pre-heated oven*, *heated swimming pool* and *centrally heated room*, sophisticated statistics are not required to corroborate obvious patterns such as

- heated <debate, discussion, argument(s), exchanges (s)> 20 %

For further discussion of such calculations, see Sinclair (1991: 69–70) and Barnbrook (1996: 92ff).

The collocates of *heated* suggest one further reason why measures of statistical significance may be of limited use. It is evident to the human analyst (though not to the computer) that the collocates of *heated* are semantically related. Consider a similar case. A small corpus produced these findings:

- distinctly <N + 1: cagey, cool, dated, dour, downbeat, iffy, inferior, meaner, muted, strange, thin, unimpressed, unwell>

No other collocates occurred at N + 1. But these collocates occurred only once each, and therefore no statistical test can be used to conclude anything about the likelihood of co-occurrence between node and collocates. A single occurrence could be due to chance. Yet, to the human analyst, there is an obvious pattern: all the collocates seem disapproving. Whatever quantitative findings or statistics are produced by the computer, they must still be interpreted by the human analyst.

3.10 Appendix 2: Further Notes on the Data-base

It is often assumed that frequency lists of the most common words in the language do not differ much between corpora. However, beyond the few hundred or so most frequent words, there are large differences in word frequency, since this depends on the topic of the texts sampled. Indeed, Moon (1997) shows that not even the top five words correspond in large corpora of spoken and written English. In a mixed spoken and written corpus, and in a spoken corpus, the top five words were, respectively

- the, of, to, a, and
- the, I, and, you, it

On average, conversational English uses a much smaller lexicon than written English. And given the mass media bias in the 200-million-word corpus, the data-base contains head-words which one would not necessarily expect in a basic word list. An example is *communique*, see above, which the Cobuild (1995b) dictionary – based on a related corpus – gives in the frequency band, for lemmas, between 6,600 and 14,700.

For each head-word (node), the software gives its frequency of occurrence in the corpus, and the top 20 collocates, with joint node–collocate frequency. These co-occurrence statistics provide an estimate of the strength of node–collocate attraction: whether a node strongly attracts a few individual words, or more weakly attracts a wider scatter of words. The handbook to Cobuild (1995b) talks of 'statistically significant' collocations, but collocates are listed simply in descending raw frequency of co-occurrence, with no adjustment made for absolute frequency of the collocates. A calculation which can be used to make this adjustment is the t-score (Stubbs 1995a).

More accurately, only collocates which co-occur more than 15 times with the head-word are given. For example, the head-word *hitherto* occurs 1,221 times; the only collocate given is *unknown* with 65 co-occurrences, in phrases such as *hitherto unknown*, *hitherto totally unknown*, and *hitherto virtually unknown*. This does not mean that it does not co-occur with other words: it clearly does, in 1,221 minus 65 times (= 95 per cent of cases). It means that there is one recurring but variable phrase, plus a wide scatter of other collocates, none of which are individually frequent. A check on raw corpus data shows several things. First, there are other roughly synonymous phrases, such as *hitherto inaccessible* and *hitherto unparalleled*. Second, many phrases have an -*ed*-form at N − 1 or N + 1 (e.g. *recognized hitherto* and *hitherto confined*). Third, the situation 'hitherto' is often reported as lacking something, as in examples such as

- which had not been recognized hitherto; hitherto barely touched by it; something she had hitherto only dreamed of

There is a restriction on the statistics. Unless a collocate happens also to occur as a head-word, the data-base does not give its absolute frequency. For example, the top collocate of *bride* is *groom*, but *groom* is not frequent enough to occur as a head-word, so we do not have its absolute frequency of occurrence. We have the statistic *bride* <*groom* 10 %>, but cannot construct the reverse statistic, and are left merely suspecting that, since *groom* is not frequent, it often co-occurs with *bride*. This seems to be correct. In a 50-million-word corpus, the word-form *bride* ($n = 737$) was over twice as frequent as (*bride-*) *groom* (348). The statistics of co-occurrence were: *bride* (*bride-*) *groom* 13 %> and <(*bride-*) *groom* <*bride* 27 %>.

Since we are dealing with around 5,000 relatively common lemmas, independent smaller corpora can be used in this way, as further evidence on individual words. This is an important general aspect of the methods. Findings from one corpus lead to predictions which can be checked − corroborated or refuted − on independent data. Approaches to language based on introspective data often run into problems of disagreement between linguists' intuitions. Work with corpora often leads to high levels of corroboration and agreement.

Around 100 high-frequency (grammatical or functional) words are not included in the head-word list. (The handbook does not specify exactly which words are in the stop-list.) There is little point in giving the 20 most frequent collocates of *the* or *to*. These stop-words are also omitted from the main collocates lists, to prevent these lists being swamped by highly frequent words. For example, base forms of verbs would almost inevitably co-occur with *to*. However, where stop-words are frequent collocates, they are separately listed (without concordance lines), and this gives evidence of frequent grammatical constructions in which the node appears. For example, the top collocates of *cases* are

- cases 22, 744 <some 14 %, many 8 %, most 6 %, such 4 %, other, number, both, few, several>

The most common stop-word is *in* (55 %), and the concordance lines confirm that the most frequent use is in phrases such as *in some cases, in many cases, in several (of the) cases*, although there are obviously other uses (e.g. *court cases*).

The data-base provides information on the probability of node–collocate pairs, but no direct information on collocations of three or more word-forms. For example, the head-word *holocaust* occurs 1,187 times; only two collocates, *nuclear* 35 and *world* 32, are given. This identifies the phrase *nuclear holocaust*. But collocations with *world* are partly due to collocations not with the word, but with the phrase *World War II*, which therefore relates to the meaning "millions of Jews killed by the Nazis".

Although longer phrases cannot be automatically retrieved, they may be immediately recognizable to native-speaker intuition. For example, the top collocates for *agent* include:

- agent 8,206 <estate, travel, secret, literary>

It is intuitively obvious that these collocates are unlikely to collocate with each other, since there are separate fixed phrases, such as *estate agent* and *travel agent*. However, the top collocates for *bodily* are:

- bodily 1,303 <harm 38 %, grievous 19 %, causing 14 %>

The second two words do not collocate directly with *bodily*, but with the phrase *bodily harm*, due to their occurrence in the legal phrase *(causing) grievous bodily harm*. In general, words often co-occur not just in collocations between pairs of individual words, but between words and multi-word phrases. (Collocations around the phrase *naked eye* are analysed by Sinclair 1996; see chapter 5.6.1.) The methods discussed here can deal with these more complex collocational phenomena to only a restricted extent: see chapter 9.

3.11 Background and Further Reading

For useful introductions to corpus methods in general, with good examples of collocational analysis, see Biber et al. (1998), and Partington (1998).

There is a very large literature on phraseology and collocations, and major bibliographies are available on the world-wide web: do a search for the words 'phraseology' and 'collocations'. Frequently cited articles include Bolinger (1976) and Pawley and Syder (1983). Descriptive work in applied areas has been done by Sinclair (1991) and others in lexicography, and by Willis (1990) and Nattinger and De Carrico (1992) in second-language learning. Weinert (1995), Skehan (1998: 29–42) and Howarth (1998) review the role of formulaic language in second-language acquisition. Moon (1998) is a substantial corpus-based study. Other work which contains many examples of phraseological units includes G. Francis (1993), Louw (1993), Stubbs (1995a, 1995b), Sinclair (1996) and Partington (1998). Cowie (1994) and Wray and Perkins (2000) provide good reviews.

The methods of investigating collocations in this chapter and the next use the simplest possible techniques: a constant span of 4 : 4, raw frequency of collocations, and unlemmatized data. For discussion of more sophisticated statistical methods for identifying the strength of attraction between node and collocates, see Church and Hanks (1990), Church et al. (1991), Clear (1993), Stubbs (1995a) and Barnbrook (1996). For discussion of software which can take into account the effect of different span sizes, different ways of calculating collocational attraction, and lemmatized data, see Sinclair et al. (1998) and Mason (1999).

3.12   Topics for Further Study

(1)   In section 3.7, I discussed the disagreement which is typically found about the appropriate uses of the word BACHELOR. Design and carry out a small experiment to test how much agreement there is on the meaning of the word ORPHAN. The prototypical denotation seems clear, "a child whose parents are dead", but the boundaries are fuzzy, and the cases to which the word can apply are not so clear. What are its core meanings? Someone who has lost both parents? Only one parent? Are the parents dead? Or just missing? Can only children be orphans? Or also older people? How old?

(2)   Design and carry out a small study to test how accurate or inaccurate native speakers' intuitions are about the use of common words. For example, compare speakers' introspective judgements and corpus data for the words: *ago*, *shoulder* and *coast*. Ask informants to give you examples of how the words are typically used, and compare their answers with a few dozen examples of usage from large corpora.

You will probably find that their intuitions about *ago* are accurate, but incomplete. You may find that their intuitions about the typical uses of the other two words correspond much less closely to attested data. Assuming that there is a mixture of such agreement and disagreement, what does this tell you about speakers' linguistic competence?

As further sources of data, you could compare the examples of usage given in collocations dictionaries. In this case, check carefully whether the dictionaries are citing corpus data or the introspective judgements of the lexicographers.

4

Words in Phrases 2: A Case Study of the Phraseology of English

In the previous chapter, I discussed the concepts, data and methods which can be used to study extended lexical units. In this chapter, I discuss the collocational behaviour of a sample of frequent English words, using data from the large data-base (Cobuild 1995b) described in chapter 3. I will present findings from a 1,000-word sample of the 10,000 head-words. (Starting from a random word in the first ten, I took every tenth word in the alphabetic list.) I will illustrate the kinds of phraseological constraints that words are subject to, show that the collocational attraction between words is much stronger than often realized, and discuss ways of representing extended lexical units more formally.

4.1 Frequency of Phraseological Units

One phenomenon, by its sheer frequency, shows the strength of phraseological tendencies across the most frequent words in the language. Suppose we take all 47 word-forms which begin with *f* in the sample. In 41 cases, the following easily recognizable combinations account for the collocation of node and top collocate. In some cases, I have added function words (which are omitted from the collocations lists); in the case of *fools* <*suffer, gladly*>, I have taken the top two collocates.

- despite the *fact* that; *faded* away; *fair* enough; short-*falls*; football *fans*; *farmer*'s wife; anti-*fascist*; mother and *father*; old *favourite*; to *feather* one's nest; *fellow* members; wire *fence*; a *few* years; *fiercely* competitive; *fighter* aircraft; semi-*final*; *finding* a way; *finish* off; said *firmly*; keep *fit*; natural *flair*; *flavour* of the month; ground *floor*; *flown* back; *focused* attention; suffer *fools* gladly; *forcing* down; rain *forest*; *former* minister; heavily *fortified*; backwards and *forwards*; *founding* fathers; old and *frail*; *free* trade; more *frequently*; close *friendships*; *fruit* and vegetables; *fuelled* speculation; more *fun*; government *funding*; the sound and the *fury*

In the remaining six cases, collocates further down the lists occur in recognizable phrases, such as:

- natural *fabrics*; animal *feed*; *filing* cabinet; space *flight*; closely *followed* by; beg (for) *forgiveness*

With many words, many more of the top 20 collocates are due to recognizable phrases. Here are examples from *fact* and *fair*:

- despite the *fact* that; as a matter of *fact*; a *fact* of life; *fact* finding; the *fact* remains that
- *fair* enough; *fair* share; a *fair* amount of; a *fair* trial; *fair* play; a *fair* chance; *fair* game

I can think of no reason why a sample of words beginning with *f* might be untypical of the whole 1,000-word sample. We therefore have initial evidence that all of the most frequent lexical words in the vocabulary have a strong tendency to occur in well-attested phraseological units.

4.2 Strength of Attraction: Word-forms, Lemmas and Lexical Sets

To estimate the extent and strength of collocational attraction across the sample of words, we can also calculate how strongly a node attracts a single word-form, its top collocate. In the following examples, the top collocate co-occurs with the node in 20 per cent and over of cases. Around 4 per cent of nodes fall into this category.

- brightly 1,467 <coloured 26 %>; calorie 846 <low 29 %>; classical 5,471 <music 22 %>; pepper 4,389 <salt 37 %>; profile 5,584 <high 28 %>; shuttle 3,453 <space 33 %>; tricks 2,202 <dirty 25 %>

In the following examples, the top collocate co-occurs with the node in between 10 and 20 per cent of cases. Around 20 per cent of nodes fall into this category.

- angrily 1,388 <reacted 18 %>; announcement 9,180 <made 10 %>; bitterly 1,782 <disappointed 11 %>; cheering 1,226 <crowd 13 %>; communique 1,060 <issued 15 %>; doses 1,687 <large 13 %>

In the following examples, the top collocate co-occurs with the node in between 5 and 10 per cent of cases. Around 40 per cent of nodes fall into this category.

- advisory 2,593 <group 7 %>; afternoon 16,204 <late 7 %>; alarming 1,711 <rate 8 %>; amid 4,649 <reports 5 %>; applause 2,207 <round 6 %>; autumn 9,307 <last 9 %>

For almost all other node-words (i.e. something over 30 per cent), the top collocate co-occurs with the node in at least one in fifty cases.

It is interesting to look also at the extremes: the relatively small number of cases where the top collocate accounts for under 2 per cent of occurrences of the node, or for 26 per cent and over. Examples include:

- continental 4,085 <breakfast 1.9 %>; explained 10,966 <never 1.2 %>; favourite 12,223 <old 1.5 %>; followed 23,270 <other 1.6 %>; issue 76,632 <rights 1.5 %>; nick 9,775 <time 1.6 %>; sun 36,118 <down 1.2 %>; victor 2,510 <emerged 0.7 %>
- backdrop 1,214 <against 33 %>; bodily 1,303 <harm 38 %>; cleansing 2,072 <ethnic 45 %>; coronary 1,228 <disease 43 %>; curriculum 4,116 <national 35 %>; efficiently 1,414 <more 29 %>; enforcement 2,990 <law 42 %>; esteem 2,021 <self 76 %>; harassment 2,731 <sexual 45 %>; hesitation 937 <without 30 %>; illusions 865 <no 35 %>; liberties 1,212 <civil 67 %>; warring 1,586 <factions 49 %>; whatsoever 1,950 <no 60 %>

Even some of the nodes with only a low probability (under 1 in 50) of occurring with a given collocate also form well-known phrases (e.g. *continental breakfast*, *an old favourite*, *in the nick of time*). The nodes with a high probability (over 1 in 4) of occurring with one single collocate are themselves comparatively infrequent, thus decreasing their likelihood of co-occurrence with a wide range of collocates. In addition, some phrases here are certainly due to topics in the British and international press in the 1980s and 1990s (e.g. *ethnic cleansing*, *National Curriculum*).

These figures show the extent to which words are co-selected in phraseological units. However, in many cases, this crude calculation will underestimate the strength of attraction of a node, since the figures show only the relation between the node and a single word-form. If the collocates list is lemmatized, then strength of attraction is immediately seen to be greater for some words, as in:

- cheering 1,226 <crowd 13 %, crowds 6 %> 19 %
- frail 944 <old 9 %, elderly 6 %> 15 %
- resemblance 1,085 <bears 18 %, bear 11 %, bore 11 %, bearing 4 %> 44 %

Nevertheless, lemmatization perhaps makes less of a difference than might be thought. I looked at all 56 words in the sample beginning with *g* and *h*. Only in 12 cases is the strength of attraction to the top lemma greater than the attraction to the top word-form. Examples are:

- golf 12,026 <course 12 %, courses> 15 %
- graphic <design 5 %, designer> 10 %
- grim 2,755 <faced 5 %, face, faces> 9 %
- himself 55,418 <found 3 %, finds, find> 6 %
- homework 1,310 <done 12 %, doing> 19 %
- honorary 1,233 <degree 9 %, degrees> 14 %

A reason for these modest increases is that the relative frequency of forms of a lemma is often very different, with the result that different forms often do not appear among the top 20 collocates.

However, what makes a much larger difference – though calculations are correspondingly more subjective – is the strength of attraction between a node and lexical sets of words which are semantically closely related to each other. Illustrative figures are:

- breakaway 1,379 <republic(s) 35 %, group, faction, party> 45 %
- cheering 1,226 <crowd(s) 19 %, people, supporters, fans, audience> 30 %
- deadlock 1,236 <BREAK 41 %, END, resolve> 50 %
- doses 1,687 <large 13 %, high, small, low, higher, lower, massive, heavy, larger> 48 %
- gathering 4,464 <information 5 %, intelligence, data, evidence> 11 %
- heated 2,470 <debate 10 %, argument(s), exchange(s), discussion> 16 %
- humanitarian 3,933 <aid 23 %, relief, assistance, help> 39 %
- obey 1,097 <orders 10 %, order, law(s), rules, command(s), instructions> 38 %
- warring 1,586 <factions 49 %, parties, sides> 73 %

In many cases it is not difficult to find a single syntactic-semantic descriptor for these lexical sets of related collocates, such as:

- deadlock <VERB meaning "end"> 50 %, often at N − 2
- doses <ADJ denoting "size"> 48 per cent, usually at N − 1

Such figures are also likely to be at least a small underestimate, since other collocates below the top 20 will also fall into these lexical sets. Occurrences of individual words may be low, but together they may provide many more semantically related words.

In summary so far: words across the whole of the everyday vocabulary of English have frequent, typical, central uses. Words are not chosen freely, but co-selected with other words in a span of a few words to left and right. After these characteristic uses, there is a long tail of word-forms which occur rarely, though these also often realize a frequent semantic pattern. The semantic patterns are typically simple and common, although the lexical realizations may be very diverse. That is, the units which this method identifies are not fixed phrases, but abstract semantic schemas, which have frequent and less frequent lexical exponents.

4.3 Lexical Profiles: Comprehensive Coverage of Data

So far I have picked out examples of node–collocate pairs which illustrate particular relations. However, a method which looks only at one or two words in the collocates list is hardly adequate, since it does not meet the important criterion of comprehensive coverage of data. For the head-words we have the following data-sets: the top 20 collocates, and 20 random concordance lines for each of the 20 collocates. We must at least account for all of these occurrences.

We would then have a profile of the characteristic uses of the node word: a lexical frame and its typical variants. The purpose of profiles (Crystal 1991) is to summarize and present information in a coherent and systematic manner, so as to facilitate comparisons and the discovery of significant patterns: a numerical dimension helps here. In principle, profiles should be comprehensive: in the present case, down to a frequency cut-off point, thereby automatically giving due weight to the most frequent cases. We are always dealing with repeated events: often hundreds of joint occurrences of node and collocate, but (given the organization of the data-base) always more than fifteen. To do this kind of analysis for each of 10,000 nodes would be a major enterprise. Every word is idiosyncratic, in the sense that its collocates are different from those of every other word. However, some initial simple examples provide a clue how to proceed more systematically.

4.3.1 Example 1: lexical profile for resemblance

Here is a case where almost all of the top collocates fit into a simple lexical schema:

- resemblance 1,085 <(bears, bear, bore, bearing) 45 %, little, no, striking, between, passing, uncanny, any, more, strong, family, remarkable, physical>

Almost all of these collocates are due to the occurrence of phrases such as:

- BEAR no *or* little resemblance to...
- BEAR a passing *or* physical resemblance to...
- BEAR a strong *or* striking *or* uncanny resemblance to...

These are not the only possibilities. Although these are the typical, central cases, BEAR co-occurs with *resemblance* in only 45 per cent of cases: it is also possible to say, for example, *HAVE a resemblance to.*

4.3.2 Example 2: lexical profile for reckless

Here is a case where all the most frequent collocates of a node fit easily into just two schemas. The node *reckless* has only five collocates with more than 15 occurrences each:

- reckless 1,045 <driving 19 %, death, causing, admitted, disregard 2 %>

It occurs in almost one case in five in the phrase *reckless driving*, and often in longer phrases such as

- admitted reckless driving; admitted causing death by reckless driving

In one case in fifty, it occurs in the phrase *reckless disregard*, and hence in longer phrases such as

- displayed a reckless disregard for safety; with reckless disregard of the consequences

Again, this obviously does not mean that all occurrences of *reckless* are in these combinations: only around 20 per cent are. It means that these are collocations which frequently recur, and that other nouns at N + 1 (as in *reckless expansion* or *reckless outpouring*) are, individually, infrequent.

4.3.3 Example 3: lexical profile for backdrop

Here is another simple case, in which only eight collocates co-occur more than 15 times with the node:

- backdrop 1,214 <against 33 %, set, provide, perfect, place, provides, form, provided>

Typical phrases are

- PROVIDE the perfect backdrop for
- TAKE place against a backdrop of
- set against a majestic backdrop of

The most frequent adjective is *perfect* (3 %). However, as well as backdrops which are:

- attractive, beautiful, dramatic, effective, epic, flattering, stunning

there are also *dismal* and *gloomy* backdrops of *disunity, turbulence, uncertainty* and *violence*.

4.3.4 Example 4: lexical profile for doses

In this example, I have grouped the top 20 collocates of the node into syntactic-semantic classes.

- doses 1,687
  <large, high, small, low, higher, lower, massive, heavy, larger> 48 %
  <daily> 4 %
  <radiation, vitamin, drugs> 13 %
  <given, taken, used, received, taking> 14 %
  <very, even> 6 %

The most frequent verb-forms are past participles. The most frequent grammatical words are: *of, in, are, can*. Typical phrases are:

- received massive doses of radiation
- given in very small daily doses

- taken in large repeated doses

The blend of collocation, colligation and semantic preference in the basic pattern can be stated informally as follows. There is typically a verb meaning "give" or "receive", often followed by a size adjective, followed by *doses of*, followed by a medical noun.

This example illustrates two points. First, it shows that even words which appear to have an independent denotation, and which are hardly ambiguous even as decontextualized individual words, may nevertheless have a strong tendency to occur within predictable lexico-syntactic frames. Second, it is a piece of evidence about the range of meanings which are typically encoded. That is, when people talk about *doses* of something, then these are the meanings which frequently get expressed. As G. Francis (1993: 155) puts it:

> [A]s we build up and refine the semantic sets associated with a structure, we move closer to a position where we can compile a grammar of the typical meanings that human communication encodes, and recognise the untypical and therefore foregrounded meanings whenever we come across them.

Corpus analysis shows what are frequent or typical uses. There are, of course, other non-medical uses, often in ironic phrases such as *large doses of sarcasm* or *can take politicians only in small doses*.

4.4 A Model of Extended Lexical Units

These examples are still presented informally. So, how might we more formally define units which are highly conventional in their semantic patterns, but also highly variable in their potential lexical realizations – which have one or more clear central tendencies, but different ranges of variation? The relations defined in chapter 3 give us the basis for a model of extended lexical units. In order to define a linguistic unit, we have to specify its possible constituents, and the possible relations between them. The constituents define the semantic content of the unit. The relations define its structure. (This section develops proposals in Sinclair 1996, 1998.) We have the following model.

RELATION	*constituent*
(1) COLLOCATION	collocate: individual word-form or lemma
(2) COLLIGATION	grammatical category

(3) SEMANTIC PREFERENCE   lexical set:
                          class of semantically related word-
                          forms or lemmas
(4) DISCOURSE PROSODY   descriptor of speaker attitude and dis-
                          course function

As Sinclair (1998) points out, relations (1) to (4) are increasingly abstract. Collocation refers to individual word-forms, which are directly observable in texts. Colligation refers to classes of words (such as past participles or quantifiers), which are not directly observable: they are abstractions based on generalizations about the behaviour of the word in the class. The classes are often small, and always closed (for example, there is a small, finite number of quantifiers in English). Semantic preferences refer to a class of words which share some semantic feature (such as words to do with "medicine" or "change"). Such a class is also abstract, and will have frequent and typical members, but will be open-ended. Discourse prosodies are even more open-ended and typically have great lexical variability.

These four relations are all probabilistic and non-directional. Two further relations specify the probabilities and the positions of occurrence. And finally, we must also say how widely our description applies.

(5) STRENGTH OF ATTRACTION. This is defined in percentage terms: given the occurrence of a node, what is the probability of occurence of a collocate, grammatical category, lexical set or discourse prosody?
(6) POSITION AND POSITIONAL MOBILITY. Relations (1) to (5) are non-directional: two constituents simply co-occur. However, it may be that one sequence always occurs (e.g. *spick and span*, but not *span and spick), or that relative position is variable.
(7) DISTRIBUTION IN TEXT-TYPES. We must specify whether the lexical unit occurs widely in general English, or whether it is restricted to broad varieties, such as journalism or technical and scientific English, or to specialized text-types, with a narrow speech-act function, such as recipes or weather forecasts.

This model brings lexis fully within the traditional concerns of linguistic theory. Much twentieth-century linguistics has assumed that lexis is not amenable to systematic treatment, because the vocabulary is merely 'a list of basic irregularities' in a language (Bloomfield 1933: 274). For much of Chomskyan linguistics, it is syntax which is concerned with general rules, whereas lexis is largely dismissed as being concerned with isolated and idiosyncratic facts. However, relations (1) to (4) correspond to the classic distinctions between syntactics, semantics and pragmatics, which were drawn by Morris in the 1930s (Morris 1938). Syntactics (or syntax) deals with how linguistic signs relate to one another (here collocation and colligation), semantics deals with how linguistic signs relate to the external world (here lexical sets and the phenomena they denote), and pragmatics deals with how linguistic signs relate to their users (here expression of speaker attitude).

The examples of collocation above also show that there is much in the behaviour of words which is automatic and not open to conscious reflection. This means that introspection about lexical meaning is often unreliable or at least incomplete. Also in terms of its automaticity, lexis is seen to be in line with many aspects of phonology and syntax (Channell 2000). In the model, lexis has acquired a primary role, and syntax a reduced role, in determining aspects of positional mobility (for example, in active versus passive variants of a unit), and in linking phraseological units to each other in running text. This revised division of labour between lexis and syntax will require much working out in detail.

A more stringent procedure – not entirely formalized, but at least a check on rank subjectivism – can be defined as follows (see Sinclair 1991: 54ff, 84ff, 105ff; 1996; De Beaugrande 1996: 515ff; and Clear 1996, for related suggestions). (1) Group the 20 collocates into semantic subsets, using criteria which are as explicit as possible. (2) Calculate what percentage these semantic subsets comprise of the whole collocates list. (3) Check the positional variability of the constitutents. The data-base averages information across a span of 4 : 4. However, positional information can easily be retrieved from the concordance lines, by using positional frequency tables: see table 4.1. (4) Check whether independent corpus data (not restricted to the top 20 collocates) reveal further uses. That is, check the recall of information (see chapter 3.6.3).

4.4.1 Example 5: lexical profile for UNDERGO

The following analysis follows this procedure. The collocational data are as follows:

- undergo 1,205 <surgery 108, tests 67, treatment 62, change 53, training 43, test 41, medical 40, before 37, changes 35, operation 34, women 31, forced 26, further 25, testing 25, major 24, examination 23, extensive 21, heart 20, required 19, transformation 17>

There is a simple pattern and discourse prosody: people involuntarily *undergo* serious and unpleasant events, such as medical procedures.

The 20 collocates can be arranged into sub-lists. Some words, mainly nouns, are medical (*surgery, treatment, medical, operation, heart*); some have to do with training and testing (*training, examination, test, tests, testing*); some concern change (*change, changes, transformations*); some adjectives concern the seriousness or extent of the events (*further, major, extensive*); some verbs concern their involuntary nature (*forced, required*). The two remaining words do not obviously fit into these sub-lists, but must also be accounted for (*before, women*).

The data-base gives 400 (20 × 20) randomly selected concordance lines, but these lines may, by chance, be selected twice, and in this case there are 343 different lines. In descending frequency: 181 involve people undergoing medical procedures, including medical tests, such as:

- major heart surgery; conventional medical treatment; mandatory drug tests

Some 72 involve people and things undergoing *changes, transformations* and *metamorphoses*. Some are explicitly unpleasant: *agonies of readjustment, malignant transformation*. Many others are by implication unpleasant, since they are

- considerable, dramatic, drastic, extensive, fundamental, major, profound, radical, significant

Some 46 involve non-medical testing, again often by implication unpleasant, since it may be *compulsory* or *rigorous*, or may involve *tough scrutiny* or *police checks*. Twenty-two involve people undergoing *training*: often military, and often *extensive, intensive* or *lengthy*, and again, therefore, not necessarily pleasant. Eleven additional cases are explicitly unpleasant: people or things undergo, for example, *cutbacks, humiliation, imprisonment, trauma*. The remaining examples are technical: see below: *bifurcations*, etc.

These exponents of the discourse prosody "unpleasant" almost always occur to the right of *undergo*. Exponents of a related prosody, "involuntary", occur mainly to the left. The lexical realizations *forced* and *required* occur in the top 20 collocates, and *must* is one of the most frequent collocates amongst the stop-words.

I have now said something about all 20 top collocates, except *before* and *women*. *Before* occurs amongst the top 10 collocates, in 3 per cent of occurrences, and provides a hint of the characteristic discourse in which *undergo* occurs. In many cases, a sequence of actions, which happen before or after surgery, tests or training, is being reported: around half the concordance lines contain references to the time when events happen, to sequences of events, or to events being planned:

- must wait 24 hours before they can undergo the procedure; undergo his fourth operation inside a year; undergo several systems checks; is planning to undergo; due to undergo; scheduled to undergo

The reason why *women* is so frequent a collocate (3%) is less obvious. It seems partly due to the frequency of mention of events such as *abortions, fertility treatment* and *hysterectomies*. It may also be partly because a sex-neutral collocate such as *patients* can refer to men or women, but when women are meant, they are explicitly mentioned.

The 343 concordance lines are not a random selection of all occurrences of *undergo*, since they all contain one of the top 20 collocates. I therefore checked an independent 2.3-million-word corpus. The word-form *undergo* is not very frequent ($n = 14$), and in this case there are no obvious differences in use across different forms of the lemma ($n = 42$), which I therefore looked at as a whole. The percentages are different, but the patterns are confirmed, and one pattern becomes clearer. In this smaller corpus, objects of the verb were from the semantic fields of "change" (16) or "medicine" (8), or were "unpleasant" (9):

- ordeals; a crisis; a savage sentence for a crime; a traumatic experience; bizarre eighteenth-century initiation rites

UNDERGO also occurs in technical English with no necessarily unpleasant connotations. Almost all other cases (8) were scientific and technical, as marked by collocates such as *bifurcations, diapause, nucleon*. The sole remaining case is *the spring-cleaning which it had undergone*: a humorous reference to a landing strip, which then *shone like black glass*.

Further corpus data reveal further specific lexical items, and show how the simple patterns can be realized by a great variety of lexis (Sinclair 1996: 95). For example, in this case, the "unpleasant" prosody is implied by the text following *pessimism*:

- why Voltaire's ideas *underwent* this *change* is not clear – possibly his new *pessimism* was a result of the great earthquake of 1755

Similarly, great lexical variety is possible in expressing the "involuntary" prosody. As well as explicit lexical items (*forced to; required to; have to; must; will have to*), the prosody may be only implied as in

- police said he would *undergo* psychiatric *examination*

Further corpus data would be certain to reveal further lexical variation, but unlikely to reveal other major semantic preferences. This is a prediction about how the word is used, and is open to empirical testing. In summary, the main semantic patterns are simple. (1) In general English, people are forced to undergo unpleasant experiences, especially medical procedures, or tests and (often arduous) training. (2) People and things undergo (usually radical and often unpleasant) changes. (3) In scientific and technical English, the word is usually neutral.

The central uses of the word, with its typical collocates, can easily be stated: see figure 4.1. The "involuntary" and "unpleasant" prosodies are usually encoded to the left and right respectively. They express the discourse function of the extended lexical unit: why is this being mentioned now? And, despite the variation, there are preferred lexical selections, down to the choice of individual words (Sinclair 1996: 88–9).

Characteristic examples from the concordance lines are:

- he was forced to *undergo* an emergency operation
- his character appeared to *undergo* a major transformation
- each operative had to *undergo* the most rigorous test
- will *undergo* extensive skills and fitness training
- forced to become refugees, to *undergo* further migration and further suffering

Concordance 4.1 shows a larger random selection of 50 concordance lines (from amongst those lines which contain one of the top 20 collocates).

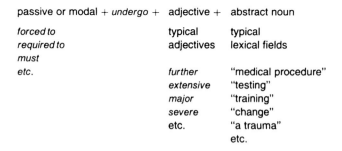

passive or modal + *undergo* +	adjective +	abstract noun
forced to	typical	typical
required to	adjectives	lexical fields
must		
etc.		
	further	"medical procedure"
	extensive	"testing"
	major	"training"
	severe	"change"
	etc.	"a trauma"
		etc.

Figure 4.1 The prototypical uses of *undergo*
The prototypical uses of *undergo* can be represented as a lexico-grammatical frame plus:
   frequent individual collocates (e.g. *surgery*)
   typical pragmatically specified adjectives (e.g. *major*)
   typical semantically specified lexical fields (e.g. "change")

1. f the Oval Test last summer to	undergo	a cartilage operation. He was not
2. and international institutions	undergo	a change – Political observers in
3. ould be aware the system is to	undergo	a historic transformation. Sometime
4. families of the nation did not	undergo	a major metamorphosis until the op
5. or the first time will have to	undergo	a means test and a needs assessmen
6. the applicants, asking them to	undergo	a medical examination, and prepari
7. court today and is expected to	undergo	a psychiatric examination. 930430
8. r – Discovery will not have to	undergo	a special fueling test because it
9. ir work, each operative had to	undergo	a stringent medical examination ev
10. m-you find romantic are due to	undergo	a transformation on the 4th, and w
11. h John Fashanu being forced to	undergo	an Achilles tendon operation. The
12. rawling estate are required to	undergo	an 'eyescan' before being allowed t
13. ge it's led dozens of women to	undergo	back-alley abortions in countries
14. arnations that the spirit must	undergo	before it can achieve release from
15. Mr Forbes subsequently had to	undergo	brain surgery, and his friends and
16. ill Clinton, style is about to	undergo	dramatic changes. Out for instance
17. former champion Pat Cash will	undergo	exploratory surgery on an injured
18. s of alcoholic beverages is to	undergo	extensive food testing. And only i
19. programme for hostages. He'll	undergo	extensive medical checks and psych
20. now in Bahrain where they will	undergo	extensive medical examinations bef
21. e championships tomorrow, will	undergo	extensive skills and fitness train
22. a hospital and insisted that I	undergo	extensive tests – There was nothin
23. baden in Germany where he will	undergo	further medical tests at an Americ
24. inal hysterectomy patients may	undergo	further surgery at a rate as high
25. Robert Mays allow Kimberly to	undergo	genetic testing. As fiction, the t
26. r Warren, who was scheduled to	undergo	his eighth open heart surgery afte
27. nd Howey may even be forced to	undergo	his fourth operation inside a year
28. h to one half of all women who	undergo	hysterectomy develop some morbidit
29. management know-how. Employees	undergo	intensive training on the shop flo
30. gories of children required to	undergo	language testing. The categories o
31. ster. Yesterday, he was due to	undergo	major brain surgery. On Friday nig
32. undergone and will continue to	undergo	major cutbacks. If Japan does not
33. atrick Buchanan is planning to	undergo	major heart surgery tomorrow – His
34. he first established prison to	undergo	"market testing" and the first for
35. s suggest that women likely to	undergo	menopause, at about age 50, ought
36. whether or not a woman should	undergo	more extensive tests where a diagr
37. t that a pioneer product would	undergo	more testing, he says. Rissler, wh
38. weapon – Police said he would	undergo	psychiatric examination before any
39. leaders could not be forced to	undergo	random drug testing in order to re
40. nly two feet in diameter, will	undergo	several systems checks before bein
41. use the family butcher shop to	undergo	significant change in appearance a
42. captain, Villiam Hyravy, is to	undergo	surgery and will take no part. The
43. wait 24 hours before they can	undergo	the procedure. Doctors must tell p
44. . So who is actually having to	undergo	the tests? An oceanographer got te
45. e. But it has not been able to	undergo	the transformation and economic mo
46. ut her ability to continue and	undergo	the treatment. It was very clear t
47. attempt last year. As recruits	undergo	training in a Fortitude Valley fig
48. d deed.' Before she agreed to	undergo	treatment and completed donor cons
49. ages are found, patients often	undergo	treatment, including bypass surge
50. e Pendennis Shipyard. She will	undergo	trials locally before sailing to

Concordance 4.1 Sample concordance lines for *undergo*

Notes: Lines from the data-base were put in random order, and every 8th line selected. These 50 lines were then ordered alphabetically to the right

Table 4.1 Positional frequency table for *undergo*, span 3:3

-3	-2	-1	node	+1	+2	+3
was [18]	forced [26]	to [219]	*	a [85]	medical [22]	and [21]
is [14]	required [21]	will [38]	*	an [26]	surgery [20]	tests [16]
be [13]	have [15]	and [9]	*	further [25]	testing [16]	examination [14]
and [11]	is [11]	must [9]	*	the [21]	treatment [15]	surgery [13]
and [11]	is [11]	must [8]	*	the [21]	treatment [12]	surgery [13]
that [8]	they [11]	he'll [7]	*	major [20]	change [9]	operation [12]
been [7]	about [10]	should [7]	*	surgery [12]	changes [9]	transformation [11]
were [7]	and [9]	who [7]	*	treatment [9]	for [9]	before [9]
where [7]	patients [7]	women [7]	*	medical [7]	heart [9]	test [9]
children [6]	that [7]	often [6]	*	heart [6]	and [8]	medical [8]
he [6]	he [6]		*	his [5]	major [8]	for [7]
in [6]	will [6]		*	testing [5]	operation [8]	in [7]
the [6]	women [6]				examination [6]	on [7]
women [6]	due [5]				extensive [6]	training [6]
will [6]	ordered [5]				transformation [6]	to [6]
for [5]					radical [5]	testing [6]
last [5]					test [5]	the [6]
not [5]					training [5]	a [5]
of [5]					the [5]	as [5]
						by [5]
						changes [5]

Notes: The node *undergo* is indicated with an asterisk. Only collocates occurring 5 times and more are shown.

Table 4.1 shows a positional frequency table, in which words in positions N − 3 to N + 3 are displayed in descending order of frequency, down to a frequency cut-off of 5 joint occurrences.

4.4.2 Example 6: lexical profile for chopped

The next example illustrates further principles. The starting data are:

- chopped 3,602 <finely, fresh, parsley, onion, garlic, tbsp, tomatoes, oz, peeled, add, off, onion(s), pepper, salt, chives, herbs, tablespoons, dried, small, tsp>

It is sometimes argued that co-occurrences between words such as *chopped*, *herbs*, *parsley* and *onions* are not real collocations, but words which co-occur simply because they correlate with states of affairs in the world. Smadja (1993: 150) argues this with reference to word-pairs such as *doctor–nurse* and *doctors–hospitals*. Kjellmer (1991: 114) points out that the phrase *glass of water* is more frequent than *cup of water*, merely because water is usually served in a glass. However, given our present limited knowledge about statistical properties of extended lexical units, it seems unwise to make firm distinctions about what is and is not linguistic. Similarly, Benson's (1990: 26) rejection of *pass the salt* as a collocation, on the grounds that one can pass all sorts of things, seems odd, since *pass the salt* is a highly stereotyped phrase.

In any case, although the extended lexical units around *chopped* are not idioms, they are idiomatic. Recipe writers could talk of ?*finely cut* or ?*finely sliced fresh parsley*, but by and large they do not. The word-form *add* occurs not only in recipes (I might add). However, when it occurs as a sentence- or clause-initial imperative, it is almost always in a recipe (or instructions for a chemical experiment). If *add* and *chopped* co-occur then the probability that this is a recipe must be near 100 per cent.

Chopped is a case where the node-word is the centre of a tight collocational cluster: the top three collocates are each 12 per cent and over, and even the last collocate is 3 per cent. In the list, 19 out of the 20 collocates are due to the use of the word in recipes.

(The exception is *off*. The collocation *chopped off* occurs almost exclusively in connection with chopping off bits of human body parts. This is confirmed by looking at all instances of *chopped* in an independent 2.3-million-word corpus. Out of 20 instances, 15 were from recipes. The other 5 all involved verb plus particle: *chopped off, chopped up, chopped at*. Four involved violence to humans. The fifth was a critical reference to music being superficially *chopped up*. So this finding seems not to be due to an over-representation of recipes in the Cobuild (1995b) data-base. I checked further by looking at occurrences from the 100-million-word British National Corpus (see Notes on Corpus Data and Software). Out of 50 random examples of *chopped*, 39 were from recipes. Of the other 11 examples, four occurred in the phrase *chopped off*, one in *chopped up*, and one in *chopped down*. Four of these were references to violence to humans. The word-forms *chop* and *chopping* are also frequent in recipes. Other phrases include *chop down trees*, *due for the chop*, *endless chopping and changing*. The form *chops* occurs mainly as a noun in other phrases, such as *lamb chops* and *licking their chops*.)

As has often been pointed out in stylistic analyses, the vocabulary of recipes is distinctive, and the collocates of *peeled* and *garnish* have a large overlap with *chopped*. The following are collocates of two or all three of these nodes:

- chives, finely, fresh, garlic, herbs, onion, parsley, pepper, slice/d, small, tomatoes

4.5 Summary and Implications

In this chapter, I have used some simple statistics to describe how words co-occur in text. The data-base (Cobuild 1995b) was produced by an entirely automatic procedure: a computer was programmed to extract the 10,000 most frequent word-forms from a large corpus together with their most frequent collocates and a random selection of concordance lines. Corpus linguistics is based on publicly available data and replicable methods: this is what is meant by empirical linguistics. Nevertheless, the output requires considerable interpretation.

A great deal of language in use consists of extended lexico-semantic units. These units are not just individual phrases which can be listed. Typical instances can be listed, but not all instances are equally representative. The units themselves are abstract: they are semantic schemas, which have default values, and typical realizations, but often no necessary or sufficient features. If we are thinking of the behaviour of a language community, then they are norms. If we are thinking of the competence of individual speakers, then they are mental models.

All of the most frequent content words in the language are involved in such patterning. This is not a peripheral phenomenon (collocations are not an idiosyncratic feature of just a few words), but a central part of communicative competence. These semantic schemas can be modelled as clusters of lexis (node and collocates), grammar (colligation), semantics (preferences for words from particular lexical fields) and pragmatics (connotations or discourse prosodies). Such a model brings the study of lexis within the mainstream of linguistic description: the units are combinations of lexis, syntax, semantics and pragmatics. The findings show that there is a level of organization between lexis and syntax, which is only starting to be systematically studied, and which is not reducible to any other level of organization.

The central problem in linguistic description is how to describe a system which is both highly complex and highly variable. Semantic schemas are general and simple patterns which have considerable lexical variation due to local context and choice.

4.6 Background and Further Reading

For references to the large literature on phraseology, see chapter 3.11. For a range of computational methods for identifying recurrent phrasal units in corpora, see Choueka et al. (1983), Yang (1986), Smadja (1993), and Justeson and Katz (1995).

4.7 Topics for Further Study

(1) It is easy to find further examples which support the claim that UNDERGO has a negative discourse prosody. However, such claims must be tested by searching for counter-examples. Can you find any? For example, study the collocation *UNDERGO training*: does this always co-occur with further collocates which imply an unpleasant experience?

You could also check examples of the collocation *willingly UNDERGO*: do they contradict the claim that people "involuntarily" undergo "unpleasant" experiences? This phrase is not frequent and you may have to search a very large text collection to find enough examples to make generalizations about its use. You might use a search engine which can find phrases in documents in the world-wide web. Here are two examples out of around 175 which I found:

- no-one, short of a severely psychotic masochist, would *willingly undergo* what she went through
- why did he *willingly undergo* forty years of hardship?

Are these uses typical? If so, what discourse prosody is there around the phrase *willingly UNDERGO*?

(2) This chapter has largely ignored the variation in collocations across different text-types. Some individual collocations may signal a specific text-

type: the phrase *finely chopped* is probably from a recipe; *warm* and *front* do not signal any text-type on their own, but *warm front* is probably from a weather forecast; *luxury home* is probably from advertising by a builder or estate agent. In general English, *time* might collocate with *spend* or *waste*; but in sports commentaries, it is likely to collocate with *half* and *injury* (Partington 1998: 17). Find other examples where a particular phrase or collocation reliably identifies a text-type, and other examples where words have different collocates in different text-types.

On the basis of such differences across text-types, Biber et al. (1998: 234) argue that 'characterizations of *general English* are usually not characterizations of any variety at all, but rather a middle ground that describes no actual text or register'. Is this criticism of the concept 'general English' justified?

(3) Words which are rough (denotational) synonyms are usually used in quite different ways: possibly in different collocations, with different connotations, in different text-types, and so on. Study the different patterns around these approximately synonymous adjectives:

- escalating, growing, increasing, mounting, rising, soaring, spiralling

For example, does *rising* have mainly positive collocates (*rising prosperity*), or mainly negative collocates (*rising costs*)? Does its discourse prosody depend on the longer phrase it occurs in? What nouns typically follow *a rising tide of*? Which nouns typically follow *mounting* or *soaring*? Partington (1998: 113–14) provides further data and discussion of these roughly synonymous adjectives.

(4) Data from the Cobuild (1995b) data-base show the nouns which typically follow *amid*, and adjectives which typically precede the nouns:

- amid 4,649 <reports 5 %, fears, speculation, allegations, signs, concern, scenes, controversy, security, claims, rumours> 28 %
- amid <growing, continuing, mounting> 7 %

Some phrases include:

- amid reports of heavy fighting; amid reports of a Cabinet split; amid tight security; amid signs of growing concern; amid scenes of blood-curdling violence; amid scenes of high emotion
- amid breath-taking scenery; amid beautiful countryside; amid romantic ivy-covered walls; amid the frantic last few days in London; amid much fanfare, the *Manhattan* tried to sail

Use these data and other corpus data to make a statement of the discourse prosody predicted by *amid*, and to discuss whether this prosody is different in different text-types.

(5) It has been claimed that 'all the forms of a verb...are often very different from one another' (Sinclair 1991: 8), in the sense that they have different collocates and therefore different uses and different meanings. However, different forms of UNDERGO are very similar in their collocates. And while *seeks* is sharply different from other forms of SEEK, *seek, seeking* and *sought* are similar in their uses and all share collocates from the semantic field of "help" (see chapter 2.2.1). Sinclair's claim is an empirical one, but I do not know of work which has investigated how often it is actually the case, and even the best-known corpus-based dictionaries (such as CIDE 1995; Cobuild 1995a; LDOCE 1995; OALD 1995) still use mainly lemmas as head-words. Investigate the different forms of some lemmas. For example, do the different forms of ACHIEVE or PURSUE share a significant number of collocates? Or do the different forms occur in significantly different phrases? What would be 'significant' in such cases?

5

Words in Texts 1: Words, Phrases and Text Cohesion

In chapters 3 and 4, I showed that knowing a very large number of collocations is a significant component of native speaker fluency. In the remainder of the book, I will show the significance of lexis in three further areas. (1) In this chapter and the next, I will show how words and collocations contribute to text cohesion. (2) In chapters 7 and 8, I will show that collocations, even of very common words, often carry cultural connotations: they are a significant component of cultural competence. (3) And in chapters 9 and 10, I will discuss some wider implications of such analysis for linguistic theory.

Most studies in corpus linguistics are concerned with the characteristics of large corpora, and therefore with patterns of the language as a whole: especially the frequency of words, phrases and collocations. However, such patterns are the norm against which individual texts are interpreted. It is therefore individual texts which are the topic of this chapter and the next.

5.1 Words and Co-text

So far, I have discussed one of the most important general findings of corpus study. It makes little sense to describe the meaning of individual words in isolation, since words are co-selected with other words, and meanings are distributed across larger units. This discovery about units of meaning can be rephrased as follows. Word and context are inseparable. If, for analytic convenience, we start from an individual word, then we can make predictions about the textual environment in which it is likely to occur. Equally, if we know something about the environment, then we can make predictions about the words which are likely to occur there (Sinclair 1992).

More accurately we are talking about word and co-text, and therefore about one mechanism of text cohesion. In this chapter, I will use corpus evidence to show some of the lexical relations which make texts cohesive. Corpora can be used to document the norms of language use, which are the background against which individual texts are interpreted. These intertextual relations between individual texts and routine language use are expressed largely in collocations: the regular co-occurrence of words in texts. Such work therefore reveals a new perspective on the relation between competence and performance: what it means to be a fluent, idiomatic native speaker of a language. It also gives a glimpse of solutions to classic problems which turn around the dualisms of langue and parole, competence and performance, system and use, creativity and routine, and macro and micro (see chapter 10).

5.2   Routine and Creativity

Words in texts are distributed according to principles which often seem strange or counter-intuitive. Most words in the language (system) occur only rarely: if you open a large dictionary at random, there will be many words on the page which you do not know, even if you are a native speaker. Most words in running text are the common ones; in particular, grammatical (function) words make up a large percentage of running text; but they will give you very little idea of what the text is about. The words which often contribute most to our understanding of the content of a given text are relatively uncommon. Thus it is often said that if you know the 2,000 or so most frequent words (lemmas) in a foreign language, then you will understand 90 per cent or more of the words (word-forms) in an average newspaper article. However, whether you grasp the point of the article is a different question, because it might well be that the 10 per cent of unfamiliar words are precisely the ones which are crucial for understanding the text (though you may be able to guess at least some of them from context).

In general, words have an extremely uneven distribution across texts. A very few words are very frequent, but most words are very rare. When rare words do occur, they tend to cluster together. For example, the word *neanderthal* might occur only a few times in a large corpus: but there is a high chance that all occurrences are in one or two texts about archaeology. As Church and Mercer (1994: 10–11) put it, content words tend to appear in bunches, 'like buses in New York City'. Suppose we divide a large corpus into 10,000-word segments, the occurrence of a given word, say *Kennedy*, will be distributed unevenly across the segments: perhaps several occurrences in two or three segments, but none at all in all the rest. This clustering is itself one mechanism of text cohesion. This chapter is about the extent to which running text consists of frequent, predictable and routine combinations of words, or infrequent, novel and creative combinations.

Consider the following apparently contradictory statements:

- '[T]exts are largely composed of...rare events' (Dunning 1993: 62–3).
- 'By far the majority of text is made of the occurrence of common words in common patterns, or in slight variants of those common patterns' (Sinclair 1991: 108).

Are these statements contradictory? Not really, if we make the following distinction. Many of the specific lexical combinations in a given text are rare events: if they were not, the text would be telling us nothing new at all. Equally, many of these combinations (at least up to three or four words in length) will be found in other texts, and many others will be specific realizations of frequent general patterns. This is the same distinction which I made in chapter 4: if we talk about extended lexical units, then this refers, not to a list of fixed phrases, but to abstract semantic units, which have typical but variable lexical realizations.

5.3 Variable Phrases and Textual Cohesion

As I showed in chapters 3 and 4, some (but rather few) phrasal units are fixed and ready-made, but the majority are much more abstract and variable. There is a continuum from a few fixed phrases to vaguer patterns which might be recognized only by some speakers (Kjellmer 1991: 126).

If we look again at the top 20 collocates of each of the 1,000 words in the core vocabulary (taken from the Cobuild 1995b data-base), then we observe that these 20 collocates are never a random list. It would be most surprising if they were, since this would mean that words occur in random contexts, with no systematic pattern in their use. So, it follows that the collocates lists always contain (one or more) sets of related words, such as synonyms, antonyms, and words from a given lexical field. For example, here are the top 20 collocates, in descending frequency, of *wife*:

- wife <children, husband, said, first, ex, man, daughter, mother, second, home, years, former, left, son, told, family, whose, old, young, died>

There are many semantic relations between the node and its collocates, including antonymous pairs, near synonyms, and other semantically related words:

- wife, husband; daughter, son; old, young; family, mother, children; ex-, former; first, second; said, told

5.4 Antonyms and Synonyms

There is a strong tendency for nodes to collocate with their antonyms. For example, in the following cases, an antonym of the node is its top collocate:

- answers <question(s) 19 %>; births <deaths 10 %>; bride <(bride)groom 11 %>; dad <mum 13 %, mom 2 %>; darkness <light 5 %>; daughters <sons 9 %>; export <import 4 %>; emotionally <physically 10 %>; father <mother 5 %>; forwards <backwards 16 %>; implicit <explicit 5 %>; indirectly <directly 28 %>; men <women 11 %>; negative <positive 7 %>; outdoor <indoor 6 %>; quantity <quality 12 %>; theoretical <practical 4 %>

Identification of antonyms is not an entirely automatic decision, but relies to some extent on intuitive judgements. For example, there might not be total agreement on whether the following are genuine antonym pairs:

- capitalist <socialist 2 %, communist 2 %>; classical <modern 1 %, contemporary 1 %>; cops <robbers 3 %>; demonstrators <police 9 %>; drink <food 7 %>

Antonyms are not decidable out of context: antonyms are not word-pairs which exist purely in the language system, but which are used in connected text, sometimes in phrases such as *cops and robbers*. Antonymy has traditionally been regarded (Lyons 1968) as a paradigmatic relation, which is permanently available in the lexicon: a phenomenon of *langue*, independent of speakers. However, the examples above show that antonymy is a syntagmatic relation, which is used by speakers to construct oppositions relevant to the current discourse. Pairs such as *conventional–nuclear*, show that antonymy is a textual relation:

- conventional < (arms, weapons) 8 %, nuclear 3 %>

Frequent textual oppositions doubtless come to have an independent existence, which can be tapped as clang responses in word-association experiments, but we have here the hint of how frequency in text (*parole*) relates to a property of the language system (*langue*). (Brazil, 1995: 34–5, makes related suggestions.)

For node–collocate co-occurrence, a figure of 1 per cent (as with *classical <modern>* above) may seem low. However, this figure is much higher than would be expected by chance (see chapter 3.9). Using quite different methods, Justeson and Katz (1991) show that the co-occurrence of antonymous adjectives is statistically highly significant. They show the tendency of several adjective pairs, such as *large* and *small*, to co-occur within a span of a few words. Examples from my data are:

- from the *large* departmental store to the *small* shoe-mender
- a *large* area of the *small* kitchen

Other general mechanisms are at work. I discussed in chapter 1.7.1 the principle that ambiguous words have one meaning per collocation. For example, the word *coffee* is ambiguous (or indeterminate) out of context, but almost always disambiguated in running text, as in:

- cup of coffee ("drink"); tin of coffee ("granules"); picking coffee ("crop of coffee beans"); a light coffee colour

Only its "drink" meaning is relevant in:

- a black coffee; coffee bar; coffee cup; poured coffee; sipped my coffee

In some occurrences, even more help with identifying the relevant meaning (here "drink") is available, since *coffee* occurs in parallel constructions, as in these attested examples with *and* or *or*:

- a coffee and tea shop
- she had ordered coffee and I had ordered beer
- come up to my house to have a coffee or a sherry
- if the coffee is too weak or the tea is too strong

The relevant sense is signalled by contrasts such as *coffee–tea* and *coffee–beer*, sometimes by the parallel syntax, and sometimes also by other contrasts such as *weak–strong*.

The principles of relational lexical semantics (see chapter 2.7) are usually applied to the language system (*langue*), but can also be applied to sets of collocates which are due to frequencies in language use (*parole*). This can also be seen with relations of node–collocate synonymy, which the data-base reveals, although in relatively few cases. Perhaps co-occurrence of synonyms is not to be expected within a small span of 4 : 4, but the textual reasons are still open to study. On the grounds that there are no true synonyms, judgements here are probably even more variable. However, examples include

- anarchy 1,057 <chaos 4 %>
- anxiety 4,961 <depression 5 %, fear, stress, tension> 12 %

- chapel 2,439 <church 3 %>
- migraine 808 <headache (s) 16 %>
- towns 6,882 <cities 9 %>
- utterly 2,689 <completely 2 %>

So, rather than regarding antonyms and synonyms as a feature of the language system, it may be better to look at things the other way round, and to use corpus evidence to show which words are antonymous or synonymous. Church et al. (1994: 156) show how little agreement there is on synonyms between major American dictionaries, and propose that lexical substitutability is itself a criterion for synonymy. More generally, co-occurrence is evidence of lexical relations.

All of these cases are examples of feature-sharing: synonyms share most semantic features with each other, antonyms share all features except the feature which is switched (plus–minus), and words in a lexical field may share a feature which is made explicit in their superordinate term. As noted in Chapter 2.4 and 2.5, closely related concepts have been proposed for the idea that semantic features are often distributed or shared across co-occurring words, and therefore for the idea that the unit of meaning is not the individual word, but an extended lexical unit. In the literature (Sinclair 1992: 17), the term 'feature-sharing' has been used for words which add little or nothing to the (default) meaning of the node. For example:

- accepted <now 3 %>; addition <new 2 %>; alternatives <other 5 %, possible, available, various> 10 %; begun <already 7 %>; bonus <added 6 %, extra 2 %>; brightly <coloured 26 %, painted 18 %>; burst <sudden(ly) 3 %>; comparisons <between 16 %>

5.5 Discourse Prosodies

In all these examples, meaning is distributed across more than one word, and thereby contributes to local textual cohesion. Such prosodies are a difficult aspect of extended lexical units to identify, because they often express speakers' relations to other people, and may depend on assumptions and worldview (see chapter 9.2). In addition, individual words and the collocations in which they occur may express quite different evaluations. For example, *flavour* can be positive, but *flavour of the month* is critical and ironic (Channell 2000: 43). Similarly, *cosy* may be positive, but *cosy little relationship* can denote "cliquey". And *little* may be positive, but *little old lady* is patronizing. These examples confirm the semantic status of extended lexical units. Or consider

- lavish <lifestyle, parties, spending, attention, hospitality>

Depending on your point of view, this might be evidence of an approving connotation of "generosity", or a disapproving connotation of "excessive wastefulness", but the collocates alone are not evidence of either attitude. This is due to methodological problems which we have already seen. First, the concordance lines may provide evidence of negative attitudes, which are not visible in repeated individual words in the collocate lists, because the lexical realizations are so diverse:

- a lavish, unnecessary lifestyle; lavish spending and immature behaviour; lavish spending and sometimes outrageous behaviour; its most lavish and ludicrous conclusion; lavish with the champers; fancy togs or lavish hospitality; lavish parties which degenerate into Roman orgies

Second, a 4 : 4 span is not always large enough to provide evidence of speaker attitude. Some collocates are embedded in longer sequences, which express stereotypes of extravagant lifestyles, or recount criminal activities. Again there are very diverse lexical collocates:

- stretch limos; private jets; he jetted off to St Tropez; pop stardom; an extravagant bash
- a callous couple milked money from a hospital charity to fund a lavish lifestyle

Most of these examples come from journalism.

The distinction between inherent, propositional meaning and connotational meaning (or discourse prosody) may in any case be based on unreliable intuitions. I am assuming that it is possible to make the following distinction. (1) Words such as *abuses, alarming, allergies, anxiety* and *assaulted* express meanings which most speakers find unpleasant. A word such as *gloom* denotes "a feeling of despair": this part of its meaning cannot be logically denied, and is not something which is merely implied or connoted. Similarly, *grim* denotes "unattractive and depressing". (2) However, a word such as *fuelled* could logically be used in positive senses, but the corpus evidence is that it collocates predominantly with words such as *fears, rumours* and *anger*.

An informal way of trying to distinguish between denotation and connotation may be to ask whether a foreign learner could produce an odd implication by using a word in the wrong collocation. For example, a phrase such as *distinctly pleasant* is presumably possible; but either neutral phrases (e.g. *distinctly different*) or disapproving phrases (e.g. *distinctly childish, distinctly odd, distinctly uncomfortable*) are more usual. Here we see the crucial difference between what is possible and what is probable.

Bearing in mind these limitations on how reliably evaluative meanings can be identified, I estimate that something over 5 per cent of the individual head-words in the 1,000-word sample have discourse prosodies, and these are sometimes relatively weak and ill defined. The following are just a few examples where the top 20 collocates of head-words are predominantly negative, sometimes neutral, but rarely if ever positive:

- amid 4,649 <fears, speculation, allegations, concern, controversy, rumours> 12 %
- associated 8,763 <problems, costs, risk(s), disease> 8 %
- attached 5,054 <stigma, blame> 2 %
- bureaucracy 2,099 <bloated 1 %, corruption 1 %>
- considerable 9,179 <pressure, damage> 3 %
- credibility 3,308 <lost, restore, gap, lack, problem, damaged, lose, undermine> 15 %
- easing 1,607 <tension(s) 9 %, sanctions 5 %, pressure 2 %>
- endure 1,256 <forced 3 %, pain 3 %>
- excessive 3,406 <force 10 %, anxiety 2 %, violence 1 %, loss 1 %, bleeding 1 %>
- hurled 962 <abuse, insults> 8 %
- impending 1,040 <doom 5 %, disaster, war, crisis, death, attack, warning, rumours> 24 %
- involving 7,390 <scandal, fraud, violence> 5 %
- load 4,140 <rubbish 5 %, old 2 %, crap 1 %>
- potentially 4,170 <dangerous 9 %, explosive, lethal, fatal, damaging, serious, disastrous, harmful> 27 %
- subjected 1,975 <scrutiny, abuse, harassment, pressure (s), torture, attacks, criticism, barrage> 13 %

The following have a tendency to co-occur with positive collocates:

- derive 767 <benefit (s), pleasure, satisfaction, comfort> 20 %
- discoveries 1,009 <new 8 %, important 4 %, great 3 %, exciting 2 %>
- expression 6,628 <freedom 5 %, artistic, creative> 7 %
- mutual 4,742 <respect, support, understanding, trust, agreement, benefit, interest> 18 %
- provided 17,619 <information, service (s), support, opportunity, care, money, training, food> 11 %

Compare negative *soaring* with positive *roaring*:

- soaring 1,568 <price(s), cost(s), unemployed, inflation, crime, deficit> 28%
- roaring 1,022 <trade, fire, success, laughter> 17%

5.6 Lexical Cohesion: Textual Examples

So far, I have shown the kinds of node–collocate relations which frequently occur in a large corpus, but have not shown how these relations are realized in individual texts. In the next section, I will use a series of text fragments to illustrate how such relations contribute to textual cohesion and to intertextual relations between texts and corpus. (Texts [1], [2], [3], [5] and [6] are from the Longman-Lancaster, LOB and FROWN corpora. See Notes on Corpus Data and Software.)

5.6.1 *Example 1:* just large enough to see with the naked eye

Sinclair (1996) analyses the lexical, grammatical, semantic and pragmatic relations within extended units of meaning. He discusses all 150 examples of the word-pair *naked eye* in a large corpus, and shows that it typically co-occurs with other lexical, grammatical and semantic units. It is almost always preceded by *the*. Further to the left is often a modal verb (*can* or *could*) plus a lexical verb (often *see*) plus *with*; or (*in*)*visible* plus *to*. Other semantically related words occur (e.g. *read* or *recognizable*). In addition, to left and/or right, there is often an expression indicating why it is difficult to see something, usually because it is very small and/or far away. In an independent corpus, I found only examples which confirm exactly these findings. They included:

- just large enough to see with the naked eye
- so small that it couldn't be seen by the naked eye
- bones so tiny that the naked eye has great difficulty in finding them unaided
- can be read, some with the naked eye, others only under magnification
- microscopic hairs, invisible to the naked eye. Each hair is so tiny that it can only be seen . . .

Below [1] is a longer context for the first example above. It is from a well-known popular text on natural history by a British author: *Life on Earth*, Collins, UK, 1979 by David Attenborough.

[1]   Other protistans feed in a different way, photosynthesising with the aid of their packets of chlorophyll. These can be regarded as plants; the

remainder of the group, which feed on them, as animals. The distinction between the two at this level, however, does not have as much meaning as such labelling might suggest, for there are many species that can use both methods of feeding at different times. Some protistans are *just large enough to see with the naked eye*. With a little practice, the creeping grey speck of jelly which is an amoeba can be picked out in a drop of pond water. But there is a limit to the growth of a single-celled creature, for as size increases, the chemical processes inside the cell become difficult and inefficient. Size, however, can be achieved in a different way – by grouping cells together in an organised colony. One species that has done this is *Volvox*, a hollow sphere, almost the size of a pin-head, constructed from a large number of cells, each with a flagellum. (emphasis added)

Note, first, the number of phrases which are related to size, very small things and difficulty of seeing:

- just large enough to see with the naked eye...with a little practice... speck of...an amoeba...can be picked out...a drop of...there is a limit to the growth...a single-celled creature...as size increases... size...cells...the size of a pin-head...cells...

The phrase *naked eye* co-occurs with a prosody of "difficulty, due to size", which is expressed in phrases distributed across several sentences. Some of these expressions are themselves conventionalized phrases, such as *the size of a pin-head*.

It is sometimes thought that lexical cohesion is mainly due to chains of (partially) repeated and semantically related words. These certainly occur in the text fragment, for example

- feed...feed...feeding
- plants...animals
- single-celled...cell...cells...cells
- amoeba...creature

In an influential critique of attempts at text analysis, Morgan and Sellner (1980: 179–80) objected that lexical chains are not a linguistic phenomenon at all, but merely 'an epiphenomenon of coherence of content'. However, Kjellmer (1991) and Hunston and Francis (1998, 2000) show that lexical cohesion is much more than a reflex of logical or content relations, and is partly due to the stringing together and overlapping of formulaic lexical combinations.

In text [1], some chunks are fixed multi-word units:

- naked eye; pond water; single-celled; pin-head

An entirely automatic method of discovering how many such combinations in the text occur frequently in the language could take every possible two-, three-, four-, five- or six-word combination in the text, and check if the same combinations occur in a large corpus. I will short-cut this procedure by taking examples of likely candidates, all in [1], and listing how many times they do in fact occur in a corpus of 50 million words:

- in a different way [126]; with the aid of [113]; can be regarded as [15]; the remainder of the [144]; of the group [508]; the distinction between [101]; the distinction between the two [4]; at this level [115]; might suggest [53]; at different times [104]; naked eye [42]; with a little practice [2]; a drop of [97]; a drop of <word> water [13]; a limit to [63]; there is a limit to the [9]; chemical process(es) [23]; hollow sphere [3]; the striking thing [2]; the size of a pin-head [4]; constructed from [35]; a large number of [391]; virtually the same [31]

(There are two occurrences of *in a different way* in the text fragment itself. The phrase *drop of* occurs in two senses, as in *a drop of water* and *a drop of fifteen per cent*. Only phrases of the first kind have been counted.)

I should perhaps make explicit that I am not in any way criticizing the text fragment for containing such phrases. On the contrary, these features are precisely what makes the text comprehensible and easy to follow.

As I keep emphasizing, extended lexical units are not merely a list of individual phrases, and some of these phrases are part of larger patterns. For example, the phrase *a large number of* is typical of the use of *large*. I studied 56,000 occurrences of *large* in 200 million words. Around 25 per cent co-occurred with words for sizes and quantities, such as *large amount*, *large proportion* and *large scale*. (See chapter 7.6.) Other phrases in the text fragment are variants on common combinations, such that certain words greatly increase the expectation that other words will occur. For example, *a limit to* occurs over 60 times in the corpus, frequently in longer related phrases such as

- a limit to how far / how much / how many
- a limit to the amount / the number

The phrase *speck of* occurs 15 times, several of those in longer related phrases such as

- a little speck of dust; a minute speck of dirt

These analyses show that native speaker intuition and observable corpus data must be combined. It was my intuition which told me which collocations to look for in the corpus. The corpus confirmed my intuition, but gave much more detailed data than my introspection could, and these data suggest an intertextual explanation for why I had the intuitions in the first place.

Here are two other text fragments, which both contain the phrase *naked eye*. Fragment [2] is from an American book on geology, published in 1974; fragment [3] is from a British science fiction novel published in 1961. I will not analyse them in detail, but have italicized the other words which relate to size and difficulty in seeing.

[2]   Minerals make up a rock just as bricks make up a brick wall, in a great variety of arrangements. In *coarse-grained* rocks the minerals are *large enough to be seen with the naked eye*. In some rocks the minerals *can be seen* to have crystal faces, smooth planes bounded by sharp edges; in others, such as a typical sandstone, the minerals are in the form of fragments without faces. In *fine-grained* rocks, the individual mineral *grains* are *so small that they can be seen only with a powerful magnifying glass*, the *hand lens* that the field geologist carries. Some are *so small that a microscope is needed to make them out*.

[3]   The sky seemed to be deserted. Alastair leant across and pressed a switch. A tiny red light sprang into life, only to fade as the screen of the second radar scanner came into operation. This was the ground *definition* unit. Although Geoffrey had relatively *little experience of interpreting* radar pictures, he *was able to recognise* the land beneath him. In *the exceptional clarity* he was *even able to make a direct comparison* between the radar *image* and the ground itself. Ahead lay the Plain of Lombardy; to the right, Turin; to the left, Milan. The directional angle of the scanner could be adjusted to cover any particular area within its range. Geoffrey turned the scale slowly to cover the ground immediately ahead. He was *able to pick out* towns, *unrecognisable to the naked eye, obscured by the ground haze* which *even on the clearest night limited angular vision*.

It is a favourite argument in many introductory linguistics textbooks that there is a vanishingly small chance of ever finding the same sentence occurring twice. The argument runs as follows. Open any book at random, and take the first whole sentence on the page. Now try and find the same sentence in a different book. You will fail. This argument is often combined with a demonstration that there is a potentially infinite number of sentences in a language. At this point, there is usually a caveat, that there are some formulaic sentences which do recur, such as those relating to common social situations (*Nice to meet you!*, *Do you come here often?*). It may also occur to you that there are other whole sentences which any native speaker knows and which are frequently repeated (e.g. *We can't get no satisfaction*). Indeed, there are some text-types (e.g. legal texts) which do use conventional phrasings which have been passed down over the centuries, for example:

[4]   This is the last will and testament of me... I revoke all former wills made by me. I direct that all my just debts and funeral and testamentary expenses be paid as soon as possible after my death.... I give the residue of my real and personal estate... unto my Trustees upon trust for sale with power for my Trustees in their absolute discretion to postpone such sale for so long as they shall think fit.

Nevertheless, so the argument runs, there are very few such sentences and they are peripheral to normal language use, which is much more creative.

The argument as it stands is perfectly correct; however, it rather misses the point. Admittedly, whole sentences (selected at random from a book) are highly unlikely to recur. However, significant chunks of sentences certainly do recur frequently, word for word, and semantic units recur: this is the normal state of affairs in running text. Text [1] contains the phrase *large enough to see with the naked eye*. Text [2] contains *large enough to be seen with the naked eye*.

5.6.2   *Example 2:* causing untold damage

The next example further illustrates the contribution of variable extended lexical units to text cohesion.

[5]   Here the Green Party has launched its Euro-election campaign. Its manifesto, 'Don't Let Your World Turn Grey', argues that the emergence of the Single European Market... will cause untold environmental damage. It derides the vision of Europe as '310 million shoppers in a supermarket'. The Greens want a much greater degree of self-reliance, with 'local goods for local needs'. They say they would abandon the Chunnel, nuclear power stations, the Common Agricultural Policy and agrochemicals. The imagination boggles at the scale of the task they are setting themselves.

Again, some of the cohesion is due to chains of repeated and semantically related words, and some chunks are fixed multi-word units:

- Green, Grey, Greens; Euro-, European, Europe; Party, election, campaign, manifesto; Market, shoppers, supermarket, goods
- the Green Party; the Single European Market; the Common Agricultural Policy; nuclear power stations

Other chunks are variants on common combinations, such that certain words greatly increase the expectation that other words will occur. This assumes that we know the norms of co-occurrence in the language, and it is these norms that can be investigated via the frequency of co-occurences in large corpora. In the examples below I have taken data from a 50-million-word corpus.

- launched its Euro-election campaign

The word-form *launched* co-occurs with restricted sets of semantically related words. Native speakers might think initially of phrases such as *launched a satellite*, or *lifeboats were launched*. However, corpus data show that a much more frequent usage (about 50 times as frequent) is with an abstract object noun, involving a plan: *campaign* is the most frequent; *appeal, bid, programme, project, strategy* also occur; and object nouns may be military, e.g. *attack, offensive, invasion*.

- a much greater degree of self-reliance

Other patterns are more variable again, but still detectable. The word-pair *degree of* is almost always followed by an abstract noun. In the 50-million-word corpus, there were about 350 examples of the pattern: *a* plus quantity adjective plus *degree of* plus abstract noun. The most frequent adjectives were *greater* and *high*, as in *a far greater degree of clarity, a high degree of support*. After *greater*, almost all the nouns expressed positive ideas: e.g. *co-operation, democracy, success*.

- the imagination boggles at

Some words are very restricted in the words they co-occur with: only *mind* frequently co-occurs with *boggles*, and is semantically related to *imagination*.

- the scale of the task

The anaphoric expression above has no single noun phrase to which it refers: it encapsulates a preceding stretch of text. The combination *the scale of the* is followed by abstract nouns which refer back to a general discourse topic (*challenge, operation, problem*), and *task* itself is often used as a metalinguistic label to summarize preceding discourse (G. Francis 1994: 89, and see below).

- the task they are setting themselves

Things one commonly sets oneself include abstract nouns, such as an *aim*, a *challenge*, an *objective*, a *target* or a *task*.

- cause untold environmental damage

In chapter 2.9.2, I analysed the lemma CAUSE and showed that its most frequent collocates are overwhelmingly unpleasant, and that it often occurs in longer combinations of verb plus adjective plus noun, such as *cause great problems*. The example in the text is: *cause untold... damage*. In turn, *untold* is usually followed by an abstract noun, which usually denotes something bad and unpleasant (*untold misery*, *untold suffering*). Most frequent is *untold damage*. Also frequent are large numbers (*untold billions*) and/or large amounts of money (*untold riches*). A few cases are positive (*brought untold joy*), but in this context CAUSE is not used. In the 50-million-word corpus, there were 10 examples such as *caused untold problems, causing untold misery*.

Finally, chunks may overlap with each other. Hunston and Francis (1998: 68) call this 'pattern flow':

- the scale of the task / the task they are setting themselves

If we now look at these chunks together, we see that several have to do with the meaning "large size". There are explicit references to size in the text fragment (*310 million, greater*), but also implicit references. If a campaign is *launched*, the implication is that it is a major event. *Untold*, *boggles* and *the scale of the* all usually co-occur with large numbers or large amounts. These patterns are not explicit in the text, but implicit in the intertextual references to norms of language use. Each individual pattern is probabilistic, but cumulatively the intertextual expectations convey "large size" as a discourse prosody distributed across the text.

We can now see that there is a discourse prosody expressing "size", across both the 'naked eye' texts [1], [2] and [3] and across the 'untold damage' text [5]. The prosodies are of indeterminate length, and expressed in different ways, but both contribute to text cohesion across several sentences.

These characteristics of language use – frequency, probability and norms – can be studied only with quantitative methods and large corpora. However, they are only one factor in text cohesion. It would be an error to identify frequency in a corpus with probability in a text. In the language as a whole, the phrase *launch a campaign* is much more frequent than *launch a lifeboat*, but if the text is about a rescue at sea, then we will expect the latter (though the former is possible). Text content is important alongside intertextual expectations.

More detail can always be added to an analysis, and networks of increasing delicacy can be shown. For example, with the lemma LAUNCH: both *new* and *first* are amongst the most frequent collocates of the three word-forms, *launch*, *launched* and *launching*, as in:

- launched a new campaign; launching a new product; launching his first single; the first time they had launched a bid

Concordance lines show other frequent time references. To LAUNCH something is to start it, and collocates such as *new* and *first* emphasize that something is beginning, but hardly add any further meaning. The phrase *launched its Euro-election campaign* in text [5] is now seen to be a typical use, implying the start of something big and important.

5.6.3 *Example 3:* causing growing pains *and* undergoing a transition

The following text fragment is from an American newspaper published in 1991:

[6] It's precisely these close-minded and socially-retarded attitudes that *cause many of the growing pains* communities in our country experience as they *undergo the transition* from big towns to small cities. If Statesboro wants the prestige and social and economic benefits... (emphasis added)

I have shown the "unpleasant" discourse prosodies around CAUSE and UNDERGO (see chapters 2.9.2 and 4.4.1), and have given their typical collocates. The collocations here fit these patterns exactly: *cause–pains* and *undergo–transition*. The phrase *growing pains* is itself a recurrent phrase. The discourse prosody is confirmed by other pejorative collocates: *close-minded* and *socially-retarded*. The fragment shows also the co-occurrence of antonyms (*big* and *small*), and of related adjectives (*social and economic*). In a corpus of 50 million words, *social* occurred over 11,000 times. In over 15 per cent of cases *social* occurred in a pair or longer sequence of adjectives, often in phrases such as *social and cultural* and *social and political*.

5.6.4 *Example 4:* undergoing rapid star formation

There is a further way in which variants of phrases are used to contruct a cohesive text. Here are a few sentences from a whole-page article entitled 'Astronomers mystified by galaxy evolution', in a serious popular science journal (*New Scientist*, 18 August 1990: 23).

[7] The Magellanic clouds, two nearby galaxies, are undergoing rapid star formation, according to an astronomer in Australia. This flies in the face of theories of how galaxies evolve. Star formation should occur rapidly at first, when a galaxy is young, then level off as gas, the raw material of stars, runs short. ... In the accepted theory of galactic evolution, gravity causes massive clouds of dust and gas to clump together to form galaxies. At first stars are born at a relatively steady rate but, as the galaxy ages, star formation begins to slow. ... Da Costa [an astronomer in Australia] tracks the rate of star formation in a galaxy over time by, first, establishing the age of its star clusters. ... [B]y looking at clusters of different ages in a galaxy, it is possible to determine how the metal ratio of the gas has changed over the life of the galaxy. The metal ratio is important because it indicates the rate of star formation in a galaxy.

This is a text about change (with a characteristic use of UNDERGO collocating with words for evolution and transformation: see chapter 4.4.1). The text contains sets of phrases which express the same propositional meaning in different syntax. The proposition that "stars are formed" is expressed variously as noun plus verb (*stars are born*), and noun plus abstract noun (*star formation*). The proposition that this happens at a particular speed is expressed variously with a verb (*star formation begins to slow*), an empty verb and an adverb (*star formation should occur rapidly*), an adjective (*rapid star formation*), a further abstract noun (*the rate of star formation*), and an abstract noun plus a prepositional phrase (*stars are born at a relatively steady rate*). Similar variants occur with:

- galaxies evolve; galaxy evolution; galactic evolution; galaxies undergo rapid star formation

These alternatives are used not merely for the sake of stylistic variation, but for a more specific discourse purpose. Processes are referred to by both verbs and nouns, often with the verbal form first in the text and the nominal form second:

- stars are born ... star formation
- galaxies evolve ... the galaxy ages ... the age of its star clusters
- the metal ratio of the gas has changed ... the change in the metal ratio
- enriching the gas with metals ... metal enrichment

The nominal form encodes the whole event as a single noun phrase, which can then be used in the discourse to build up more complex noun phrases:

- the rate of star formation in a galaxy
- the rate of metal enrichment

These noun phrases can, in turn, be used as the subject or object of other verbs. Once the concept of speed of formation has been encoded in a single noun phrase, then different rates can be compared with each other:

- *the change in the metal ratio* over time is a pretty good indicator of *the rate of star formation*

Halliday (1993b: 55–6, 69) points out that the sequence in which grammatical variants are used in a text may mirror the sequence in which they were developed in the history of the language. Complex noun phrases are formed so that they can be used to refer to complex phenomena. He analyses a similar example in a text on how stress in glass causes it to crack. The following phrases occur in the text, in this sequence:

- glass cracks; a crack grows; the rate at which cracks grow; the rate of crack growth; the glass crack growth rate

5.7 Collocations and Coherence

In chapter 1, I distinguished between cohesion, which is formally marked in the text, and coherence, which is inferred from background knowledge. Various terms are used for talking about background expectations: frames, schemas, scripts, prototypes, and stereotypes. For example, we have widely shared expectations about recurring events such as going to the dentist, going to school, going on a picnic, or being involved in a traffic accident. These events all involve typical actors, equipment and activities: these are the default values of the schema, which are taken for granted, and can normally be left unsaid, because they can rely on group knowledge. They can therefore support inferences by default (Johnson-Laird 1983: 370–1; 1988: 245), and these inferences can provide textual coherence.

However, expectations do not arise from nowhere. Brown and Yule (1983: 62) discuss how the background assumptions we make about the normality of the world contribute to our understanding of coherent discourse. They argue that 'we assume that' doors open, hair grows on heads, dogs bark, the sun shines. In English, hair is blond, trees are felled, eggs are rotten (but milk is sour, and butter is rancid), we kick with our feet (but punch with our fists, and bite with our teeth). The examples which Brown and Yule use involve precisely such collocations, which are available to intuition, and it is their very banality which contributes to our sense of a predictable and stable world. In an influential sociological discussion, Berger and Luckmann (1966) point to the importance of frequent 'institutional formulae' in the construction of a taken-for-granted everyday reality.

Such collocations reveal some of our stereotypical knowledge of the social world, but they may not correspond to actual usage. For example, the very fact that KICK implies FOOT means that the two words tend not to collocate in running text: they have no need to. In a corpus of 50 million words, I found the following, for a span of 10 : 10:

- KICK 8,742 <FOOT 0.3 %>; FOOT 3,827 <KICK 0.8 %>

That is, KICK and FOOT collocated only about 30 times. There was one example of the tautologous *she kicked at him with her foot* (what else could she have kicked at him with?). A few examples specified some part of the foot (*kicking with the inside of your foot*). Other examples were not really references to kicking at all:

- she swam without haste, in a slow and easy motion, with *kicks* of her thick webbed hind*feet*, and strokes of her tail

So, the collocations which are accessible to introspection must be distinguished from those which actually occur in running text. It is not that the introspective examples are somehow wrong, but that they reveal prototypical concepts.

Due to their default interpretations, words often make general predictions about the content of surrounding text. In a famous experiment, Loftus and Palmer (1974) showed that words can trigger different assumptions, and affect perception and memory. When witnesses to a film of a traffic accident were questioned in different ways (*How fast were the cars travelling when they bumped into each other?* versus *when they smashed into each other?*), they gave systematically different estimates of the speed. Such assumptions do not arise from nowhere, but are created by recurrent collocations in text. In a large corpus, I studied the collocates of past tense forms in the semantic field of "hit". Collocates of HIT itself show its wide range of uses, often metaphorical and/or in fixed phrases (*hit for six; hit rock bottom*):

- HIT <areas, badly, bottom, car, earthquake, flooding, hard, hardest, jackpot, recession, sales, six, target>

In contrast, BUMP has connotations of clumsiness, COLLIDE is used predominantly with large vehicles, SMASH has connotations of crime and violence, and STRIKE has metaphorical uses or is used with natural disasters:

- bumped <accidentally, car, head, lurched, stumbled>
- collided <aircraft, car, jet, lorry, mid-air, plane, ship, tanker, train, trawler, vehicle>
- smashed <bottles, broken, bullet, car(s), glass(es), looted, police, windscreen, window(s)>
- struck <blow, disaster, earthquake, lightning, tragedy>

Pagano (1994: 257) points out that one test for the background expectations of schemas is what can plausibly be denied. Thus one might say (invented example):

- the cars smashed into each other but (oddly enough) there was no broken glass [I]

But the following sounds strange:

- ?the cars bumped slowly into each other but there was no broken glass [I]

In chapters 7, 8 and 9 I give other examples of how recurrent phrases convey cultural connotations (see also Moon 1998: 245, 257–60).

In summary: Corpus study shows recurrent lexico-semantic units, whose scope does not correspond to traditional syntactic units. Syntagmatic lexical patterns both provide a perspective on text cohesion, and also have implications for a theory of communicative competence. In much linguistic theory, a parallelism has often been assumed between syntagmatic/paradigmatic and syntactic/lexical. Lexical items have been seen as filling paradigmatic slots in syntactic chains. This corresponds to aspects of linguistic competence which are tapped by introspection and elicitation, but it does not always correspond to actual behaviour. Corpus study has shown that this slot-and-filler model is inadequate: syntagmatic organization is much stronger than often realized, and there are rarely, if ever, free paradigmatic choices of lexis.

Corpus studies show that the great majority of words typically occur in simple semantic patterns, whose lexical realization can be highly variable. We can predict the semantic patterns, and we can even predict the percentage of occurrences with a given lexical realization, but we cannot predict the outcome in individual cases. That is, we can make predictions relative to a corpus, but not to a text. This clarifies a common confusion about *parole*. Many features of an individual text (= *parole*) are idiosyncratic: if they were not, the text would convey no information and there would be no point in reading it. But a corpus is not mere performance: as a sample of language use, it reveals typical and repeated patterns (see chapter 10).

5.8 Summary and Implications

The main analysis in this chapter of texts [1] to [7] illustrates several principles, some of which we have seen before.

(1) Collocational facts are linguistic. They cannot be reduced to content or logic.
(2) Many phrases are idiomatic, but are not idioms. This is because, although the combinations frequently occur, they are not entirely fixed, and/or they are compositional and semantically transparent. More accurately, they are not idioms of decoding, but are idioms of encoding (see chapter 3.1).
(3) Many phrases have conventional meanings. For example, the combination *naked eye* is not entirely semantically transparent. It could mean all kinds of things, such as "with unprotected eyes" or "without spectacles", but, as Sinclair (1996: 84) points out, it is conventionally used to mean "without the use of telescope, microscope, etc."
(4) A theory of language use must find a balance between creative and routine language use. Much linguistics, especially post-1960, has emphasized the creative aspects of language, and ignored the predictable combinations which constitute a large percentage of normal language use (though see Bolinger 1976; Pawley and Syder 1983; Allerton 1984; Sinclair 1991; and Miller 1993). These combinations have implications for our concept of fluent and idiomatic native-speaker competence.
(5) Syntagmatic patterning is much more fine-grained than is generally shown in grammars. Semantic units stretch well beyond words and short phrases, and are a relatively unexplored mechanism of text cohesion.
(6) Analysis cannot be restricted to isolated texts. It requires an analysis of intertextual relations, and therefore comparison of individual instances in a given text, typical occurrences in other texts from the same text-type, and norms of usage in the language in general.

One topic which I have largely ignored is that preferred mechanisms of cohesion differ in different text-types. For example, scientific research articles often mark anaphora by repeating whole noun phrases, whereas popular accounts use pronouns. Scientific text-types have been thoroughly described (for example, Myers, 1994, compares scientific research reports with popular accounts of the same topics by the same authors, and Atkinson, 1999, is a study of the historical development of scientific genres), but little comparative analysis of cohesion in different genres has yet been done.

5.9 Background and Further Reading

The classic work on lexical field theory was done on German in the 1920s to 1940s, by Trier (1931) and Weisgerber (1950). It is probably best known to English-speaking linguists via Ullmann (1957) and Lyons (1977). Porzig (1934) also did early influential work on collocations.

Most of the large literature on cohesion lays little emphasis on the role of collocations. For example, Halliday and Hasan (1976), the standard reference, has only four pages on collocations, which are said to be 'the most problematical part of lexical cohesion' (p. 284). On the other hand, the literature on phraseology usually regards word combinations in their own right as linguistic units, and not from the point of view of their contribution to text cohesion. However, for work on collocations and text cohesion, see Kjellmer (1991), Moon (1994), and Bublitz (1996, 1998).

Other work has identified classes of words whose function is primarily to organize text. General nouns, which refer to whole topics (such as *affair, business, claim, matter*), general verbs (e.g. *happen, occur*), and words which contribute to logical structure (such as *conclude, fact, reason, subsequent*) are discussed by Halliday and Hasan (1976), Partington (1998: 92ff), and Winter (1977). Other examples of 'procedural vocabulary' and prospective rhetorical devices are discussed by Widdowson (1983) and Tadros (1994).

Some studies have used computational techniques to study the contribution of lexis to textual organization. G. Francis (1994) uses large corpora to identify the nominal groups which are typically used to encapsulate and often evaluate discourse topics, and which often use common collocations (as in *this far-sighted recommendation; this thoughtless and stupid attitude*). Yang (1986) shows how technical and sub-technical words can be identified on the basis of their statistical behaviour: technical vocabulary is restricted to texts on particular specialized topics, whereas sub-technical vocabulary is both frequent and evenly distributed in academic texts, independent of their specialism (for example, words such as *accuracy, basis, decrease, effect, factor, result*). Phillips (1985, 1989) uses automatic methods of lexical analysis to study the distribution of lexis in science textbooks, and how words therefore contribute to cohesion within chapters.

5.10 Topics for Further Study

In a study of corpora of written and spoken English, Erman and Warren (2000: 53) estimate that between 40 and 60 per cent of running text may consist of ready-made combinations of words. Such estimates depend on the methods used in the calculation, especially on the texts sampled and on the exact definition of 'ready-made' (for example, as strings of word-forms or abstract semantic units). Erman and Warren (2000) talk of conventionalization and of 'prefabs', Hunston and Francis (2000: 215ff) talk of 'pattern strings' and of 'pattern flow', and Biber et al. (1999: 993) talk of 'lexical bundles'. But the general conclusion, as throughout this chapter, is that a significant proportion of language use is routinized, conventionalized and idiomatic.

(1) Decide on a definition of 'ready-made' language.

(2) Select some text fragments and estimate the extent to which they consist of 'ready-made' extended lexical units.

(3) It might be possible to range texts along a continuum from those which are highly routinized to those which are highly creative. Some types of legal text would be towards the routinized end of the continuum: see text [4] above. Some types of poetry might be at the creative end (though literary creativity is certainly not restricted to such aspects of idiomatic language use). Give examples of more and less routinized texts, and consider reasons for such variation.

(4) What implications does this view of routinized language use have for theories of language comprehension and production?

6

Words in Texts 2: A Case Study of a Short Story

The main aim of this chapter is to show how computer-assisted methods can be used to study lexical patterns in texts. The main data are from a single short story by James Joyce, and as comparative data I have used two different reference corpora of one million and two and a half million running words. One main argument throughout the book is that text analysis must always be comparative: we can interpret patterns in an individual text only if we know what is to be expected in the language as a whole. In addition, since no single corpus can be a perfect sample of language in use, it is often wise to use two or more independent corpora in comparisons.

6.1 Public Data and Replicable Experiments

An essential feature of computer-assisted text and corpus linguistics is that both data and methods are publicly accessible. Here, the data are a well-known short story and publicly available corpora. Also, computational procedures can be explicitly defined: they may, for example, be embodied in commercially available concordance software (such as Scott 1997a), or defined in student textbooks on corpus linguistics (such as Barnbrook 1996) or more specialized articles (such as Stubbs 1995a).

When data and methods are publicly available, then findings can be replicated. If language study is based on introspective data from the individual linguist, a genuinely reproducible experiment is rarely possible, since neither data nor methods are independent of the analyst. However, in many academic areas, replication of experimental results is taken for granted as an essential procedure for checking and refining knowledge. One scholar presents results, and describes the data and the research method which were used. A second scholar, independently, uses this description to reproduce the experiment, to check whether the method is feasible, and whether the same results can be obtained.

It is sometimes necessary to check an analysis by replicating it on exactly the same data, but it is also necessary to check the findings on different, but comparable, data, in order to see whether they were an artefact of one single data-set. Such comparisons are becoming increasingly possible in corpus linguistics, since findings from one corpus are a prediction about what will be found in other independent corpora. The methods, data and findings are in the public domain, where their reliability can be tested, confirmed, criticized and developed by independent witnesses, who repeat and refine experiments using comparable procedures on different data-sets.

I will illustrate these points by discussing how words are distributed in texts. First, I will discuss some features of word frequency and word sequence, which are very simple but can nevertheless reveal interesting properties of textual organization. Second, I will discuss some features of vocabulary distribution, based on a more sophisticated analysis proposed by Youmans (1991). I will replicate Youmans's analysis, using one of the same texts as he does, and developing some points in his argument.

There is a difference between findings (however produced) and their interpretation. Computer-assisted methods of text analysis cannot interpret texts for us, but they can provide, for subsequent human interpretation, new kinds of evidence. I will show that quantitative methods provide empirical ways of studying the lexical patterns which make texts cohesive, but the emphasis is on semi-automatic or computer-assisted methods.

6.2 Lexis and Text Structure

A text is a semantic unit of language in use. Examples of written texts include short stories, newspaper articles and school-books. For a text to be comprehensible, it must be lexically cohesive: it must contain chains of repeated and related words, distributed across the text, in patterns of old and new information. The large literature on text and discourse analysis contains relatively little on how lexis contributes to textual organization (though see the references in chapter 5.9). This is a surprising omission, because it is only the vocabulary which can tell the reader what a text is about.

Analysts have been pessimistic about finding linguistic markers of structural boundaries in long texts, such as whole novels, or even short stories. In a review of this topic, Paltridge (1994) argues that patterns of cohesion are of little help in formally identifying boundaries, since chains of lexical cohesion run across the boundaries which readers intuitively identify. He concludes that sections of texts are distinguished on semantic grounds: that is, by reference to their content, and not to their form. It is certainly correct that it is often meaning and content which lead to judgements about textual boundaries, but topics are, after all, signalled by vocabulary, and it should therefore be possible to study how they are formally marked. Much work has been done on the structural organization of academic articles, and the different stylistic features of abstract, introduction, main text and conclusions (Swales 1990). However, as Paltridge (1994: 293) notes, once a certain level of complexity is reached, titles, sub-titles and the like are generally used to keep track of textual structure. Structural markers of this type are, however, not used in fictional texts. Short stories are not divided up into sections such as 'exposition' and 'introducing the main characters', yet literary critics regularly identify such sections in narratives. So, again, it should be possible to find the formal basis for such judgements.

In order to test how far we can push the idea that lexis contributes to textual structure, I will treat a text in the most simplistic way imaginable: merely a string of word-forms, which are in turn merely strings of characters separated by spaces or punctuation. The computer software has no access to any other structural information at all: it is unable to group word-forms into lemmas, grammatical classes or lexical sets, and it has no access to tagged or parsed versions of the text. Therefore, it will treat as entirely different words: members of a lemma such as *go*, *goes*, *going*, *gone* and *went*, as well as pairs such as *mother* and *father*, or *house* and *home*.

Lists of word frequencies and plots of word distributions can give only hints as to how a text can be interpreted, but they may help in identifying major topics and textual boundaries, and thus provide an empirical basis for interpretation. If these techniques are applied to a diverse sample of texts, this may reveal general mechanisms of text cohesion. A major advantage of computer-assisted analysis is that it transcends the very limited human capacities of memory and observation, and can help identify patterns across large corpora of language use. However, in order to have confidence in a method, we must also check its results on small texts which are within the narrow limits of human observation.

My main example, the short story 'Eveline' from *Dubliners* by James Joyce (1914), is convenient as a main illustration. First, it is short, a little over 1,800 words. Second, the story is well known, and widely available to readers who want to check my analysis. Third, it has been the subject of many literary critical and stylistic analyses (such as Hart 1969; Chatman 1969): we can therefore compare the computer's results with the interpretations of trained critics. Fourth, it is one of Youmans's (1991) main examples: I can illustrate his methods, and compare his findings with mine. (Along with other stories from *Dubliners*, the text is available in machine-readable form, in the Longman-Lancaster corpus. See Notes on Corpus Data and Software.) A summary of the story will make my argument easier to follow:

A young woman (Eveline) is sitting at home, looking out of the window, watching passers-by, and remembering incidents from her childhood, including a difficult relation with her father, and the death of her mother. She is thinking about a possible future life: whether to leave home, and to go to South America with a man called Frank whom she has recently met: 'Was that wise? She tried to weigh each side of the question.' She gets up 'in a sudden impulse of terror', with the thought that she must escape from her restricting home life, and goes to the harbour where a boat to Buenos Ayres is waiting to sail. Frank is there: he pleads with Eveline to leave with him, but she finds it impossible to go.

6.3 Analysis 1: Frequency Statistics (Descending Frequency Order)

6.3.1 Frequency of function words: statistics

An essential starting point for many quantitative text analyses is a word frequency list, and even the frequencies of the most common function words in a text can be revealing, if they are compared with the most frequent words in general use. The ten most frequent words in the LOB corpus (see Notes on Corpus Data and Software) of one million words of general written English, and in 'Eveline', in descending frequency, are:

[1] LOB: the of and to a in that is was it
[2] 'Eveline': the her she to had of and he a was

The most frequent word in both corpus and text is *the*. This is only to be expected: it is usual to find that the single word *the* makes up a large percentage of any running text. Here, its frequency as a percentage of the total running words is slightly higher in the corpus than in the text: LOB 6.8 per cent, 'Eveline' 5.6 per cent.

However, there are words which occur in [2], but not in [1]: *her*, *she*, *had* and *he*. This shows simply that these four words occur higher in the frequency list from 'Eveline'. In order to estimate how much more frequent they are in the story than in the language as a whole, we can compare their frequency, as a percentage of the total running words, in the corpus and in the text:

[3] LOB: her 0.40 %, she 0.39 %, had 0.54 %, he 0.88 %
[4] 'Eveline': her 5.25 %, she 4.54 %, had 2.57 %, he 2.46 %

Relative to text length, *her* and *she* are over ten times as frequent in the text as in the corpus. This difference in relative frequencies becomes even more striking if we compare their frequencies to the most frequent word, *the*. Thus, for example, we take the absolute frequencies, in the text and in the corpus, of the words *her* and *the*, and calculate one as a percentage of the other. For 'Eveline', we have *her* 96, *the* 103: 96 is 93 per cent of 103.

[5] LOB: her 6 %, she 6 %, had 8 %, he 13 %
[6] 'Eveline': her 93 %, she 81 %, had 46 %, he 44 %

These statistics begin to show the kind of lexical selection which Joyce has made.

6.3.2 Interpretation

To the human analyst, it is obvious that [3], [4], [5] and [6] contain three third-person singular pronoun forms: *her*, *she*, *he*. We might wonder whether completing the pattern, by looking at the other third-person singular pronouns, *him/his* and *it*, would also be revealing. However, the differences in relative frequency here are much smaller. As percentages of *the*, they are

[7] LOB: him/his 13 %, it 15 %
[8] 'Eveline': him/his 19 %, it 11 %

A check back with the text shows that almost all instances of *her* and *she* refer to Eveline; instances of *he* and *him/his* are split mainly between Frank and Eveline's father (only a few refer to other peripheral characters, such as a man whom Eveline sees from the window). The form *had* is frequent since Eveline is remembering past events (*they had all gone for a picnic*) or thinking over the present (*in her home ... she had shelter and food*).

There is a second pattern. The forms *her* 96 and *she* 83 are more frequent than *he* 45 and *him/his* 18. But for the female character, the subject pronoun is less frequent than other pronouns, whereas for the male characters, the subject pronoun is more frequent. This is a story in which Frank wants Eveline to act, but in the end she cannot act (as he wishes).

6.3.3 *Frequency of content words: statistics*

The 100 most frequent words in a large general corpus will be almost all function (grammatical) words. The figure of 100 is an arbitrary cut-off point, but after this point frequency lists for large corpora contain mainly content words (nouns, verbs, adjectives and adverbs: see chapter 2.8.1). A frequency list for 'Eveline', which ignores the 100 most frequent words in LOB, therefore identifies the most frequent content words in the story:

[9] father 11, used 11, home 10, life 7, not 7, Frank 6, go 6
[10] always, away, come, felt, Harry, money, mother, mother's never, no, see (all frequency 5)

(The content words which do occur in the 100 most frequent words in LOB, with their frequencies in 'Eveline', are: *then* 8, *like* 6, *now* 5, *other* 4, *people* 4, *time* 4, *said* 3, *first* 2, *made* 2, *man* 2, *new* 2, *two* 2, *years* 2, *Mr* 0.)

6.3.4 Interpretation

In [9] and [10], several keywords (see below on this concept) have now risen to the top. The words *father* and *home* signal important topics in the story. The word *used* (all in *used to*) occurs because Eveline is remembering her childhood or meetings with Frank. Other words in the lists identify further key topics.

If we give our procedures information on different types of word-groups, the patterns are not changed, but some become more striking. If we lemmatize the word-forms, then several words become more prominent, though this may not be particularly revealing:

[11] GO (go, going, gone, went) 14; FATHER (father, father's) 12; MOTHER (mother, mother's) 10; SAY (say, saying, said) 10; HOUSE (house, houses) 8; KNOW (know, known, knowing, knew) 7; GIVE (give, given, gave) 7; PEOPLE (people, people's) 5; PLAY (play, played, playing, player) 5

More revealing might be to group the words so as to show semantically related sets, such as

[12] father('s) 12, mother ('s) 10, brothers 2, sisters 2, children 4: total 30
[13] home 10, house (s) 8: total 18

In a literary critical analysis, Hart (1969: 52) points out that 'the words *house* and *home* occur no fewer than 18 times', but he does not explain why he cites only this single statistic. One could equally well point out that the semantically related words in [12] occur a total of 30 times.

In themselves, these statistics hardly tell us anything which is not evident from reading the text. After all, the story recounts a relationship between Eveline and two men, her father and Frank. However, even modest initial facts about word frequencies can be of interest. (1) They show that central topics of the story are reflected in simple facts about word frequency. (2) The statistics are features of the text, which require subjective human interpretation, but the facts themselves were not brought into existence by the interpretation. (3) Although a human reader can observe the frequency of pronouns in a single short story in a rough and ready way, this would not be possible with a longer text, and the comparative facts (the norms represented by the general corpus versus the selections in the individual text) are certainly not open to direct observation. (4) Combined with a knowledge of the text, statistics help in selecting features for further study.

6.4 Analysis 2: Frequency Statistics (Keywords)

In [2] I gave the ten most frequent words in 'Eveline'. The next ten most frequent words are as follows. (Eleven are listed, since the last four all have the same frequency of 11.)

[14]   in, that, would, with, on, for, out, father, his, it, used

This list now contains the word *would* ($n = 18$): see below. It also contains two lexical words, *father* ($n = 11$) and *used* ($n = 11$), which have already occurred in [9] above. In LOB, *would* is at rank 43, and *father* and *used* are not in the top 100.

So far, I have made simple comparisons between the text and a corpus. It is possible to generalize these procedures, and to compare a text with a reference corpus in order to see which words occur significantly more frequently (according to standard statistical tests) in the text than in the corpus. This type of analysis is proposed by Scott (1997b, 1997c, 1997d) and it can be carried out using software which he has written (Scott 1997a). The analysis compares two frequency lists from the text and from the corpus, and, controlling for the size of text and corpus, generates a list of words which occur with unusual frequency in the text. I am here only looking at words which are high in frequency in the text. More accurately, Scott (1997b) defines as keywords those words in a text whose frequency is either unusually high or unusually low, in comparison to a reference corpus. The statistical test of significance used is a log likelihood test (Dunning 1993).

Using this software, I compared 'Eveline' with a different corpus of around 2.5 million words of written British English, both fiction and non-fiction. The comparison showed the following words to be significantly more frequent in the story. (The probability of error was less than one in a million for all items.)

[15]   her, she, had, Frank, Ernest, Ayres, Harry, he, home, Buenos, father, avenue, mother's, used, would

As Scott (1997b: 51) points out, keywords usually 'give a reasonably good clue to what the text is about'. As here, proper nouns will often be frequent in a specific text, but rare in a large corpus (Ernest and Harry are Eveline's brothers). Otherwise, there is a large overlap with words we have already identified in raw frequency lists. The words *her, she, had*, and *he* occurred in the first analysis: see list [2]. The words *Frank, Harry, home, father, mother's* and *used* occurred as soon as we ignored the top 100 words: see lists [9] and [10].

One word which has been picked out by the keywords procedure, in [15], is *would*. It occurred in [14] but not in earlier lists, and it is worth looking at it in more detail. It occurs 18 times, and in the context of the story, it does indeed seem to be significant. This is a story in which Eveline is thinking about – but in the end failing to act on – hypothetical possibilities for her future. Examples from the text (emphasis added) are:

[16] [Eveline is thinking about leaving home] Perhaps she *would* never see again those familiar objects.... But in her new home, in a distant unknown country... she *would* be married – she, Eveline. People *would* treat her with respect then. She *would* not be treated as her mother had been... Frank *would* save her. He *would* give her life, perhaps love, too.... Frank *would* take her in his arms.... He *would* save her.... If she went, tomorrow she *would* be on the sea with Frank.

6.5 Analysis 3: Frequency Statistics (Order of Occurrence)

The methods so far tell us nothing about how the words are distributed in the text: they might be spread evenly throughout or clustered together.

6.5.1 Statistics

An alternative to presenting words in descending order of frequency is to present them, with their frequencies, but in their order of occurrence in the text (Sinclair 1991: 30; Barnbrook 1996: 48–50), and this can give the first hints about text structure. For example, the first paragraph of 'Eveline' is:

[17] She sat at the window watching the evening invade the avenue. Her head was leaned against the window curtains and in her nostrils was the odour of dusty cretonne. She was tired.

A frequency list sorted in text order of occurrence therefore begins like this:

[18]   she 83, sat 2, at 10, the 103, window 4, watching 1, evening 4, invade 1, avenue 4, her 96, head 4, was 40, leaned 1, against 2, curtains 1, and 46, in 33, nostrils 1, odour 2, of 47, dusty 2, cretonne 2, tired 1

A well-known fact about texts of many kinds is that a few words occur frequently, most words occur rarely, and about half of the word-types occur once only. We can see from [18] those lexical words which occur in the opening paragraph, and which then occur more than once:

[19]   sat, window, evening, avenue, head, odour, dusty, cretonne

With such a list for the whole text, we can see which words are introduced for the first time only late in the story. For example, *Eveline* herself is not named (except in the title) until almost a third of the way through the story, and the words *Frank* and *him* occur for the first time at almost exactly the mid-point. Frank has been mentioned once earlier (*a fellow*), but not named. The paragraph in which he is first named is, intuitively, a new topic in the story. Here is the paragraph, in which the software has marked (>) the words which occur for the first time:

[20]   She was about to >explore >another life with >Frank. Frank was >very >kind, >manly, >open-hearted. She was to go away with >him by the >night-boat to be his >wife and to >live with him in >Buenos >Ayres where he had a home waiting for her. >How >well she >remembered the >first time she had >seen him; he was >lodging in a house on the >main >road where she used to >visit.

The corresponding frequencies of the 'new words' are:

[21]   explore 1, another 2, Frank 6, very 4, kind 1, manly 1, open-hearted 1, him 9, night-boat 1, wife 1, live 2, Buenos 3, Ayres 3, how 1, well 1, remembered 4, first 2, seen 1, lodging 1, main 1, road 1, visit 1

In [21] the new lexical words, with a frequency greater than one, are:

[22]   another 2, Frank 6, very 4, live 2, Buenos 3, Ayres 3, remembered 4, first 2

This procedure also shows which new words are introduced only in the closing paragraph of the story:

[23]   He >rushed >beyond the >barrier and >called to her to >follow. He was >shouted at to go on, but he still called to her. She >set her white face to him, >passive, like a >helpless >animal. Her >eyes gave him no >sign of love >or >farewell or >recognition.

6.5.2   Interpretation

Since *she* is the first word of the story, see [17], it has no anaphoric referent. (Only once we know the story, are we sure that it refers to the name in the title.) In addition, the first sentence contains definite articles in *the window* and *the avenue*, which also have no anaphoric referents. The opening forces the reader to forgo all preliminary information, to make inferences about who *she* is, to accept that *the window* and *the avenue* are familiar to this unnamed female character, and to adopt her (non-omniscient) point of view.

In an influential discussion of narrative techniques, Stanzel (1984: 158ff) points out that only a fictional text could begin in this way, and that this use of referentless pronouns and definite articles is a signal of a story which starts *in medias res*. He cites another short story which begins in a similar way, Somerset Maugham's 'The force of circumstance':

- *She* was sitting on *the* verandah waiting for her husband to come in for luncheon.   (emphasis added)

Joyce himself uses the same device in the opening sentences of other stories in *Dubliners*, for example (emphasis added):

- There was no hope for *him* this time: it was *the* third stroke.   ('The sisters')
- Eight years before *he* had seen *his* friend off at *the* North Wall and wished him God-speed.   ('A little cloud')
- Two gentlemen who were in *the* lavatory at *the* time tried to lift *him* up: but *he* was quite helpless.   ('Grace')

It might be thought that because of these features of the fictional text, the frequency of the definite article would be higher than average in 'Eveline'. In fact, the frequency of *the* and *a* in 'Eveline' is slightly lower than in the reference corpus. (As a percentage of running words the figures are LOB: *the* 6.8, *a* 2.3; 'Eveline': *the* 5.6, *a* 2.2.) We can make such inferences about text-type and point of view only from the order of occurrence of the words, and not from their frequency alone.

6.6 Analysis 4: A Vocabulary-management Profile

The techniques illustrated so far are described, along with related methods, in textbooks on corpus work (Barnbrook 1996: 43–64) and other articles (Scott 1997c, 1997d). I now discuss a more powerful method, described by Youmans (1991), which can tell us about the overall structure of the text.

6.6.1 Types and tokens, vocabulary and text

This method makes use of the distinction between (word-) types and (word-) tokens, and of a statistic known as the type–token ratio. Each word-form which occurs in a text is a word-token. When we say that a story is 1,800 words long, we are referring to word-tokens, but the story will not consist of 1,800 different words, since some words will be repeated, some quite frequently (see chapter 2.2). When we are talking of the number of different words in a text, we are referring to word-types. So, if the word *home* occurs ten times in the story, then this is ten word-tokens, but only one word-type.

The type–token ratio is the ratio of the number of different words in the text to the number of running words. As a text becomes longer, the type–token ratio becomes lower. This is because the number of word-tokens continues to rise at a constant rate, but the number of word-types rises more and more slowly, since words tend to get repeated more and more often. If the text was very long indeed, the speaker or writer would eventually run out of new words: everyone's vocabulary is finite. So, eventually, there would be no new types, only new tokens. Therefore, the type–token ratio is a measure of the lexical diversity of a text. It depends on the size of an author's vocabulary, and on the way in which the words in this vocabulary are used in the text. As speaker-writers produce a text as a linear sequence of word-forms, they must continually choose between using 'old' words (which have already occurred in the text) or 'new' words. Not all of these choices are conscious, and many will be influenced by grammatical rules. (A general model of text production based on these ideas is set out by Tuldava 1998: 84–6.)

As the text gets longer, the probability of new words steadily declines. The speaker-writer is under two opposing pressures. New words are needed in order to develop and broaden the topic, otherwise the same things are being continually repeated. And old words are needed in order to make the text cohesive, otherwise the text will become impossibly diverse and incomprehensible. (This is often expressed by saying that a text must have a certain level of redundancy.) In any case, for syntactic reasons, a small set of function words must be constantly repeated. This second tendency places limits on the lexical diversity of the text.

There are different limits for lexical and grammatical words. As a text gets longer, the number of different lexical word-types gets larger, subject to the constraint of what the text is about, and subject to the ultimate constraint of the size of the author's vocabulary. But the number of grammatical word-types is limited and quite small. Although 30 to 40 per cent of the running words in written texts are likely to be grammatical word-tokens (see chapter 2.8.1 on lexical density), these will be realizations of a small set of word-types which keep recurring. So, in creating the text, the speaker-writer makes choices from the available vocabulary, and alternates between repeating old words and introducing new words (with different patterns of repetition for lexical and grammatical words). These opposing pressures operate not only over whole texts, but cyclically over smaller sections of texts. Texts turn out to have distributions of old and new vocabulary, which show both regularities and breaks. In short text fragments, the patterns of old–old–old–new–new–old can be seen in several of my examples above, such as [20].

These ideas have implications for topics such as measures of reading difficulty (a text which contains a high percentage of 'new' words may be more difficult to understand), or authorship attribution (authors vary in the extent to which they repeat the same words from a relatively small vocabulary or use words from a large diverse vocabulary). They also have implications for estimating how adequately a corpus represents a language, since this depends not only on its size (in running words of text), but also on the size of the vocabulary on which it draws. Again see Tuldava (1998: 82ff).

6.6.2 *Youmans's method*

Youmans (1991) has proposed a computational method of text analysis based on these ideas. Usually, the type–token ratio is calculated as a single statistic for whole texts, but Youmans's method is to calculate the type–token ratio separately for different segments of text. I have not had access to his software: based on the description in his 1991 article, the software has been rewritten from scratch (see Acknowledgements, above). For purposes of replicating findings, it is better in any case to reconstruct a method from first principles.

The software identifies points in the text at which new words are used for the first time, by sampling the type–token ratio within a moving span of running word-tokens. The moving span proceeds token-by-token through the text: for example, from word 1 to 35, 2 to 36, 3 to 37, and so on. The program keeps track of all word-types in the text so far. For each new span, it checks whether the words in the current span have already occurred earlier in the text (old words), or whether they are occurring here for the first time (new words). The span size can be altered to any value, and a larger span will show broader patterns across a longer text. Within the span, it calculates the ratio of new words to old words. This ratio is stored along with its position in the text, taken as the mid-point of the span. On a given run of the program, the span (of word-tokens) remains constant, say 35, but the number of new word-types varies. If every word-token in the span is a new word-type, the type–token ratio is $35/35 = 1$: in practice, this is highly unlikely. If every word has occurred before, the type–token ratio is $0/35 = 0$: in relatively short texts this is also unlikely, but in long texts, the ratio can move to zero, especially if smaller spans are set.

For any normal narrative or discursive text, the ratio will be higher at the beginning of the text, where most words are new, but it will quickly decrease. The only exceptions will be texts with 'odd' structures: for example, a shopping list might be cohesive due to a list of semantically related words (e.g. *butter, cheese, mince, tomatoes*), but it could consist of a sequence of words which each occur once only: the number of word-tokens equals the number of word-types.

(The program can be given a stop-list of high-frequency words which are ignored in the checking of word types. After the first few words, non-content, grammatical words are likely to be evenly distributed throughout the text. Therefore, as Youmans (1991: 766) points out, a stop-list will affect the distribution curve for the first few spans, but make little difference subsequently.)

So, the program reads in a text, and prints out the type–token ratios with their text positions, the mid-points of the moving span. Output is in three columns: word, token, type–token ratio. Word is the current word in the running text; token is a number, its position in the running text; and type–token ratio is defined above. These figures can then be converted into a type–token curve using any convenient software.

6.6.3 'Eveline'

Here, I will illustrate the power of the technique to identify significant boundaries in the text. (See Youmans 1991, 1994, for more detailed discussion.)

Outputs from runs of the program on 'Eveline' are shown in figures 6.1 and 6.2, with the span set at 35 and 151. The curves start high: at the beginning of the text all words occur for the first time. But soon, words start to be repeated: if this were not so, then the text would not be cohesive at all. The smaller span in figure 6.1 shows more jagged ups and downs, and, as Youmans (1991: 783) points out, it shows quite regular peaks where new vocabulary is introduced every 100 words or so. The larger span in figure 6.2

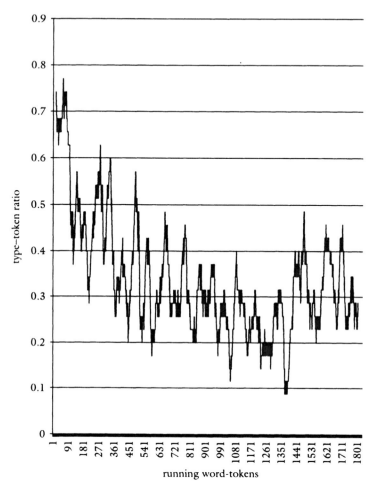

Figure 6.1 'Eveline', span 35

shows more clearly the overall structure: a steady down-slope, with small intervening peaks, until three-quarters of the way through the story, where there is the longest up-slope in the whole curve.

Care needs to be taken in interpreting such curves, and data on many texts will have to be compared before the principles are well understood. The down-slopes tell us relatively little about the text structure. First, there is a general tendency for the type–token ratio to decrease over the whole text: figures 6.1 and 6.2 show this clearly. Second, for a given down-slope, we do not know whether old words have occurred much earlier in the text or only recently. (An adjustment to the program would allow 'old' words to be

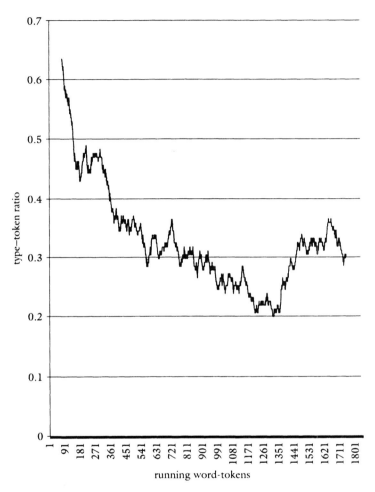

Figure 6.2 'Eveline', span 151

treated again as 'new' if they have not occurred for some given stretch of text, say 2,000 words. This might be particularly revealing in longer texts, such as whole novels. Later work by Youmans [personal communication] uses this adjustment to the technique.)

However, up-slopes are easier to interpret: these are the points at which new lexis is being used for the first time (Youmans 1991: 77; 1994: 118ff). If a prominent up-slope occurs late in the text, then this is likely to signal a major boundary. The new words have, as it were, had the chance to occur during the whole story so far, but they have not occurred till now. Although late in the text, a burst of new vocabulary is introducing a new turn in the story. I will concentrate on the lowest point and the following single most prominent rise in the curve in figure 6.2.

A feature of the text which would surely not be missed by any alert reader is that Joyce uses almost identical lexis at two points in the story: in the opening sentences and towards the end, as Eveline's time is 'running out':

[24] [token 1] >She >sat >at >the >window. . . . >Her >head >was >leaned >against the window >curtains >and >in her >nostrils was the >odour >of >dusty >cretonne.

[25] [token 1316] Her time was >running out but she >continued to >sit by the window, >leaning her head against the window >curtain, >inhaling the odour of dusty cretonne.

Section [25] corresponds precisely to the lowest point on the curve, three-quarters of the way through the story.

The exact coincidence between this sentence and the lowest point of the curve is an artefact of the chosen span of 151. With a span of 35, the lowest point on the curve comes around 50 words later. (Youmans, 1991: 783, uses a span of 35 to identify the deepest valley and its following major peak in the curve for 'Eveline': his findings correspond exactly with mine.) Longer spans are less sensitive to local variations in vocabulary, but much work requires to be done on how the span size affects the details of the analysis. As Youmans (1991: 76) puts it, vocabulary curves correlate with information flow, but they act like a wind-sock, 'surprisingly effective in telling us which way, and even how hard, the wind is blowing, although it typically lags slightly behind (or jumps slightly ahead) of major changes in the weather'.

Up to this point in the story, there has been no external action. Eveline has been sitting at the window, remembering incidents from her childhood and the more recent past with her father and Frank. Now, she hears a street organ outside and this reminds her of a street organ playing on the night of her mother's death. The curve remains low across the next sentences:

[26] [token 1342] Down >far in the avenue she could >hear a >street >organ >playing. She knew the >air.

The curve then starts to rise, as her mother's death scene is described:

[27] [token 1358] >Strange that it >should come that very night to >remind her of the >promise to her mother, her promise to keep the home together as long as she could. She remembered the last night of her mother's >illness; she was again in the >close >dark room.

The curve continues to rise to high points between tokens 1430 and 1480, the point in the story which describes her mother's final madness and death:

[28] [token 1431] She remembered her father >strutting back >into the >sick-room >saying: '>Damned >Italians! Coming over >here!' As she >mused the >pitiful >vision of her mother's life laid its >spell on the very >quick of her being – that life of >commonplace >sacrifices >closing in >final >craziness. She >trembled as she heard again her mother's >voice saying >constantly with >foolish >insistence: '>Derevaun >Seraun! Derevaun Seraun!'

Here the curve is higher than it has been since around token 735. The story has reached a lexical high point. The curve remains high, as the text continues with Eveline's first physical action in the whole story:

[29] [token 1493] She >stood up in a >sudden >impulse of >terror. >Escape! She >must escape! Frank would >save her.

The curve dips slightly, but stays high as she goes to the harbour, and meets Frank. The peak reaches its highest point between tokens 1590 and 1620, where she sees the boat which is to take her to South America, and between 1630 and 1680, where her indecision reaches its climax:

[30] [token 1594] Through the >wide >doors of the >sheds she >caught a >glimpse of the black >mass of the >boat, >lying in beside the >quay wall, with >illumined >portholes. She >answered >nothing. She felt her >cheek >pale and >cold and, out of a >maze of >distress, she >prayed to >God to >direct her, to >show her what was her >duty. The boat >blew a long >mournful >whistle into the >mist. >If she went, >tomorrow she would be on the >sea with Frank, >steaming >towards Buenos Ayres. Their passage had been >booked. Could she still >draw back after all he had >done for her? Her distress >awoke a >nausea in her >body and she >kept >moving her >lips in >silent >fervent >prayer.

In the last fifty words of the story, there are shifts to the narrator's point of view, and then, for the first time, to (what could be read as) Frank's point of view. As noted above, these shifts are also signalled by new vocabulary in the final sentences: see [23].

In a literary critical interpretation, Hart (1969) identifies 'three main parts' in the story: a long first part in which Eveline thinks about the past and possible future; a second 'brief interlude', in which she 'reasserts her decision to choose life'; and a third part which ends in her 'psychological failure'. These three parts correspond astonishingly closely to the troughs and peaks identified by the program. In addition, the evidence from the program can at least partially explain Hart's otherwise subjective impression of 'a general flatness both of vocabulary and sentence-structure' in the first section, which contrasts with 'the almost frenzied conclusion'. The literary critic's impressions are quite correct, but they can now be given an objective textual basis.

It will take considerable work before we know just what can be discovered with the method. For example, is there an optimum span setting for discovering finer and coarser units in texts of different lengths? Are there identifiable recurring vocabulary curves for short stories? Do different types of texts have predictably different kinds of lexical organization?

6.7 A Further Note on Replication

At the beginning of the chapter, I made the point that computer-assisted corpus analyses are replicable, because they are based on data and methods which are public. However, replication means something more complex than doing exactly what someone else has already done, and strict replication of an experiment is probably rather rare in all sciences. With computer-assisted work, it could be pointless: if you run the same data through the same computer program, you will get the same output each time. This will tell you nothing about whether the program is working correctly, or whether the procedure is sensible. However, I did not do exactly what Youmans had done. First, I used different computer software, which was re-written on the basis of his general description. Second, the software contained different features, which allowed me to track the first use of words in a text.

In other types of linguistic work, it is often not possible to carry out a strict replication. Suppose that you do a psycholinguistic experiment, in which you test a group of people on their reactions to a list of vocabulary ('Tell me as quickly as possible the opposites of the following words'...). Even if I can get the same group of people together again, I cannot carry out the same experiment. First, I am doing it and not you, and the experimental subjects may react differently to a different experimenter. Second, they are doing it for the second time, so their reactions will almost certainly be different. The best I could do would be to test the same people with comparable words, or comparable people with the same words. In any case, it is of little interest how one group of people react to a task of this kind. What is of interest is generalizations about behaviour. So the results of any single experiment are a prediction about how other people will react in comparable circumstances.

A replication will therefore generally be aiming to check whether compatible results arise if some variable is altered, such as the age of the persons tested, or the kinds of words used.

In this chapter I have shown that the story 'Eveline' is structured in a particular way. The real interest of the analysis is the possibility that this is an individual instance of a general phenomenon. The analysis predicts that we will find comparable organization in other texts: for example, that there is a general pattern in texts of many kinds, such that new vocabulary tends to be introduced in cycles of around 100 word-tokens. A deeper form of replication requires testing the procedures on different texts, and therefore cannot be a mere repeat of the original experiment. This then opens up many other questions, such as whether there are characteristic vocabulary profiles which we might be able to identify in different text-types.

6.8 Limitations on the Analyses

I have also emphasized deliberate limitations on the analyses. My analyses all assume that the relevant lexical units are single word-forms: strings of characters separated by spaces or punctuation marks. Thus, I noted in [9] that the word-form *used* occurs eleven times, but the analysis cannot recognize that *used* can have quite different meanings, which are disambiguated by the surrounding phraseology. In fact, in 'Eveline' all eleven occurrences are in the construction *used to* plus verb, and all refer to habitual past action (e.g. *used to play, used to go, used to visit*). The major contribution of phraseology and predictable collocations to text cohesion was the topic of chapter 5.

I am well aware of other limitations on my analyses. The distributional methods which I have used are designed to remain as close to the surface of the text as possible, and to make no reference to any other structural organization. They treat a text as a statistical and lexical unit, whose unity is due to the simplest possible mechanism of patterns of unlemmatized word-forms. So, there are many other (purely lexical) features of texts which these methods are unable to capture. For example, following *she*, there are few action verbs and many mental state verbs, such as:

- she heard; she looked; she had consented; she knew; she remembered; she felt; she mused; she wanted; she caught a glimpse

When Eveline does take some action, it is sometimes parts of her body which are the subjects of verbs and which seem to be acting on her behalf (Chatman 1969: 28):

- her head was leaned against the window curtains; her hands clutched the iron; her eyes gave him no sign

In addition, the computer software I have used cannot identify fine details of the lexis, which any skilled reader would interpret as having potential symbolic value. For example, whereas Frank lodges *in a house on the main road*, Eveline lives on the edge of town: when she stares out of the window, she watches a man *out of the last house* passing in the street. And perhaps Frank's name is significant (*frank* = "open"), in that he stands for life, as opposed to Eveline's stuffy inability to act. Füger (1980) provides a concordance for all words in *Dubliners*: this is a convenient source of data for studying such patterns.

6.9 Summary and Implications

No single method can do everything. The aim is not to replace other methods, but to identify one important marker of larger textual units. If you are unsympathetic to the kind of analysis I have illustrated, you will probably think that any interpretation placed on the findings is a post hoc justification of number-crunching. If you are more sympathetic to the approach, you may think that such methods can

> identify textual features which deserve close interpretation;
> explain some intuitive reactions to texts;
> identify some text-types and narrative points of view;
> lead to generalizations about the distribution of old and new information across long texts.

I have presented findings on some of the formal lexical features of a literary text. These features are visible only with computational help (this is certainly true of longer texts than I have discussed here), but the features really exist: they have been discovered, but not created, by the computer. In a study of the most frequent words in the novels of Jane Austen, Burrows (1987) formulates an elegant defence of such work:

> Computer-based concordances, supported by statistical analysis, now make it possible to enter hitherto inaccessible regions of the language [which] defy the most accurate memory and the finest powers of discrimination. (pp. 2–3)

In a useful review of Burrows's book, Paterson (1987) emphasizes that statistical and literary patterns are not the same thing. As Paterson puts it:

'presumably [Burrows] is not suggesting that henceforth we need a microcomputer at our side when we read a novel.' In work of this kind, we have to consider the appropriate balance between computational findings and human interpretation. As I emphasized at the beginning of the chapter, such interpretations are computer-assisted.

Perhaps it seems disappointing that the analysis of 'Eveline' confirms what literary critics have said about the division of the story into sections: the method seems to add little to what an intelligent reader knows already. However, I think we would be rightly suspicious of a technique which was completely at odds with the interpretations of trained readers. In addition, although the computer produced results compatible with those of a trained reader, it produced them in a very different way. We may therefore have the beginnings of an explanation of the human reader's interpretation, because we can make explicit some of the textual features which a human reader (perhaps unconsciously) attends to.

We must distinguish between the formal features which the computer finds in the text and the human reader's interpretation of the text, and we must assess the literary significance of what the computer finds. The computer's findings (frequencies, comparisons or graphs) are not an interpretation of the meaning of the text, but a presentation of some of its formal features. The computer presents these textual features in a convenient form, which the human reader can more easily interpret. Sometimes, the computer may discover very fine-grained patterns indeed, and the question then arises as to whether even a highly trained human reader can register equally fine patterns.

There are therefore difficult questions here about how much of our linguistic behaviour is conscious. It is absurd to imagine readers calculating comparative frequencies of lexical items, but it is less absurd to consider how patterns of repetition affect their interpretation. Similarly, presumably Joyce did not consciously attend to type–token ratios when he wrote the story. It would be odd to imagine him composing the story, and thinking to himself: 'It would produce a neat literary effect if I distributed this word evenly throughout, but used that word several times in a little cluster towards the end.' It is less odd, however, to imagine him saying to himself: 'I won't name *Frank* till about half-way through the story: that would maintain a little suspense, and maybe hint that Eveline wants a lover/husband, but does not care too much about Frank as an individual.'

Youmans's (1991, 1994) work is a neat example of an all too rare event in linguistics: a previously unknown phenomenon which can be observed with a relatively simple technique (Ziman 1978: 57). His method works, and provides replicable findings, in a small area of the social world which was previously thought to be closed to systematic study. It makes visible a kind of linguistic patterning which was previously invisible and unsuspected.

In summary, in this chapter, I have used the analysis of a short story in order to discuss different concepts which are central to corpus semantics: (1) an important lexical statistic: type–token ratio; (2) word frequencies and their distribution as objective evidence of textual structure; (3) a text as a semantic unit which can be seen as both product and process; and (4) the relation between instance and norm (here between an individual text and a reference corpus). The most general methodological point concerns the possibility of applying replicable methods to observable data.

6.10 Background and Further Reading

On basic text statistics see Sinclair (1991) and Barnbrook (1996). For more specialized discussion, see Youmans (1991, 1994). For readers of German, a very useful discussion of more advanced statistics is Tuldava (1998).

6.11 Topics for Further Study

In this chapter I have looked only at the contribution of individual word-forms to textual organization, but have not looked at collocations. However, Joyce's story contains many phrases which contain recurrent collocations. Here are a few from the opening paragraphs:

- on his way home; there used to be; her brothers and sisters; was not so bad; a long time ago; a school friend

Use the methods illustrated in chapter 5 to study the contribution of such phrases to the story.

7

Words in Culture 1: Case Studies of Cultural Keywords

This chapter and the next are about words and phrases which have particular cultural significance.

Several scholars have proposed that it is possible to identify, in different languages, a relatively small number of words whose meanings give insight into the culture of the speakers of those languages. Benveniste (1954: 336) proposed that the whole history of modern thought and the principal achievements of Western intellectual culture are linked to the creation and development of a few dozen essential words. Williams (1976/1983) produced exactly such a dictionary of culture and society for something over a hundred words and associated phrases in English. Similar dictionaries have been produced for other languages: for example, Strauss et al. (1989) for German. And in a series of books and articles, Wierzbicka (e.g. 1999) has argued that the lexicon of a language can be regarded as a key to history, culture and society, and that cultures can be understood through their keywords. For example, she studies *Heimat* and *Vaterland* ("homeland" and "fatherland") in German, and *dusha* and *toska* ("soul" and "yearning") in Russian. These are only rough translations, of course, since the argument is that such culturally significant words are embedded in complex cultural assumptions and do not have exact equivalents in other languages. In this chapter, I will discuss how corpus methods can provide systematic evidence about the significance of a few such keywords in English. In chapter 8, I will show how cultural significance may derive from the history of words which have been borrowed from other languages.

My examples in this chapter are from discourse which expresses evaluative moral views about different groups of people. Case study 1 discusses labels for different social groups, such as *ethnic* and *racial*. Case study 2 discusses a text about the need to *care* for the *heritage* of a nation. Case study 3 discusses the connotations of phrases such as *proper language* and *proper behaviour* in the discourse around *standards* of education. Case study 4 discusses the dissemination of cultural values via a well-known fairy tale, *Little Red Riding Hood*, which has been influential in setting out what is regarded as *proper behaviour* for children (especially girls).

Much debate in such areas is emotive, and in some cases different interpretations of words have led to legal disputes. Bayley (1997) discusses a case involving the terms *ethnic* and *racial* in the 1976 Race Relations Act in the UK. A Sikh boy had been excluded from a school because he refused to remove his turban and cut his long hair. The decision of a lower court was that Sikhs were defined by religion, not by race, and that the Act therefore did not apply to them. So, judges in a higher court were required to take decisions about the meaning of phrases such as *racial group* and *ethnic or national origins*, as these were used in the Act and in other legal texts, and defined in dictionaries: this included evidence that the meaning of *ethnic* has changed in recent English.

It is therefore important to look closely at the nature of the evidence and arguments used. It is initially difficult to see how discourse in this sense can be studied systematically at all, and there are certainly severe problems of sampling and representativeness. It is obvious in a rough and ready way that values are conveyed by the way in which words are used, but the questions for corpus semantics are: can the analysis of connotations be made systematic, and can the linguistic mechanisms involved be made explicit?

As I have argued, especially in chapter 5, individual texts can be interpreted only against the background of the usage of many speakers in the speech community. We can evaluate individual instances only if we know how topics are usually or often talked about. This is part of what is meant by culture: the repertoire of shared meanings which circulate in a community. Therefore the analysis must be comparative and intertextual. I will try to show that relations between texts can be studied with replicable, quantitative methods. As in the book as a whole, the analysis is based on two major principles of semantics, developed by scholars such as Saussure, Wittgenstein and Austin. First, meaning is use. Second, meaning is relational. Words acquire meanings from the collocations in which they occur in individual texts, but also from the collocations in which they frequently occur in texts of many kinds across the usage of a speech community. Such uses and relations are open to study in large historical and contemporary corpora.

7.1 Data and Citation Conventions

In order to study keywords and their connotations, I use three main types of data: individual text fragments, etymological data from a large historical dictionary, and corpus data on the contemporary language. (I will also briefly illustrate the possibility of making parallels with related words in another language.) In citing the keywords being analysed, I will place them in capitals, both in the data quoted and in my discussion. So, a word in capitals means that it is a lemma: for example, CARE is realized by *care, cares, cared* and *caring* (see chapter 2.2). In this chapter, it also means that it is a keyword, in the sense discussed below. The capitalization in the text samples is therefore my added emphasis. As elsewhere in the book, italicization indicates word-forms and cited words and phrases.

7.2 Text and Discourse

I have already shown that speakers often say what others have said countless times before: they use extended lexical units which are conventionalized in their semantics, and often predictable in their lexis. Speakers usually do not express themselves 'in their own words', but in words which are endlessly recycled in their speech community. Native speakers conform not only to rules of grammar, but also to norms of idiomaticity, and perhaps even to norms of what they might be expected to say. In chapters up until now, I have used 'text' and 'discourse' to mean naturally occurring instances of language in use: individual spoken and written texts. However, 'discourse' is also used in a different sense to mean conventional ways of talking (such as academic discourse), which form constellations of repeated meanings. In this sense, individual texts are a realization of widespread discourse patterns.

7.3 Case Study 1: ETHNIC, RACIAL and TRIBAL

A great deal of the language which circulates in the social world is a reformulation of other texts. Krishnamurthy (1996) shows how such language use can be analysed, by studying one aspect of the 'language of racism' in the uses of words such as ETHNIC, RACIAL and TRIBAL. He begins (p. 129) by posing a classic question about the relation between language and thought:

> Each one of us is exposed to a wide variety of language input in our daily lives, some of it our own choosing and some not. This input helps to shape our knowledge and understanding of both the language and its users. However, the predominant attitudes and opinions expressed in the language may also shape our thinking.

His argument runs as follows. We are usually exposed to a great deal of mass media language every day. The media therefore have 'a substantial influence on the language community they serve', partly because the same language is recycled several times a day, in news and current affairs programmes. This daily exposure to the same words and expressions 'might cause us to unwittingly adopt their attitudes and opinions' (p. 147). The argument that language use influences attitudes is plausible, although Krishnamurthy provides no direct evidence of whether people's views are in fact changed by media language. However, he does provide evidence of the use and frequency of words and phrases, not only from individual newspaper articles, but also from dictionaries, and from a 120-million-word corpus of contemporary English, mostly post-1985, both British and American. The analysis is careful and detailed, and I give here only a brief summary of some main findings.

The article discusses words which apply to groups of people, referred to as

- clans, communities, minorities, nations, races, tribes

As Krishnamurthy points out (p. 133), there is the danger in such discourse that people are thought of only as groups, and not as individuals. In his classic discussion of 'orientalist' discourse, Said (1978: 287) makes the same point:

> In newsreels or newspapers, the Arab is always represented in large numbers. No individuality, no personal characteristics or experiences. Most of the pictures represent mass rage and misery, or irrational (hence hopelessly eccentric) gestures. Lurking behind all of these images is the menace of the *jihad*.

In Krishnamurthy's corpus data, pre-1985, RACIAL was the most frequent of the three adjectives, but post-1985, ETHNIC is almost twice as frequent as RACIAL and four times as frequent as TRIBAL. ETHNIC has also become most productive morphologically, with terms such as *ethnicity, multi-ethnic* and *inter-ethnic*. (Williams, 1983, added ETHNIC and RACIAL to his list of keywords: they were not in the 1976 edition.)

All three terms connote "violence", but other associations differ. ETHNIC collocates with

- groups, minorities; clashes, cleansing, conflicts, tensions, unrest, violence

but also with *studies*, and is the preferred term in academic discourse. RACIAL has additional ethical and bureaucratic associations:

- equality, discrimination, commission (Commission for Racial Equality); abuse, harassment, prejudice, tension, violence

TRIBAL often refers to group organization:

- assembly, chiefs, leaders; conflict, fighting, violence, warfare

It is frequent in tourist brochures, since *tribal dancing* and the like are presented as tourist attractions.

Phrases such as *ethnic group*, *racial group* and *tribal group* could all denote the same social phenomenon: groups of people who share a cultural, geographical or religious identity. However, the phrases are used in different ways, with different collocates, in different text-types, and acquire different connotations. They are also used with reference to different parts of the world: for example, ex-Yugoslavia has *ethnic groups*; many areas of Africa have *tribes*; but South Africa is still (post-apartheid) an area where journalists talk about *race*. The term *ethnic* is also used with reference to Britain, but here *ethnic minority* means "black" or "black and Asian" (Krishnamurthy 1996: p. 134).

In summary, terms such as *ethnic group* and *tribe* do not denote inherent properties of the social groups, but express speakers' attitudes toward those groups. Phillipson (1992: 38–9) notes the use of a range of terms in colonialist discourse (we are a *nation*, they are a *tribe*), and Partington (1998: 74–5) notes a range of words which are used to refer to other people, but not to ourselves:

- cults, extremists, fanatics, fundamentalists, militants

So, representations circulate in the social world. The world could be represented in all kinds of ways, but certain ways of talking about events and people become frequent. Ideas circulate, not by some mystical process, but by a material one. Some ideas are formulated over and over again, such that, although they are conventional, they come to seem natural. Both the representation and the circulation are profoundly affected by the mass media, which recycles the same phrases over and over in newspapers, on radio and television, and in news broadcasts, commentaries and talk shows. Corpus analysis is one way in which the propagation of phrases can be studied: both changes over time and distribution in different texts. This is the concept of culture put forward by Sperber (1996: 1): 'Culture is made up, first and foremost, of such contagious ideas.' Krishnamurthy (1996) presents an excellent study of ways in which ideas about groups of people are constructed through language use. He shows something of the linguistic mechanisms involved (repeated collocations) and of the dissemination of language use (to large mass media audiences).

7.4 Case Study 2: HERITAGE and CARE

The concept of HERITAGE has had considerable commentary from cultural analysts (see K. Thompson, 1997, for several examples). In a study of how contemporary Scotland is represented in the media, especially in tourist advertising, McCrone et al. (1995) analyse the membership of the National Trust for Scotland, its social class make-up and the political beliefs of its members, and also give examples of their discourse, collected in interviews, about their concept of HERITAGE.

In much discourse in the UK, selected history is reinterpreted as HERITAGE, and such concepts have been used in a discourse around national unity. For example, in a speech on English teaching in 1991, Prince Charles contrasted cultural HERITAGE with recent TRENDS in education. Some phrases from his speech are:

[1] cultural roots; cultural tradition; our great literary HERITAGE; Shakespeare's land; fashionable TRENDS towards the 'relevant'; too great an emphasis on the child-centred approach; the cultural HERITAGE of our country (*The Times*, 23 April 1991)

Raban (1989: 23), in an analysis of a speech by Margaret Thatcher, notes that she also uses words from this semantic area, and that 'two of her most cherished words [are] *history* and *roots*'. (HISTORY is one of Williams's 1983 keywords.)

7.4.1 *Keyword:* HERITAGE

The *OED* cites American uses such as *a priceless heritage* (of folk music) from the 1930s, and British uses such as *Britain's cultural heritage* from the 1940s. A slightly earlier British use is the phrase *this heritage of the English-speaking peoples* (1934, cited by Pennycook 1994: 131). These senses seem to increase from the 1960s. This 1967 American citation collocates different keywords:

- a call for... people in this country to unite, to recognize their HERITAGE, to build a sense of COMMUNITY

HERITAGE seems to have entered widespread use in the UK in 1975, which was European Architectural Heritage Year (K. Thompson 1997: 27, 63). The idea of Heritage Centres dates from 1976; in 1980 a National Heritage Bill went through parliament; and by the 1990s the British government had set up a Department of National Heritage. It is an inherent part of this meaning of HERITAGE, that heritage is in danger: in the face of a decline in values, it must be preserved and protected. There has been considerable debate on the pros and cons of this concept (K. Thompson 1997). Critics of the *heritage industry* (the title of a 1987 book) have seen it as an aristocratic plot to save country houses, as a nostalgia whose selective memory creates a past that never existed, or even as 'retro-chic' whose ever-widening range turns everyday household junk into something worth preserving. Defenders of the concept have argued that it has value as a genuine, locally based, grass-roots movement. Ayto (1989) records the proliferating use of HERITAGE, especially with respect to tourism in the late 1980s, and notes the often ironic use of *heritage* and *retro-chic*. HERITAGE merges history (often represented by buildings) and geography (landscape).

I checked the most frequent collocates of HERITAGE in a large corpus of contemporary British English. It sometimes occurs in ironic phrases such as *the heritage lobby* or *heritage industry*. There is nothing inherently critical about the isolated word *industry*, but in collocations such as *race relations industry* and *fitness industry*, and in references more generally to social or political activities, the word can imply criticism of useless activity (Cobuild 1995a). However, most collocates of HERITAGE show its positive connotations. The most frequent collocates and some characteristic phrases are:

- cultural, national, rich
- cultural heritage; valuable natural heritage; maintained its colourful heritage; steeped in heritage

Other frequent collocates signal positive connotations and the need for heritage to be preserved, and also the state intervention now involved in its preservation:

- architectural, artistic, common, industrial, musical, natural, priceless; care (for), celebrate, explore, guard, preserve, protect, save
- centre, department, English, foundation, fund, Minister, national, state

In a single year's editions of *The Times* and the *Sunday Times* (1995), the word HERITAGE occurred over 1,500 times – an average of four times per day – largely in its "state intervention" uses (as in *National Heritage Secretary* and *Heritage Minister*).

7.4.2 *Keyword:* CARE

The word HERITAGE has obvious political and ideological connotations, and has received much explicit commentary by cultural analysts. One of its collocates (see above) is CARE, which is perhaps less obvious as a cultural keyword, though these implications can be seen in the following extract from an editorial in the magazine of the National Trust for Scotland. The title of the magazine is *Heritage Scotland*. The title of the editorial, *Who Cares?*, is a play on words. The expression usually conveys extreme lack of interest. Here, the question is taken literally, and answered in the editorial. The first paragraph (my emphasis added) repeats an argument, which, as it says, is frequently repeated: we 'regularly read': in the newspapers that moral standards are falling; nevertheless, there are people who try to protect the community and preserve such values.

[2] We regularly read newspaper headlines denouncing the 'moral sickness' within society. It is therefore important to all of us to know that there are CARING organizations like the National Trust for Scotland, which not only preserves and protects buildings, landscape and inanimate objects, but also CARES for the people and the communities at its properties. (from *Heritage Scotland*, 1993: 10, 2)

Since around the 1960s, CARE has developed important ideological and political implications in contemporary British English, as in recurring phrases such as *health care, care in the community* and *caring society*. One might say, rather cynically, that these uses signal an uncaring society, conceived of mainly in economic terms. They occur in parodies of psycho-babble by social satirists such as Dame Edna Everage (Barry Humphries), who says things such as *I mean that in a very caring way*.

However, the only way to substantiate rough observations of this kind is to use a corpus. I studied the historical changes in the word across the 4,800 occurrences of the lemma CARE in the *Oxford English Dictionary* on CD-ROM, and its contemporary uses by studying around 40,000 occurrences in a 120-million-word corpus of British English. The combination TAKE–CARE, is frequent, often in longer combinations with an adjective before CARE:

- take considerable care; take great care; take proper care; the utmost care was taken

Since around 1900, the noun *care* has undergone a change from predominantly personal uses (to *take care* of someone) to frequent institutional uses (*child care*). Institutional uses occur from the early 1900s, but have become particularly frequent since around the 1950s:

- from 1900: children's care committee, care of the aged
- from 1920: spiritual care, pastoral care
- from 1930: medical care, health care, baby care

- from 1950: child care, hospital care, dental care (frequent)
- from 1980: health care (very frequent)

There are many compound items, such as:

- children in care; taken into care; residential care; community care; day care; intensive care; skin care; specialist care; child care workers; health care workers; health care plan; after-care services; hospital-based home care programs; outpatient or ambulatory care services; antenatal and well-baby care; well-women care

The grammar of particular word-forms has changed. The word-form *caring* is attested from the sixteenth century, often as a verb, and often in negative contexts, such as

- not caring how; seldom caring whether; past caring

Only since the 1960s does it occur as an adjective before a noun (*a caring society*), often in combination with other adjectives:

- good, caring, committed television; a loving; caring home; a caring society; friendly, caring atmosphere; involved and caring father; caring, concerned and aware

The phrase *caring professions* occurs only from the 1970s, and the word *carer(s)*, as in *professional carers*, occurs only from the late 1970s (see also Ayto 1989: 60–1). (See chapter 1.7.4 on the word *caring* in lonely hearts ads. For an independent corpus study of CARE, see Johnson 1993.)

These changes in British English are part of much wider European or even global changes (Fairclough 1992). In a smaller study (Stubbs 1997), I have investigated some of the changes in the German word PFLEGEN (= CARE), to show that it is also a keyword in contemporary German society. I studied over 4,000 occurrences of the lemma PFLEGEN in the German language corpora held at the Institut für Deutsche Sprache in Mannheim. (See Notes on Corpus Data and Software.) Like CARE, the lemma PFLEGEN has acquired new meanings which are politically significant, especially in medical and financial areas. The word has several uses which fall into distinct semantic fields, some of long standing, such as caring for parts of the body, caring for language and culture, or cultivating political relationships:

- Haar pflegen = "groom hair"; eine Sprache pflegen = "cultivate a language"; Kontakte pflegen = "foster contacts"

Very frequent collocates of PFLEGEN in contemporary German include uses in medicine and in finance, because of its connection to hospital bills and insurance payments:

- Pflegeberufe = "caring professions"; Pflegeversicherung = "care insurance", i.e. a compulsory insurance which covers home care or hospitalization if necessary in old age

7.4.3 *Keyword:* COMMUNITY

Another keyword discussed by Williams (1983) is COMMUNITY. Debates around this word were an important theme of both Conservative and Labour parties in the UK in the 1990s. Text [2] above discusses the need to protect *communities*, and a later paragraph in the editorial comments explicitly on the word:

[3] The dictionary definitions of COMMUNITY include 'joint participation or ownership'; 'community of property'; 'community of interests'; 'interacting relationships'. Taken together, these definitions describe the essential elements of the Trust's involvement in, and obligations to, the COMMUNITY. We work both with and for others in the preservation and presentation of the HERITAGE and ENVIRONMENT of Scotland.

So, these examples illustrate how analysis can relate a text fragment about caring for the environment to changes in uses of the word CARE in the UK, and to wider cross-language changes in this semantic field.

7.5 Case Study 3: PROPER STANDARDS

There were several keywords in the controversial debates around Standard English in British culture and education in the 1980s and 1990s. The politicized nature of this debate is evident from the huge number of texts of different kinds which it generated: several government reports on English teaching, culminating between the late 1980s and early 1990s in extensive, and several times revised, legislation around English in the socalled National Curriculum; widely reported speeches on English teaching by Prince Charles, and commentary by leading politicians in the mass media or in autobiographies (e.g. Thatcher 1993); and the massive coverage of the debate in the mass media. Standard English must be a topic of deep symbolic importance when public figures intervene in the debate.

7.5.1 Keyword: STANDARD

Again, the question is how text and corpus analysis can contribute to social analyses. In the first volume of her autobiography, Margaret Thatcher (1993) devotes several pages to the National Curriculum, and asserts her belief in a place in the English curriculum for

[4] STANDARD English, the traditional learning of grammar and learning by heart (Thatcher 1993: 595).

These links, between STANDARD English, grammar, learning by heart, and tradition (compare HERITAGE), seem obvious to many people, if not to linguists. Such collocations can be observed and empirically studied.

The word STANDARD is possibly the most ambiguous of all the keywords discussed by Williams (1976), who analyses its changing senses from the twelfth century to the present. Meanings include a flag and symbol of authority (*royal standard*), or an erect and upright object (*standard lamp, standard rose*), and then by extension an authoritative example of correctness, especially in the context of weights and measures (*standard foot*) or of an authoritative book (*standard textbook*). A *standard of living* means a level which people strive to or can expect to attain as a right. Levels of competence may be referred to as *standards*. The plural *standards* is usually positive, but *standardization* is often negative.

Williams's analysis is based mainly on historical evidence from the *OED*. Implicit in his account is the principle that different meanings are associated with different phrases, and the high probability that different meanings are associated with different collocations and different syntax can now be studied in much more detail, using corpus data. The top collocates for STANDARD from a 200-million-word corpus (Cobuild 1995b) are as follows. The first set are shared by both forms of the lemma, singular and plural.

- STANDARD <living, high, set, new, double, any, higher, international>
- standard <rate, model, gold, many, sub, practice, such, become, bearer>
- standards <safety, meet, even, trading, national, quality, own, minimum, service, highest, environmental, same>

Several fixed phrases and correspondingly different senses are evident from these lists alone, for example: *standard bearer* (= "flag or national symbol"), *gold standard* (= "accepted measure"). Other senses are signalled by different collocates as follows (this illustrative list is not complete).

Sense 1. One of the most frequent phrases is *standard(s) of living* or *living standard(s)*, which almost always occurs in longer phrases, with collocates which indicate the meaning "acceptable or expected level of achievement":

- attain, better, comply with, conform to, declining, decreased, exacting, gone up, high(er), improving, increased, live up to, low(er), maintain, measure up to, poor, preserve, reach, rigorous, rising, stricter, tougher

Sense 2. The meaning "judging one thing relative to another" is signalled by the word *by* followed by plural *standards*:

- by the standards of the seventeenth century; by today's standards; judged by the standards of ordinary daily life

Sense 3. The meaning "usual" or "normal" is signalled by abstract nouns immediately following singular *standard*, such as

- method, pattern, practice, procedure, routine, technique, treatment

Sense 4. The meaning "moral principles" occurs in phrases such as *double standards*, or in *standards of* followed by abstract nouns such as

- conduct, decency, fairness, morality

As Williams says, there is 'an active social history' in the development of these uses, which show how the phrase *Standard English* combines – and confuses – concepts of measurement, normality, expectation, attainment, judgement, authority, correctness, morality, and symbol.

7.5.2 *Keyword:* PROPER

Much discussion on educational topics hinges on what is seen as PROPER. Here is part of a statement from a prominent member of the British Conservative party:

[5]   We've allowed so many STANDARDS to slip ... teachers weren't bothering to teach kids to spell and to punctuate PROPERLY (Norman Tebbit, Radio 4, November 1985: cited by Graddol and Swann 1988: 102).

And here is part of a statement made by Prince Charles immediately after the publication of a government report on English teaching. As the *Daily*

Telegraph put it, he 'launched a scathing attack on STANDARDS of English teaching'.

[6] We've got to produce people who can write PROPER English. It's a fundamental problem: All the people I have in my office, they can't speak English PROPERLY, they can't write English PROPERLY.... I do not believe English is being taught PROPERLY. You cannot educate people PROPERLY unless you do it on a basic framework and drilling system (Prince Charles, 28 June 1989).

Such statements can only strike a chord or ring a bell, as we say, if they fit into wider ways of talking. In this short statement, Prince Charles uses *proper* and *properly* five times. It is also 'one of Mrs Thatcher's keywords' (Raban 1989: 38): in the text by Thatcher which Raban analyses, she talks of *a proper attitude to work*, *proper respect* for people from other cultures, and the *proper place* of religion in the school curriculum. In both 4,300 examples of PROPER from the *OED* and in 9,100 examples from contemporary data, the most common noun phrase is *proper place*. This phrase occurs as early as a 1489 citation from Caxton. Other frequent phrases are *in its proper position* and *in their proper order*. Both *proper* and *properly* are amongst the 3,500 or so most frequent words in contemporary English (Cobuild 1995a).

PROPER has complex social meanings: it denotes what is considered appropriate, real and genuine, according to the standards of some social group:

- a proper job; doing a job properly; proper behaviour; a proper course of action; the proper authorities

Indeed, one can talk of *proper standards*. Such uses do not state explicitly what this norm is. The listener is supposed to know: the ultimate cultural knowledge.

Lexical patterns often seem obvious once they have been pointed out, so I will say immediately that the patterns I am about to illustrate are not explicitly recorded even in corpus-based dictionaries (Cobuild 1995a; CIDE 1995; LDOCE 1995; OALD 1995). The examples given in dictionaries confirm my data, but the principles underlying them remain inexplicit. The main pattern is that *proper* typically occurs with

 negatives, such as *no*, *not*, *never*, *can't*;
 words such as *fail*, *need*, *without*;
 words which imply warnings and criticisms.

These characteristic patterns of co-occurrence can be seen in the following attested examples:

- *no* time yet for a *proper* examination of the map
- he *couldn't* get it to work *properly*
- put forward *without proper* consideration of your needs
- printed in the press *without properly* researching the subject
- the crying *need* is for a *proper* international airport
- the *need* to be *properly* immunized
- two out of five people *lack* a *proper* job
- *failed* to give it a *proper* look
- alleged *failure* to use procedures *properly*
- *hinders proper* training
- *totally outside proper* democratic control
- *make sure* you cook them *properly*
- it is *harmless when* used *properly*
- *unless proper* care be taken to improve it

Diachronic data show that these uses go back a long way. The last example, from the *OED*, dates from 1745. The following example (from Francis et al. 1998: 366) shows that, even in cases where there is no explicit negative form, there may nevertheless be a criticism of something lacking:

- my family tell me that I should stop dreaming and get myself a *proper* job

In summary, the words are most frequently used in criticisms or warnings. A frequent collocation is *TAKE proper care*. Keywords often inter-collocate, and ideas gain stability when they fit into a frame.

Many everyday ideas about language fit very firmly into a frame which contains terms such as

- standard, standards, accurate, correct, grammar, proper, precise

For linguists, the same terms mean something quite different because they fit into an entirely different lexical field, which contains terms such as

- dialect, language planning, high prestige language, social variation

These fields are systems of meaning, which use particular vocabulary, take particular things for granted, appeal to different states of knowledge (for example, lay and professional), and therefore allow only particular argumentative moves. Much of the public debate is a struggle over competing definitions, and some of the history of this debate is documented in Crowley's (1991) book on language, history and cultural identity, which is entitled *Proper English?*

The positional frequency table (table 7.1) shows the top 20 collocates, in a span of 3:1, for 2,333 occurrences of the node *proper*, in a corpus of 50 million running words (part of the Bank of English).

Table 7.1   Positional frequency table for *proper*, span 3:1

N−3	N−2	N−1	node	N+1
to	in	a	*	job [42]
>not	get	the	*	place [42]
it	>not	its	*	care [32]
>n't	to	>without	*	way [29]
there	have	their	*	name [25]
must	is	>no	*	medical [19]
is	had	works	*	use [20]
>failed	>without	and	*	names [18]
give	into	with	*	time [21]
they	right	first	*	relationship [14]
>never	prim	provide	*	training [14]
up	>lack	quite	*	channels [11]
would	make	get	*	perspective [11]
do	for	take	*	treatment [11]
>failing	like	perfectly	*	course [12]
things	provide	given	*	respect [10]
which	with	some	*	balance [10]
>needed	be	give	*	authority [10]
>cannot	director	have	*	food [10]
>haven't	good	for	*	assessment [9]

Examples of attested phrases:
   get a proper job
   not in its proper place
   failed to take proper care
   do it in the proper way
   without proper medical supervision
   did not make proper use of
   ensure that all staff receive proper training

Notes: The data are from 50 million words of the Bank of English (CobuildDirect).
The node *proper* is indicated with an asterisk.
Collocates are ordered by t-score: i.e. descending frequency, corrected for absolute frequency of collocate. The frequency of collocations with the right-hand collocates is in square brackets. Negatives and related words amongst the left-hand collocates are marked with an arrow.

7.5.3 Keyword: TRENDY

One theme in the discourse on education is the value of history and heritage: another is a corresponding distrust of trends and fashion. The first citations for TRENDY in the *OED* are from 1965. It is most frequently used to describe what are regarded as superficial fashions, especially places to eat and drink, and clothes. Collocates include:

- bars, boozers, café, night club, restaurant(s)
- boutiques, clothes, fashion, gear, jeans, trainers

Uses often express disapproval:

- a trendy eatery; slightly odd, trendy clothes; in danger of becoming a trendy area; hanging out with the trendy crowd; a loony policy of trendy lefty politics; a trendy new form of kitsch; jumping on the trendy AIDS bandwagon; if stripped of their trendy trappings

The word TRENDY is surprisingly (to me) frequent even in the quality press. It occurred nearly 250 times (i.e. on average four or five times per week) in one year's editions of *The Times* and the *Sunday Times* (1995), in the same kind of collocations, and largely in connection with fashion and entertainment:

- trendy righties; funky coolness, costumes from trendy outfitters; the young and trendy; a trendy W1 night-club; Soho's trendy coffee-shop; twenty-something trendy crowd

TRENDY often co-occurs with other words ending in *-y* or *-ie*, which often themselves express pragmatic meanings of childishness (*bunny, nanny, teddy*), of informality (*comfy*), or are insulting (*loony lefty*) (Stubbs 1996: 206–8):

- the designs are variously casual, racy, sporty – or kicky, trendy, funky [Canadian 1973]
- trendy intelligentsia... arty intelligentsia [British 1982]

Many uses involve what are seen as superficial educational fashions:

- Prince Charles is furious at *trendy teaching* which has axed Shakespeare from many schools [British tabloid newspaper]

- today's *trendy teaching methods* are not getting the three R's through [British tabloid newspaper]
- the *left wing canker of trendy theories*, low expectations and poor achievement [American newspaper]
- [he] blames *half-baked trendy theorists* who claim that learning standard English is a waste of time [British tabloid newspaper]

(The last example is quoted by Graddol and Swann 1988: 111, who discuss such discourse.)

The quote below, from a 1998 newspaper article, makes explicit the speech acts in which the word typically occurs, a sneer or a complaint:

- The commonest response...was to dismiss what goes on in new universities such as [name of university] as 'trendy'. Implicit in this sneer is the original complaint about....

7.6 Case Study 4: *Little Red Riding Hood*

There is a tendency to think of cultural keywords as words which have obvious political or ideological meanings. These are the kinds of examples discussed by Williams (1976/1983): ALIENATION, BOURGEOIS, COMMUNITY, DEMOCRACY, ETHNIC, and so on. However, even the most common words in the language, such as LITTLE, especially when they occur in frequent phrases, can have strong cultural connotations.

I have argued that studies must be comparative and intertextual. In a socially influential case of the same story told from different ideological points of view, Zipes (1993) has published 38 English-language versions, from the seventeenth century to the present, of *Little Red Riding Hood*. He discusses the textual and social history of the story, including versions by Perrault (late seventeenth century) and the brothers Grimm (early nineteenth century), which had huge circulations and a large influence on the education of children. He analyses the techniques and discursive strategies by which violence is represented, both in the texts and in their illustrations, and also in the frequent intertextual references in contemporary advertising and films. In short, he gives a great deal of concrete historical detail about the adaptation, dissemination and reception of the most widespread and notorious fairy tale in the Western world, with its themes of adolescence and obedience, and how it has been used to control gender roles and social norms. Such a case study illustrates Foucault's (1980) theses on social control, sex and education.

Sperber (1996) uses *Little Red Riding Hood* as his main example of a text which has been very successful in getting itself widely distributed, in a causal chain of telling and retelling, over the centuries, in different versions, adaptations and translations: 'millions of mental representations causally linked by millions of public representations' (p. 63). Sperber's analysis is similar to Zipes's (1993: xi) analysis of the 'power of the commonplace' in the transmission of this tale and its reception, and his analysis emphasizes the essential role of repetition in the construction of the social world. (See also Berger and Luckmann 1966; Giddens 1984; Bourdieu 1991.) Sperber's general theory of mental and public representations and of their distribution is that some ideas propagate successfully, and culture is made up of those ideas which are so contagious that they become widely distributed, long-lasting, stable representations. However, we have to explain how it is that some ideas are so successful: why is it that they get communicated repeatedly? We could use corpus methods to start to answer Sperber's question: 'what formal properties make *Little Red Riding Hood* more easily comprehended and remembered' (p. 63) than other texts?

A keyword in many of the versions is LITTLE, and a look at some of its uses in the language in general will illustrate one small part of the propagation process: the cumulative effect of micro-processes at the level of words and collocations. I studied 300,000 occurrences of the word-forms *little*, *small*, *big* and *large*, and found that they occur in largely complementary distribution, and have quite different uses and collocates. In particular, *little* has strong cultural connotations. In data from a 200-million-word corpus (Cobuild 1995b), the most frequent noun to co-occur with *little* is *girl*, and the most frequent adjective to co-occur with *girl* is *little*. The frequency of different phrases, normalized to frequencies per million words, was as follows:

little girl(s) 15.5   little boy(s) 10.0
small girl(s)   0.5   small boy(s)   2.2

We have to explain why the phrase *little girl(s)* is 30 times as frequent as *small girl(s)*, whereas *little boy(s)* is less than 5 times as frequent as *small boy(s)*. Evidence comes from the mutual attraction and repulsion between the two adjectives and their immediate collocates. *Small* most often collocates with formal words concerning quantities. These rarely co-occur with *little*.

- small <N−1: comparatively, exceedingly, infinitely, numerous, relatively>
- small <N+1: amount(s), degree, fraction, number(s), portion(s), proportion, quantity/ies>

Words which immediately precede *little* often convey the speaker's evaluation: either approval that someone or something is "cute", or disapproval that someone or something is "strange" and/or repulsive in some way. These words do not occur before *small*.

- little <N−1: beautiful, charming, cute, dainty, dear, good, lovely, neat, nice, pretty, sweet, tiny; curious, dirty, funny, poor, wretched>

Words immediately following *little* can also convey "cuteness", but these words also occur after *small*.

- little <N+1: boy(s), child(ren), girl(s); fellow, man; animal(s), bird(s), boat, creature, house, room, town, village>

The forms *large* and *big* are also in mostly complementary distribution. *Large* typically collocates with words for quantities and sizes (e.g. *amount*, *extent*, *number*). *Big* can also mean "large in physical size": *big city*, *big house*. However, *big boy* can connote "grown up": *big boys don't cry*. In general, there is a strong tendency for *big* to have metaphorical meanings (as in *Big Apple* = "New York", *Big Bang* = "origin of the universe") and often ironic or pejorative meanings (*big head*, *big mouth*, *big time*). These are all probabilistic statements, expressing strong statistical tendencies: *small* also occurs in metaphorical and pejorative phrases, such as *small fry* and *small beer*.

What follows from these data? First, paradigmatic oppositions (such as *little–big*, *young–old*) are usually thought of as being permanently available in the structure of the vocabulary, but words are co-selected, and this limits choices in syntagmatic strings. There are stereotyped phrases such as *little old lady* and *little old man*, but combinations such as ?*little young lady* or ?*small old lady* are impossible or very unlikely. There is the frequent phrase *a pretty little girl*, but *a pretty big girl* could only mean "a girl who is fairly big". Second, one of the most frequent words in the language can convey cultural stereotypes: especially in combination with other words, however, LITTLE conveys strong expectations. Of over 70 instances of *little old* before a noun in a 50-million-word corpus, over half were in the phrase *little old lady/ies*, or similar phrases such as *little old grandma*. The combination *little old* is either cute and folksy, or critical and patronizing, as in

- this frail little old woman; the dear little old church; little old thatched villages; a ramshackle little old van; any weedy little old man

The combination can even be used purely pragmatically and non-literally, as in *little old New York, little old me* (an atypical case of adjectives modifying a pronoun); or in this example from a novel:

- Mattie sneered: 'Oh, you and your little old committees.'

The combination *little man* has two distinct uses, one pejorative, one admiring:

- a ridiculous little man; an evil, nasty, frightful and revolting little man [A]
- the little man against the system; little man versus Big Business; a victory for the little man

In terms of communicative competence, all words, even the commonest in the language, contract collocational relations. In terms of cultural competence, culture is encoded not only in words which are obviously ideologically loaded, but also in combinations of very common words. One textual function of recurrent combinations is to imply that meanings are taken for granted and shared (Moon 1994). The data suggest an intertextual explanation of why the word LITTLE has the connotations it does in the phrase *Little Red Riding Hood* (and also in *Little Miss Muffet* and *Little Jack Horner*).

In summary, it is possible to combine analyses of the historical development of different versions of a text, its dissemination (publication history, sales, etc.), and its use in social control and education. These are topics which are discussed by Zipes (1993). It is also possible to analyse the intertextual background of a text, in the sense of the connotations of its keywords. These intertextual relations presumably go both ways. The phrase *Little Red Riding Hood* both fits into very widespread patterns in the language, and also contributes to those patterns.

7.7 Discursive Formations

In this chapter, I have used the term 'discourse' to discuss ways in which language is used, often implicitly, to evaluate people, and to construct arguments which are based less on logic than on association. There is a danger that this concept of discourse (which is very different from uses in earlier chapters) is hopelessly vague, but I have argued that we can study how associations are formed by using techniques of comparative collocational analysis. Not all arguments depend on sequential logic, but may depend on a web of associations, and simplistic oppositions, such as good English versus bad English, and high standards versus crime. The main idea is that certain representations circulate widely in a society at a given time. It is individuals who produce individual texts, but these texts are not produced with complete freedom.

Foucault (1980) makes the following points about the power of discourse to construct knowledge. Not all topics exist prior to being talked about: they are brought into existence by the discourse itself. For example, 'care', 'community' and 'heritage' are not things which exist independently in the external world, and are then named by language: they are topics which are created by being named. Suddenly, as we say, 'everyone seems to be talking about them'. These topics can then, in turn, produce huge amounts of discourse. For example, the related topics 'proper English', 'falling standards' and 'trendy teachers' have generated enormous amounts of language use, including government reports, debates amongst educationalists, and commentary in the media. The topics are inseparable from the power of speakers, since a set of keywords can be reinforced by prominent public figures. If speakers constantly refer to 'ethnic minorities' or 'proper behaviour', then they create social identities and position the speaker inside or outside group boundaries. Foucault's term for all the things that are said about a given topic at a given historical period is a 'discursive formation': the means which are available to people to make sense of a topic, including the keywords and phrases which are in widespread circulation.

These ideas have everyday counterparts. It is a common enough observation that we have to use words in ways which are usual in our speech community: if we did not, then we would not be understood. So, there is widespread recognition that things can be represented differently. A term for this notion, which appeared quite suddenly in the late 1980s, is *spin doctor*. Algeo (1991: 235) records *spin doctor* in American usage from 1986, along with related terms such as *spin control*. Ayto (1989) records *spin doctor* in British newspapers in 1988, though still sees it as an American usage. These expressions had become more frequent in British English by the mid-1990s, but I remember still being unsure of their exact meaning, and asking British and American colleagues, in 1994, what they meant: they were also not quite sure. The terms then became very frequent in connection with what was seen as a new kind of politics in Britain, which made sophisticated use of the mass media. Here, the term *spin doctor* was frequently used to refer critically to the advisors of leading members of the Labour government which was elected in 1997. Usages such as *give a story a particular spin* also became frequent. (Benson et al. 1997: vii, 313, record these uses.)

7.8 Summary and Implications

Studies of language in culture raise large and difficult questions, and I have certainly not answered them all in this chapter. They include questions about different concepts of discourse, objectivity and subjectivity of interpretation, and the relation of language and thought.

(1) *Discourse.* In phrases such as 'academic discourse' and 'racist discourse', 'discourse' means recurrent formulations which circulate in a discourse community. This may seem a rather mystical notion, and there are certainly problems associated with it.

(2) *Instance and norm.* However, I have used the same basic method as in previous chapters – searching for patterns revealed by recurrent collocations – to show that empirical methods can be used to study discourse in this sense. And I have used different kinds of data – individual text fragments, corpora and dictionaries – to show that some aspects of meaning can be explained only with reference to relations between an individual text and its intertextual background.

(3) *Linguistic and cultural stereotypes.* Since we can fully understand only a small fraction of the social world, we all work with strong expectations about what is typical or normal. Much of the time, we work with frames and scripts (see chapter 5.7), for example of going to school, of teacher–pupil relations, and of TRENDY teachers. These cultural stereotypes are a source of conventional knowledge: cues to build a familiar world (Brown and Yule 1983). These stereotypes do not arise from nowhere, but are continually constructed and reinforced by descriptions which circulate in the social world. A community's value system is built up and maintained, at least partly, by the recurrent use of particular phrasings in texts. As Thompson and Hunston (2000) argue: 'a very large corpus can mimic, though not of course replicate' the experience of coming across thousands of instances of a collocation.

(4) *The limits of introspection.* Some analyses of keywords may seem to confirm the obvious. However, although the ideological (even legal) significance of some keywords (such as ETHNIC and RACIAL) is perhaps evident, the significance of others (such as HERITAGE and CARE) has changed rapidly, and the significance of others again (such as PROPER and LITTLE) is less obvious. Even if the complex meanings of words such as PROPER seem obvious in retrospect, they are not open to unaided introspection, and are only very incompletely, if at all, recorded in dictionaries. Only empirical studies can systematically document cultural transmission, reproduction and change.

(5) *Objectivity and subjectivity.* The fact that I have used computer methods to identify patterns in large corpora does not make the analysis objective. One problem is selection: I have focused on only a few words, and one might ask why I picked those and not others. This problem in the original book on *Keywords* by Williams (1976/1983) is pointed out by Ruthven (1989: 112–14), who discusses the danger of proceeding from a handful of keywords to cultural generalizations. There may be merely 'the illusion of lexicographical rigour' in trying to go from individual words to the attitudes held by members of a culture: attitudes cannot be read directly off the use of words.

(6) *Criteria for selection.* My own selection of keywords was certainly partly intuitive, but was not based merely on my personal opinion. Some of the words have received wide commentary from cultural analysts, or have appeared in book and magazine titles, and I have shown that they occur widely, in the mass media, and sometimes in prominent statements by prominent speakers. Indeed, a defining characteristic of some keywords, but not all, is that they are well documented by explicit linguistic commentary in the mass media. Statistical methods can also be used to identify words which occur more (or less) frequently than would be expected in different text-types. I have not used such methods in this chapter (though I used them briefly in chapter 6.4). They are discussed in detail by Scott (1997b, 1997c, 1997d).

(7) *Replicable analyses.* Keywords, and texts in general, have no definitive meaning which can be stated once and for all. However, interpretations can be grounded in evidence, and the availability of large corpora has substantially changed the nature of this evidence. Most important, the results are based on publicly available data. You can test my generalizations on comparable but different data, in order to check that they were not an artefact of the specific texts which I happened to use.

(8) *Linguistic and encyclopedic knowledge.* Much recent linguistics assumes that there is a clear distinction between linguistic knowledge and encyclopedic knowledge. However, as Hudson (1996: 245–7) points out, no convincing arguments have ever been put forward for this distinction. If you know the meaning of the word TRENDY in British English, you know not only its denotation (what kinds of things the word typically describes: restaurants, clothing, and so on), but also its connotations (that people find these superficial). There seems no way to insulate the linguistic from the cultural knowledge.

(9) *Evaluative connotations.* Work on recurrent collocations suggests that many more words have evaluative connotations than is often realized. I discuss this in more detail in chapter 9.

7.9 Background and Further Reading

Language has been an important topic in British cultural studies since the 1960s. Turner (1990) gives a useful history, with references to work by Richard Hoggart, Stuart Hall, and others. The most famous work on 'keywords' is Raymond Williams's (1976/1983) explicitly politicized dictionary, *Keywords: A Vocabulary of Culture and Society*, which was based on diachronic information from the *Oxford English Dictionary*. The *OED* as a source of documentary evidence about national culture was clear to its originators: see chapter 8.

The background to educational change in the UK is set out by Brumfit (1995: x–xvi), who summarizes curriculum legislation and annotates a list of the corresponding government reports between 1975 and 1993; and by Stubbs (1989), Cox (1991) and Cameron (1995), who discuss the political and ideological background.

On corpus methods for studying keywords, see Krishnamurthy (1996), Stubbs (1996) and Scott (1997c, 1997d). Using examples of keywords in educational policy, Piper (2000) shows how corpus methods can provide replicable analyses of publicly available data.

7.10 Topics for Further Study

(1) Consider the words capitalized in text [3] above, COMMUNITY and ENVIRONMENT, and collect data on their connotations. COMMUNITY is discussed in Williams (1983). He mentions ENVIRONMENT under the entry for ECOLOGY.

(2) I have looked at only one keyword in *Little Red Riding Hood*. Since many versions of the story are widely available (Zipes 1993), including modern parodies and radical adaptations, this is a convenient text for further comparative analysis. Here are a few suggestions.
(a) Study how words such as *little*, *girl* and *maid(en)* are used in different versions of *Little Red Riding Hood*.
(b) The German for *Little Red Riding Hood* is *Rotkäppchen*. The diminutive suffix *-chen* denotes smallness and/or connotes cuteness (*Häuschen* = *little house*). The word for *girl* (*Mädchen*) has this ending, but the word for *boy* (*Junge*) does not. Study the denotations and connotations of the words for *Little Red Riding Hood* in other languages.
(c) Study the connotations of the word *path*. For a modern reader, this word may make intertextual references to phrases such as *stray from the right path*, *take a wrong path*, or *keep to the straight and narrow*.

(d) Study the connotations of the word *wolf*. For a modern reader, this word may make intertextual references to phrases such as *werewolf*, *wolf-whistle*, and *keep the wolf from the door*. Zipes (1993: 36) points out that, apart from the Bible, the fairy tales of the brothers Grimm (published 1812 to 1815) was the most widely read book in nineteenth-century Germany. The following may have intertextual meaning for some modern readers: 'Beware of false prophets, which come to you in sheep's clothing, but inwardly they are ravening *wolves*' (Gospel according to St Matthew, 7: 15).

(e) In a study of children's early reading books Baker and Freebody (1989) found that the adjective LITTLE was frequent, and that the phrase *little girl*, was significantly more frequent than *little boy*, and argue that these collocations convey ideological messages about the social world. Frequent associations make some features of the world conceptually salient, but since the associations are implicit, they are difficult to discuss and negotiate, and appear to be a constant, shared and natural feature of the world. Carry out similar analyses on significant words in texts written for children.

(3) Specialized dictionaries such as Algeo (1991) and Ayto (1989) contain many other keywords which students could investigate. Algeo (1991) documents new words in mainly American English from 1941 to 1991. His citations for some 2,500 words in their earliest known uses provide evidence of public preoccupations over this period, including

- appeasement, apartheid, back-to-basics, toy-boy, user-friendly

Ayto (1989) records words and meanings which became current in British English in the mid-1980s, and discusses how they reveal social trends. These include:

- downsize, ecstasy, ethnic monitoring, kiss-and-tell, perestroika

8

Words in Culture 2: Case Studies of Loan Words in English

In chapter 7, I pointed out that cultural connotations are sometimes due to the layers of meanings which are deposited on a word over long periods of time (one example was STANDARD). Relations between vocabulary, culture and history were a major impetus for the originators of the *Oxford English Dictionary*, who were in no doubt about the cultural importance of an exhaustive record 'of the appearance of each word in the language'. It was argued that words 'embody facts of history', and are 'a record of great social revolutions, revolutions in nations and in the feelings of nations'. Much may be learned, it was argued, 'by noting the words which nations have been obliged to borrow from other nations' (Trench 1851, 1858).

In this chapter, I will discuss the historical origins of words which English has acquired from other languages, and the changes in meanings which accompany this process of borrowing. As in the book as a whole, I will emphasize that words should be studied in the collocations and the text-types in which they typically occur, and I will show that the history of words is another area where corpus methods can provide new data and methods for studying word meaning.

8.1 Data

I will give examples from both raw corpora and also from dictionaries based on corpora. Some large corpora have been designed specifically for linguistic study: here I will use a 50-million-word section of the Bank of English (see Notes on Corpora Data and Software, above). In addition, there are large text collections which have been prepared for other purposes, but which can be studied for examples of contemporary usage: here I will use *The Times* and the *Sunday Times* for 1995 on CD-ROM, that is, all editions of a British up-market national daily newspaper for a complete year.

Major innovations in dictionaries since the 1980s also provide new ways of studying words which have been borrowed into English. Some dictionaries are based on large computer-readable corpora: for example, the *Collins COBUILD English Dictionary* (Cobuild 1995a) was prepared from the evidence of a 200-million-word corpus of contemporary English. A measure of which words are frequent in contemporary English is whether they occur in this dictionary, since it contains only words which were thought frequent enough in the corpus to be of use to advanced learners of English as a second language. 'Frequent enough' is defined by five frequency bands: 700, 1,200, 1,500, 3,200 and 8,100 words each. These words make up 95 per cent of running text in the corpus. Outside this total of 14,700, I estimate that the dictionary lists a further 15,000 head-words.

Other dictionaries are available in machine-readable form with search software. The *Oxford English Dictionary* (henceforth *OED*) is a traditional dictionary, in so far as it gives words and their meanings, and also their etymologies. In its CD-ROM and internet versions it is a relational database, which can be searched in many ways, often within seconds. It is possible to search for all words borrowed from a given language, all words first recorded in a given time period, or a combination of the two: for example, all German loans first recorded in English after 1900. It would take years to find such words in the tens of thousands of pages of the printed *OED*. (For further details, see Jucker 1994, and Simpson and Weiner 2000.)

A combination of sources makes it possible not only to study the origins of words, but also to study how frequently they are used in different text-types in contemporary English. These sources and many others are publicly available, and mean that students can do their own projects.

8.2 The Etymological Fallacy

Linguistics is traditionally divided into diachronic and synchronic study. A diachronic study is a historical one, of how languages change over time, and a diachronic study of the origin and history of words is called 'etymology'. All languages are constantly changing, but for some purposes it is convenient to ignore this. A synchronic study is a deliberate simplification, which looks at a language at a point in time, and ignores language change.

Diachronic linguistics in general is an important sub-branch of linguistics, but etymology has long been out of fashion with many linguists, and many dictionaries, especially those designed for foreign learners of English, do not record any information on the origin of words. This neglect is often due to the argument – largely correct as far as it goes – that native speakers only rarely know the origins of words in their language, that origins are only rarely of relevance to their meaning and use nowadays, and that historical facts are therefore equally irrelevant to foreign learners.

Speakers do often complain that words are wrongly used, that they were formerly used to mean something different, and that this earlier meaning is their proper meaning. For example, some people complain that *decimate* is used nowadays in an imprecise way to mean "destroy a very large number of", whereas it really means to "put to death one in ten", because it comes from the Latin word *decimare*, which is related to *decem* meaning "ten". (This meaning is preserved in English *decade* and *decimal*.) However, this argument is, in turn, generally rejected as follows. First, words change in meaning over time, this is a natural process, and nothing can be done to stop it. Second, speakers use this argument highly selectively. They do not complain, for example, that *nice* really means "silly" (which it used to: it comes from Latin *nescius* = "stupid"), or indeed that *silly* really means "saintly" (which it used to: it is cognate with German *selig* = "blessed"). Furthermore, any search for the earliest meaning of a word is doomed to failure. The Latin word *nescius* itself must be derived from other words which themselves had even earlier meanings. In fact, it derives from *ne-scius* meaning "not know" (compare *science*). But then where did the *scius* part come from? Such arguments become involved in an infinite regress, and stopping at any given point earlier in time is arbitrary. Linguists call this faulty line of argument the etymological fallacy: precisely because words change in meaning over time, the meaning of a word cannot be established from its etymology. The *OED* also records that the word *black* has a 'difficult history', and was sometimes confused in Old English with a similar word which meant "shining" or "white", but speakers would be ill-advised nowadays to use *black* to mean "white".

Often people's complaints about changes in meaning are restricted to individual words, rather than considering coherent sets of words, and their complaints tend to be inconsistent. I gave the example above of *decimate*. Another well-known example is *gay*, which now almost always means "homosexual", whatever it previously meant. But I have not come across anyone complaining about changes in the meaning of *cowboy* (Crystal 1995: 138). This word used to have positive, romantic associations, and is still used in phrases such as *cowboy films* and *cowboy boots*, but it is now frequently used (especially in British English) with strongly negative connotations, in phrases such as *cowboy operators* and *cowboy companies*, to mean untrained and incompetent people who run an unreliable business, as in *cowboy builders* and *cowboy security firms*. (Perhaps there is a lobby group of cowboys who are protesting against this use.)

Even these isolated examples are useful in so far as they show how unstable word-meanings are: many words and their meanings have changed considerably over time, and word-meanings are inherently variable. Williams (1976) shows, for example, that *culture* has nowadays a variety of different meanings because of semantic extensions in the past, which have left layers of meanings deposited over time. Early meanings, concerning "tending crops or animals" (*agriculture*), were extended to human development (early sixteenth century), and to the abstract general process (late eighteenth century), when the word acquired social class connotations. As a result, we now have different uses, such as *sugar-beet culture, germ culture*, and culture in the sense of "music, literature and the arts".

However, the etymological fallacy disposes only of some poor reasons for studying etymology. If etymology is restricted to a few individual words, it is probably doomed to the study of idiosyncratic accidents of history, and it is difficult to see how generalizations could emerge. It is more interesting to look at sets of words, such as words in particular lexical fields, or words borrowed from different languages, or to look at how loan words are differently distributed in texts and text-types. In other words, we can follow the principle, on which this whole book is based, of looking at words in their discourse contexts.

8.3 Language Change

Because it generally happens so slowly, we usually cannot observe diachronic change directly. We might be aware that a few words are used only by older speakers, and that younger speakers use a different word, as happened, for example, with *wireless* and *radio*. In these cases, we can observe the synchronic variation, which is the result of diachronic change. It is only occasionally that individual speakers are placed in circumstances where they realize how much vocabulary does change over a few decades. In 1951 Monica Baldwin published her autobiography: *I Leap over the Wall*. She had entered a strict convent in 1913 and left in 1941, after 28 years, the entire interwar period, cut off from radio, films, newspapers or new people to talk to. When she left the convent, she did not understand many words and phrases, including

- cocktail 1806, hard boiled (outlook) 1886, to have a hunch 1904, nosey parker 1907, it's your funeral 1908, jazz 1909, mutt (= "fool") 1901, close-up 1913, streamlining 1918, plus fours 1920, cutie 1921, robot 1923, it's your pigeon (= pidgin = "business") 1925, parking 1926, Hollywood 1926, believe it or not 1929, belisha beacon 1934, striptease 1936

The dates are the first uses recorded in the *OED*, and are indeed mainly in the interwar period or just before. Some words seem to have taken a few years to become current, and Baldwin did not know them when she entered the convent. The word *cocktail* is attested from 1806, but it was mainly used in American English. Some of these words and phrases have, in the meantime, gone out of fashion again. It is important to cross-check etymologies in independent sources where possible, and in these cases Baldwin's anecdotal account confirms that the *OED* dates are correct. (There are, for example, some differences between Pfeffer's 1987 study of German loans and dates given in the *OED*. For words which entered English post-1941, the *OED* can be compared with Algeo 1991.) One problem with datings in dictionaries is that they necessarily rely almost entirely on written language, but a word is often current for years in the spoken language before it appears in published texts.

8.4 Terminology

It is usual to talk of 'loan words' being 'borrowed' from one language into another. These are slightly odd terms, since the words are not given back to the source language. A 'loan translation' means that parts of a word or phrase in the source language have been separately translated. For example *Christmas tree* is a loan translation of German *Weihnachtsbaum*. (This is also called a 'calque'.) The term 'false friends' means that words which are similar in different languages in fact mean something subtly or completely different. For example, German *aktuell* does not mean "actual", but "contemporary" or "up-to-date".

So, we can make statements such as the following. There are many English loan words in German, such as *Smoking*, *Snackbar* and *Snob*. Some loans are false friends: in German *ein Smoking* means "a dinner jacket". Relations can involve words which are apparent borrowings, but which do not exist in the source language. A common phrase in German is *im Partnerlook*: this refers to two people who are recognizably together because they are similarly dressed, in matching pullovers or whatever. The word *Pullover* is an English loanword in German, but German also has the word *Pullunder*, meaning "sleeveless pullover", which does not exist in English. (By the way, *loan word* and *loan translation* are both loan translations from German *Lehnwort* and *Lehnübersetzung*.)

When words are borrowed into a language, they may become assimilated or integrated into the new language. Many words which were borrowed at some time in the past into English are fully integrated, in the sense that native speakers regard them simply as English words, and do not realize that they are loans. For example, the words *dollar*, *Christmas tree*, *folk-song* and *poodle* were, as a matter of historical fact, borrowed or translated from

German, though probably only a few English speakers know this. Often when words are borrowed into English, they are adapted to English word-structure, irrespective of how they were used in the language of origin. For example, the word *helicopter* is from two Greek words *helix/helikos* (= "screw") and *pteron* (= "wing"). So, etymologically, the word structure is *helico*-plus-*pter*, but in English the word is reanalysed as *heli*- plus -*copter*, which leads to abbreviations such as *copter* and *helipad*. Presumably English speakers find the phoneme structure in *pteron* un-English (though it has survived in *pterodactyl*), and many probably reinterpret *heli*- as being analogous to other prefixes such as *demi*-, *semi*- and *hemi*-. (The "spiral" or "twisted" sense of *heliko*- survives in English phrases such as the *double helix*, as a term for DNA.)

At the other extreme, loans may not be integrated at all, but spelled and pronounced as they are in the foreign language, so that they are not so much borrowed as quoted, as in these loans from French:

- crime passionel, déjà vu, femme fatale, mot juste, sauve qui peut, coq au vin, nouvelle cuisine

The following deliberately self-contradicting paradox is from a letter to the editor of *The Times* (11 September 1995):

- English will always provide the *mot juste*.

It received several follow-up letters including this one (18 September 1995):

- [English will also provide] a certain *je ne sais quoi* in keeping with, inter alia, the Zeitgeist of the age.

8.5 Words, Politics and National Stereotypes

Lack of assimilation (in pronunciation, spelling or word structure) can therefore be used as a resource to connote "foreignness". In such cases, a knowledge of where words come from is an essential part of their meaning in the contemporary language. Often words are created or borrowed in response to world political events, and such loans give at least a sidelight on history and cultural contacts between nations. For example, here are the dates of the first attested uses of a few words recorded in the *OED* or Algeo (1991):

- cold war 1945, sputnik 1957, Watergate 1972, -gate 1973, perestroika 1987, intifada 1988

The whole point of using a set of German loan words such as

- Nazi 1930, Third Reich 1933, Nazism 1934, Führer 1934, Gestapo 1934, Luftwaffe 1935, Anschluss 1938, Blitzkrieg 1939

is to signal a set of meanings concerned with Nazi Germany before and during World War II. In contemporary German, *Luftwaffe* is a common noun which means "airforce", but in English it means "the airforce in Nazi Germany", and is on the hazy boundary between proper names and common nouns. In addition to these historically significant cases, loan words often confirm national stereotypes, and symbolize the foreign and the strange. From German, English has borrowed *blitzkrieg, kitsch* and *lederhosen*. From French, *bistro, gigolo* and *mot juste*. From Italian *allegro, forte* and *pianissimo*, and *pasta, pizza* and *spaghetti*. Such words are perhaps just the ones which would occur first to English speakers, and, as I will show below, a more systematic search for German loans in English does something to balance crude national stereotypes.

However, there is no doubt that loans in English are often used to signal exoticness, and there is a clear connection between loan words and culture. The *OED* gives around 1,200 twentieth-century loans and loan translations from French into English. Most are rare, and not known to most native English speakers at all, but ones which are frequently used come mainly from a small number of areas, especially cooking (i.e. cuisine!), clothing and fashion, the arts, plus a few from political and/or military fields:

- anorexic, après-ski, arriviste, bikini, bistro, blouson, brassière, cagoule, calque, camouflage, conurbation, courgette, Dada, dirigisme, discothèque, dressage, embourgeoisé, exocet, franglais, frigidaire, gaffe, gaga, garage, gigolo, hotelier, limousine, mannequin, microfiche, pacifist, plonk (<vin blanc?), profiteer, questionnaire, racism, sabotage, surrealism, Third World

There are only a few words current in contemporary English from Arabic, Chinese and Japanese, and they denote areas of meaning which (for many English speakers) are (stereo)typically related to these cultures. The *OED* gives about 50 loans from Arabic, though few are in common use. *Ayatollah* (from Arabic via Persian), *Allah* and *mullah* are frequent enough in contemporary English to be given in the Cobuild Dictionary (1995a). Many native speakers probably also know *felafel, Hezbollah, mujahidin* and *tahina*. The *OED* gives about 80 loans from Chinese, though few are in common use. *Chow mein, kung fu* and *wok* are frequent enough to be given in Cobuild (1995a). Many native speakers may also know other words such as *dim sum* and *mah jong*. Most linguists know the word *pinyin*. Some of these words are from Cantonese, not modern standard Chinese (i.e. the variety known in the West as Mandarin). The *OED* gives about 120 loans from Japanese, though few are in common use. *Bonsai, karate* and *origami* are frequent enough to be given in Cobuild (1995a). Many speakers may also know *kendo* and *sukiyaki*. Most linguists know the word *kanji*. Most native speakers also know other items such as *Honda, Kawasaki* and *Suzuki*.

Given the globalization of commerce, many etymologies are more international than they appear. In English, the name *Sony* (as in *Sony Walkman*) connotes "Japan". The name of the company was originally *Tokyo Tsushin Kogyu Kabushiki Kasha*. It was thought, understandably, that this name would not be memorable, and the word *Sony* was deliberately coined, both to recall Latin *sonus* (= "sound"), and also because it could be pronounced in many languages (Du Gay et al. 1997: 48).

Jucker (1996) discusses how loan words can provide both positive and negative local colour. One of his examples is the use, in a British newspaper, of *a German autobahn*, rather than *motorway*, to connote high speed, 'so that the reader can be astonished at what strange things happen in foreign countries'! (*Autobahn* is in Cobuild 1995a.) So, a knowledge of etymology can be relevant to understanding the meaning (or at least the connotations) of words.

Jucker (1996) also points out that loans can have quite different functions in different languages. Thus German loans in English can have the function of expressing local colour, foreignness or even anti-German stereotypes, though German loans occur much more widely than this (see below). However, English loans in German do not necessarily convey connotations of Britishness or Americanness, but rather modernity and internationalness. Sometimes, this seems to reach extremes. For example, German telephone bills in 1998 used the following words to refer to local and long-distance calls: *CityCall* (= local), *RegioCall* (= up to 50 km), *GermanCall* (= long-distance within Germany), *GlobalCall* (= international long-distance). The German for "telephone call" is *Anruf*, but this was not used. It was possible to use a *Tarif-Hotline freecall* to get further information about prices. Word-forms, word-structure and capitalization are all un-German (and not quite English either). Customers seem to have found some of these terms rather absurd, and by 1999 they had been changed. For example, *Call* had largely been replaced by *Verbindung* (= "connection"), and *GermanCall* had been altered to *Deutschlandverbindung*!

8.6 Fields of Knowledge and Text-Types

The examples above show not only the history of individual words, but the beginning of generalizations about how sets of words function in texts. If the history of words is investigated with an eye to lexical fields and associated text-types, then there are important generalizations to be made about etymology. If we go back pre-1066 to Old English, then the vocabulary was just Germanic, with only a few words from other sources. However, the Norman invasion of 1066 led to a broad division right across the English vocabulary. The indigenous population spoke the Germanic language, but the incoming ruling class spoke Norman French, so for many years the different social classes spoke different languages, and bilingualism must have contributed to the enormous influence of the incoming Romance language on the native Germanic language. There was a large influx of Romance vocabulary into those areas of society which were controlled by the newly arrived ruling class: government, law, religion and academic areas. So, there was an intimate connection between the etymology of words, the social class of speakers, and the text-types in which words of different origins were used.

The mix of the two languages has led to many sets of doublets and triplets in English, such as *help* and *aid*, cognate with German *helfen* and French *aider*. Compare:

- go down, descend; mean, signify; get, obtain; motherly, maternal; kingly, royal, regal

In general, it is the Romance words which are less frequent and more formal (Granger 1996). Such doublets are seen in fixed phrases which derive from early legal English where the old Anglo-Saxon and the new Latin or French words were used alongside each other. Clerks of the court were unsure whether the two terms meant the same, so they used both, for safety. Examples include phrases such as *breaking and entering* (where *breaking* is cognate with German *brechen* and *entering* is cognate with French *entrer*), and *last will and testament* (German *der letzte Wille*, French *testament*).

In addition, large sets of words, borrowed over time from particular languages, are now used in particular fields of activity. For example, many scientific and technical terms are formed from Latin and Greek roots, and text analysis shows very different percentages in different text-types.

8.7 A Case Study of German Loan Words in English

The six languages which have contributed the largest number of loan words to English are Latin, Greek, French, Italian, Spanish and German. Jucker

(1994) used the *OED* on CD-ROM to investigate the relative contributions of these languages to English from 1500 to the present. English is a language which, in the past, has absorbed a large number of words from a large number of languages. However, Jucker finds that the rate of borrowing fell off sharply in the twentieth century. Nowadays, most new words in English are not borrowed from other languages, but formed from language-internal resources. I checked the *OED* for words first recorded in the 1970s and 1980s. Some are borrowings, as with these loans and loan translations from Russian: *glasnost, perestroika, Kalashnikov, refusenik*. But most are created from within the language, as acronyms or new combinations of old morphemes, often in analogy to old combinations:

- aids, ageist, backslash, camcorder, chairperson, download, flexitime, kissogram, microchip, popemobile, shambolic, televangelist, up-market, yuppie

Jucker (1994) studied periods of 70 years between 1497 and 1986. In the last two periods, 1847 to 1916, and 1917 to 1986, he finds that loan words from Latin, Greek and French drop from thousands to hundreds. The contributions of Italian and Spanish are also considerably less in the twentieth than in the nineteenth century. The contribution of German has also declined but has remained more constant than other languages over the last 500 years (with a peak in the nineteenth century), and German is the language which has made the largest contribution to English in the twentieth century. For example, the following are German loan words or loan translations pre-1900, which are all frequent enough in contemporary English to be listed in the Cobuild Dictionary (1995a), although mainly not within the top 15,000 words.

- angst, aspirin, bum (= "lazy person"), chic (<*French* ?*German* schick), Christmas tree, dachshund, death-wish, delicatessen, dollar, doodle, drill (= "cotton cloth"), dumb (= "stupid"), ecology, eiderdown, enzyme, ersatz, fahrenheit, fife (<Pfeife), folk-song, hamburger, hamster, handbook, heroin, hinterland, hock (= "Rhine wine"), kaput, kindergarten, kohlrabi, lager (= "beer"), larch, noodle, plunder, poltergeist, poodle, rucksack, spanner, swindler, waltz, Yiddish, yodel, zeitgeist

English does not have many German loan words in common use, but this list already shows that those it does have are a more mixed bunch than stereotypic lists (of *nazi*, etc.) might imply. As in many areas of language study, intuitions about loan words are unreliable. Native speakers can usually produce examples of loan words from various languages, but they are often stereotypes.

German has been a major language of scholarship in the nineteenth and twentieth centuries, especially in chemistry and other natural sciences, but also in the humanities and social sciences, hence loans such as:

- biology, chromosome, gauss, gestalt, gneiss, Hertz (Hz), leitmotif/v, marxism, quartz, umlaut, weltanschauung

The intellectual influence of German-language work can be seen in linguistics: via work, in the eighteenth and nineteenth centuries by Herder, Humboldt, the brothers Grimm and others, in the late nineteenth century by the Junggrammatiker, and by Max Müller, Hermann Paul and Hugo Schuchardt (on creoles), and in the twentieth century by, for example, Karl Bühler, Franz Boas and Leonard Bloomfield (a Germanist, of Austrian descent, and greatly influenced in his early work by the German psychologist Wilhelm Wundt). Henry Sweet (1845–1912) spent a year studying at Heidelberg University, emphasized all his life the importance of German linguistic scholarship, and published an English book for German learners: *Elementarbuch des gesprochenen Englisch*. Pfeffer and Cannon (1994) list 101 borrowings in linguistics. The following are all fairly widely used in English-language linguistics.

- ablaut, Ausbausprache (= "developed language"), formant, Grimm's Law, High German (<Hochdeutsch), isogloss, neo-grammarians (<Junggrammatiker), loan translation (<Lehnübersetzung), loan word (<Lehnwort), Mischsprache (="mixed language", hybrid language), Plattdeutsch (= "Low German"), Rhenish fan (<Rheinischer Fächer), schwa (*Hebrew* sheva; 'in German books spelt *schwa*', OED), sound shift (<Lautverschiebung), Sprachbund (= "linguistic area"), Sprachgefühl (= "linguistic intuition"), Stammbaum (= "family tree"), umlaut, Ursprache (= "original language", protolanguage), Urtext (= "original text", earliest version of a text), Verner's Law, Wernicke's aphasia, Yiddish

If the *OED* software is instructed to search for all loans from German after 1900, it finds about 1,250 items. However, this figure is misleadingly high for different reasons. A search certainly finds words which are current in contemporary English, including

- abseil, allergy, bakelite, diktat, festschrift, flak, kitsch, nazi, realpolitik, schizophrenia, snorkel, spritzer, stratosphere

If we are generous about what we include, a search finds up to 75 words which are widely known to native speakers, but this includes many proper names, such as

- Alzheimer's [disease], Bauhaus, Dobermann, Geiger [counter], Jugendstil, Rottweiler

It also includes words which are certainly widely known, but where the etymology is only indirectly German (e.g. *quiche* < French < Alsace dialect *Küchen* < German *Kuchen*). In general, many loan words have multiple origins, and not a single source in one language. A few words name specifically German cultural phenomena, and stereotypes at that, though perhaps *dirndl*, *lederhosen* and *loden* are the only three which are current (though not common enough to be in the Cobuild Dictionary, 1995a).

If the *OED* software is similarly instructed to search for all German loans from 1800 to 1900, it finds over 2,400 items, but again relatively few of these are current in contemporary English. The following are in the *OED* but not in the Cobuild Dictionary:

- dummkopf, edelweiss, liebfraumilch, ouija (< oui + ja!), riesling, schadenfreude, weltanschauung, weltschmerz

The *OED* on CD-ROM is a powerful research tool, which makes possible entirely new investigations of aspects of vocabulary. However, incautious use of the software may produce quantitative results which look superficially plausible, although it may turn out that the computer was not acting intelligently, because the pattern-matching is limited. I have therefore also used other corpora and specialist dictionaries (Algeo 1991; Williams 1976/1983), including the essential historical dictionary by Pfeffer and Cannon (1994), which lists loans not only alphabetically, with etymologies, but also chronologically, and by semantic areas.

The figure of 1,250 loans since 1900 found by the *OED* software is just a rough statistic to start from, since it does not distinguish between intuitively very different cases, as follows.

(1) *Historically motivated words*. From the *Nazi*-set above, the Cobuild Dictionary (1995a) gives only *blitzkrieg* and *Nazi (sm)*. The German origin of such loans is certainly recognized by English speakers: indeed, that is the whole point of using them. In that sense, they are not English words at all, but German words which can be quoted in English to refer almost exclusively to a specific historical period. If we are generous about

this category, and include other political and military terms (some, I suspect, common only amongst fans of British war films), there are about 25 items, including

- gauleiter, herrenvolk, lebensraum, messerschmidt, panzer, stalag, stuka

In their earliest uses, *blitz*, *blitzkrieg* and *flak* had only a military sense, but they now have general meanings, as in these examples from Cobuild (1995a):

- there is to be a blitz on incorrect grammar
- a blitzkrieg of media hype
- attracted more than their fair share of flak from the press

(2) *Names*. Dictionaries are often uncertain how to deal with proper names for people and places, titles of works of art, and so on. The *OED* software finds about 80 items in this category, only a few of which are widely known to educated speakers, and their status as words in English is perhaps dubious. They include

- Hitler, Humboldtian, Leibniz, Nietzschean, Rheingold (the opera and express train), Schumannesque

(3) *Technical terms*. The largest category by far (about 750 out of 1,250) is technical terms, unknown to most native English speakers. From a random sample of 125 of the 1,250 loans post-1900 found by the *OED* software, only 7 were in Cobuild (1995a). Even if we assume that twice that many are probably widely known by native speakers, this still means that only about 10 per cent of these 1,250 loans are current in contemporary English. The largest sub-categories (over 30 per cent together) are mineralogy and chemistry, and many other words come from biology, geology, botany, medicine, physics and mathematics. Pfeffer and Cannon (1994) estimate over a longer time period that 50 per cent of German loans are specialist, technical or scientific words. In chemistry, German-language publications had declined in international influence by the 1990s. Earlier loans include

- adduct, biotin, dehydrase, emulsoid, heterophile, indigoid, lactol, mutase, perbunan, polyaddition, pterin, sabinene, stigmasterol, uridine, zwitterion

However, it is problematic to call these German loans at all. Many were coined in German from Greek and Latin, and are indistinguishable from other Greco-Latin technical terms in English, which have been formed according to the conventions of professional academic groups, and are largely independent of national or language groups. They are part of an international vocabulary, which makes the notion of etymology as origin in a single given language rather dubious.

(4) *Loan translations.* This category includes

- anti-body < Antikörper; pecking order < Hackliste (nowadays < Hackordnung); power politics < Machtpolitik; rainforest < Regenwald; space-time < Raumzeit; superman < Übermensch

The *OED* notes other cases as merely parallel in German and English: *breakthrough* (*Durchbruch*), *delouse* (*entlausen*), *hookworm* (*Hakenwurm*). If we allow both sets, the software finds about 25 items in this category.

(5) *Indirect loans.* The *OED* software does not distinguish between words loaned recently from German, and words with a more complex history. For example, some words passed from much earlier forms of German into Yiddish, though there may still be comparable words in modern German, and usually via American into British English. There are over 30 examples, such as *bagel, glitzy, nosh, schlep* and *schmal(t)z*. See Rosten (1971).

There can be no definitive list of the words which are in English. The vocabulary of a language is an open set, with words coming and going all the time. This is discussed in a famous passage in the original introduction to the *OED*: the vocabulary of English is 'not a fixed quantity circumscribed by definite limits', but rather a 'nebulous mass [with a] clear and unmistakeable nucleus [which] shades off on all sides ... to a marginal film that seems to end nowhere'. (See chapter 2.8.2 on core vocabulary.) The vocabulary also shades off into obsolescent and archaic words. Etymological dictionaries contain information on the first sighting of a word (usually in a written text), and loans referring to world political events (such as *sputnik* and *Watergate*) can often be precisely dated. But we cannot see words die: many of them just crawl away quietly, and hide in large dictionaries, where their last resting places are labelled 'obsolescent' or 'archaic'. Although words may have a sudden onset of use, they often die out gradually, which is why the language of older speakers may sound old-fashioned. This decreasing frequency can only be recorded in large corpora: for example, *sputnik* arrived in English and many other languages in 1957, but is no longer recorded in Cobuild (1995a).

8.8 Frequency in the Vocabulary versus Frequency in Texts

If we look at all the words borrowed from German over the last 500 years, the number is surprisingly large. Pfeffer and Cannon (1994) collected data from the *OED* plus 'all major dictionaries in English', and found over 6,000 German loans from 1500 to the present day. Even this large number is only 1 or 2 per cent of the English vocabulary as recorded in the *OED*, which contains over 320,000 head words and 616,500 word-forms, including derivatives and phrases (Algeo 1990). However, Pfeffer and Cannon point out that only some 10 per cent of these loans are in everyday use. The list of 6,000 contains words which are attested in English-language texts, but many are rare or obsolete. If we look at the German loans which are actually used in contemporary English – and if we further exclude indirect loans, proper names and the like – then we are left with a much smaller number. In addition, we should probably consider separately the many highly specialized technical words, which occur only in a narrow range of texts. Therefore, in general corpora, the text frequency of German loans is much lower again. As with the vocabulary as a whole, a few words occur frequently, but most words occur rarely.

I searched for all the nineteenth- and twentieth-century German loans listed above, including their derivatives (e.g. *ecology, ecological, ecologist*), in a corpus of 2.7 million words, which contained samples from over a thousand different texts, spoken and written, fiction and non-fiction of many genres, all post-1900, mostly post-1960, and including over 500,000 words from British and American newspapers. Only 15 loans occurred more than 10 times:

- antibody, blitz, biology, diesel, dollar, ecology, enzyme, handbook, hinterland, lager, marxism/t, nazi(sm), space-time, waltz, Yiddish

Most occurred fewer than five times or not at all:

- angst, eiderdown, rucksack, snorkel (fewer than 5)
- ersatz, kindergarten, poltergeist, zeitgeist (not at all)

Even if we include words such as *biology* (and all its derivatives, frequency 140) and *dollar* (frequency 80), the combined frequency of occurrence was only about 650. This is fewer than one occurrence every 4,000 words, or about 0.025 per cent of running text.

The text frequency of words depends on the content of the texts in the corpus. For example, there were 12 occurrences of the loan translation *space-time*, all from a single text on astrophysics, and 38 occurrences of *Nazi* (nearly 6 per cent of the total of 650), many from texts on German history, though the word is distributed throughout the corpus. Its frequency does not seem to be an artefact of my data, since the Cobuild Dictionary (1995a) records *Nazi* in its third frequency band: amongst the 3,400 most frequent words in English. Even *Nazism* gets into the top 15,000.

A few recognizably German loans with their frequency of occurrence in *The Times* and the *Sunday Times* in 1995 include

- angst 189; blitz 210; diesel 306; eiderdown 7; ersatz 49; hinterland 68; lager 198; kindergarten 54; nazi, nazis, nazism, etc. 459; poltergeist 4; rucksack 49; waltz 114; Yiddish 28; zeitgeist 56

8.9 False Friends: *Flak*, *Blitz* and *Angst*

One principle of etymology is the etymological fallacy (see section 8.2 above): the 'real' meaning of a word cannot be established from its history. Thus, even words which are borrowed from German, and recognized as such, may not mean the same in German as in English. In fact, they are most unlikely to mean exactly the same, since they are used in a quite different linguistic context, and loan words can create false friends. For example, two words which were originally military terms in German have undergone changes of meaning in English: *flak* (occasionally spelled *flack* in English) and *blitz*.

In German, *Flak* was a World War I abbreviation of *Flieger-* or *Flugzeugabwehrkanone* (= "anti-aircraft gun"). The abbreviation occurs in words such as *Flakartillerie* (= "troop armed with anti-aircraft guns"), and the word occurs in modern German only in discussions of military history. In English, the word still has a military meaning, although the sense has shifted from the gun to the bullets, often in the phrase *flak jacket*. However, it has acquired an extended sense, which does not exist at all in German, of "severe criticism". Only this "criticism" sense was considered frequent enough to be included in the Cobuild dictionary (1995a). The word *flak* occurs in 140 articles in *The Times* and the *Sunday Times* in 1995, both with its military meaning, but also frequently with a critical or ironic meaning, and often in phrases preceded by a colloquial verb and a quantifying expression, as in

- take all the flak; arouse considerable flak; attract political flak; catch most of the flak; come in for a lot of flak; cop the flak; draw considerable flak; escape the flak; face the flak; get a lot of flak; pick up some flak; run into more flak

- a new generation of Flak Catchers staff are trained to deal with consumer complaints

One reason why *flak* is frequent in newspapers is that it is short. For example, a newspaper headline used the phrase *Union Flak*, followed, in the body of the article, by the phrase *criticism from teaching unions*. In summary, the word typically occurs in informal phrases such as *TAKE a lot of flak for*, and is often used to refer to public criticism of public figures.

In German, *Blitz* means "lightning", and it is also used in several compound words, which denote a rapid and surprising action of some kind, for example *Blitzaktion*, *Blitzstart* or *Blitzkrieg* (which has also been borrowed into English). In English, *the Blitz* was given the narrower meaning of the German bombing of British cities, especially London, in World War II. However, *blitz* has also acquired new meanings, especially in the media. In *The Times* and the *Sunday Times* in 1995 it occurred in 210 articles, still frequently in its original sense (e.g. *the London Blitz*), but also frequently, usually as a noun, but also as a verb, as in

- advertising blitz; legislative blitz; marketing blitz; media blitz; merchandising blitz; promotional blitz; propaganda blitz; publicity blitz; blitz of TV ads
- I trust the motorway police will have a blitz on these idiots
- a drugs clean-up... or blitz on illegal immigrants
- the Tories are to blitz seats in Scotland
- the marketing campaign [began] with a blitz of cardboard Michael Jackson cut-outs
- launched another 'bumph-busting' blitz to get rid of millions of unnecessary pieces of paper
- in a blitz in the Naples hinterland... police seized goods

This second meaning has complex connotations. It means a major, sudden, and therefore surprising, effort to deal with something which has been badly neglected; an attempt to catch people unawares, either in connection with a marketing campaign (*launched an advertising blitz*), or with a campaign to clean up anti-social or criminal activities (a *blitz on drink-driving*). This informal use is most frequent in spoken English and in journalism.

I will take a third example in more detail: *angst*. In everyday German, *Angst haben* means "to be frightened of". However, the sense borrowed into English comes from psychology and philosophy. Wierzbicka (1999: 123–67) gives a detailed analysis of its meanings as a cultural keyword in German. There is an *OED* citation from 1849, but the first main citations are from Freud [1922] and Heidegger [1941], where the word has the meaning of "existential dread, metaphysical guilt and fears". However, in more recent everyday English, it has acquired strong evaluative connotations, with the pejorative implication that the dread is about trivial things. It often occurs in semi-fixed phrases, about 10 per cent in *angst-ridden*, and a further 10 per cent in *teen(age) angst*, plus related phrases such as *adolescent angst* and *high school angst*. It is something which is *pandered to* or *thrashed out*; people are said to be *riddled with* or *riven with* angst. The following examples (from the Bank of English) are evidence of its highly critical connotations:

- piffling, sniffling pseudo-angst
- nasal whining or chestbeating angst
- the usual teen-angst, punkthrash, grungefest boogaloo
- tawdry angst-ridden verses [recollect] his inglorious past
- a tasty mix of angst and vinegary pop thrills
- what lurks at the bottom of the Angst Barrel, be glad we're here to scrape it for you
- self-adjusting cruise control could take much of the Angst out of the Autobahn
- genuine tortured souls or mere designer angst merchants?

In the last example, note the use both of *designer* (as in *designer drugs*, *designer stubble*), in the sense of "superficially fashionable and trendy"; and also of *merchant* in the colloquial sense of someone who is engaged in a disreputable activity (*gossip merchant*, *speed merchant*). Meanings are typically distributed across phrases, not tied to one word-form.

These examples show strong evaluative connotations which the word does not have in German. Its main use in English is when other people's behaviour is being evaluated in ironic or highly critical ways. *Angst* is something typically suffered by adolescents, or by middle-aged, middle-class, introspective, sensitive, suburban souls, who have no genuine worries. It is one of a large set of words in English (especially in British culture?) which are deeply critical of people for trying to appear more important than the speaker thinks they are. Channell (2000) discusses other examples such as *grand, pontificate, self-important, social climber*. The Cobuild Dictionary (1995a) notes that *angst* is 'used mainly in journalism'. I checked its occurrence in *The Times* and the *Sunday Times* in 1995. It occurs in 190 articles, but is much more frequent in the Sunday edition than in the weekday editions. It appears on average in two articles in each Sunday edition. This carries many more articles on artistic and cultural topics, and the word is often used in reviews of books, music and films, often mocking people for their essentially trivial, fashionable concerns. Examples include:

- the angst of hiring baby's first nanny
- middle-class angst is instantly lampoonable
- the teen rebel angst that is de rigueur in the anglo world
- arguing... that angst was out, self-pity was passé
- his male-angst mid-life-crisis novels
- childhood angst and the first stirrings of puppy-love
- liquor, wife-swapping, existential angst and hypocrisy
- drink, drugs and post-adolescent angst
- the controversy, the backbiting and the hand-wringing angst
- Brecht's late-life, angst, schadenfreude, weltschmerz and many other nasty German words-laden classic [from a review of *The Caucasian Chalk Circle*]

In the last example, note the other German loans. *Schadenfreude* occurred in 45 articles, though *weltschmerz* occurred only in two. The concordance lines (see concordance 8.1) give a few examples of the most frequent collocations.

Together, the three examples illustrate the complex changes which can take place when words are borrowed across languages. All three have formed false friends. Their uses in German and English are quite different: this includes the strong tendency of the words to occur in typical phrases in English (such as, *take a lot of flak, launch a blitz on, teenage angst*). All three are most frequent in journalism. Speakers of English as a foreign language should perhaps be especially careful in using the word *angst*, which often has an ironic and insulting discourse prosody.

8.10 The *OED* and Cultural Keywords

Archbishop Trench (1851), one of the proposers of the *OED*, saw language as 'fossil history', and Raymond Williams (1976), in his famous *Vocabulary of Culture and Society*, uses the same geological metaphor. Using data from the first printed version of the *OED*, Williams investigated the history of over 100 keywords in British culture: nodes around which ideological battles are fought. He uses a more modern (Marxist) idiom than Trench, but his idea is essentially the same: that words embody facts of history, and that they can be analysed diachronically to reveal unconscious assumptions of their community of users.

Williams also shows that many words in English were influenced by cognate words in French and German. Words are borrowed back and forth between languages, and although a word-form may not have been borrowed from German, many meanings have been greatly influenced by German-language philosophy, psychology and sociology. In many of his entries,

1. t she has re-created herself as angst-ridden 15-year-old Lettie Chubb in
2. H> Paw are yet another bunch of angst-ridden Americans who deal in guita
3. ght. Box 26615. – Lesbian, 30s, angst-ridden and fed up. Loves music, fr
4. trols fans Limebirds – Magpie – angst-ridden but stylish fuzz boys Razor
5. anything is difficult, but for angst-ridden control freaks like us who
6. 845 514212). – Mothers who have angst-ridden days wondering about what h
7. rner) – From all-action hero to angst-ridden everyman, Harrison Ford's c
8. cal reviews where I'm like, the angst-ridden genius and stuff, and the p
9. xperience-Newman because of his angst-ridden good looks and stunningly a
10. at Radiohead who, despite their angst-ridden image, actually inspired th
11. u're looking for a fine line in angst-ridden indie pop with future poten
12. teralism of El Penitente or the angst-ridden introspection of Herodiade?
13. o she had been telephoned by an angst-ridden parent seeking help for her
14. that such lyrics aren't simply angst-ridden personal confessions. – The
15. e. It's easy to assume that his angst-ridden postures are the product of
16. ted by archetypal sounds and an angst-ridden post-colonial search for fr
17. was, however, disturbed by the angst-ridden quality of German policy du
18. ovember '83. After two years of angst-ridden soul searching and worrying
19. as a role model by hippies and angst-ridden teens, determined to set th
20. aken seriously. Here, in tawdry angst-ridden verses, he recollects his i
21. So begins the dating game, the angst-ridden weeks of plotting and polit
22. ran film-maker and doyen of the angst-ridden, filed suit against his lon
23. hed notion that all artists are angst-ridden, sensitive souls. Unpretent
24. unk as f-and the soundtrack is angst-ridden, spastically groovy, punk r
25. l female band as long as you're angst-ridden / ranting / heartbroken /meekly
26. ause for Verve for keeping teen angst alive, adding drily – They don't h
27. r Flash Liquid. – June 30: Teen angst evening with The Shangri-Las. – Th
28. their fusion gawky energy, teen angst, rap urgency, heavy-duty rhythms,
29. n repetition emblematic of teen angst. Like Understanding. You don't und
30. If you treasure the early teen- angst movies of Mcdowell, you must immed
31. ip paper, and is the usual teen- angst, punkthrash, grungefest boogaloo,
32. zy pop melodies, simple teenage angst and boundless, unstoppable enthusi
33. intensity, hiding their teenage angst and depression under a pile of hoo
34. neers Clive – We're the teenage angst fiery West midlands guitar band, a
35. Thrashing out all that teenage angst has meant she's come to know herse
36. autobiographical line, Teenage angst has paid off well, now I'm bored a
37. o' is Kurt's revenge. – Teenage angst has paid off well. Now I'm old and
38. perfectly with Rollins' teenage angst lyrics. He plays these high-pitche
39. s the new kid in town – Teenage angst, love, fights, summer camps – they
40. loop of somebody else's teenage angst. They move the goal posts altogeth
41. dy time pouring out her teenage angst. Whatever Rosie's problem, Pamela
42. the latest addition to teenage angst. 'I do think about spots, but line
43. ult is some truly awful teenage-Angst poetry ('I must write/I must live
44. vampire film with teenage biker angst and Kathryn Bigelow's lovely and e

Concordance 8.1 Sample concordance lines for *angst-ridden* and *teen(age) angst*
Note: The data are from the Bank of English.

Williams notes the influence of major thinkers such as Freud, Hegel, Herder, Marx and Weber. Cases where Williams notes German–English relations include

- aesthetic, alienation, anthropology, bourgeois, capitalism, class, community, culture, dialectic, ecology, ethnic, existential, folk, formalist, genius, history, humanity, idealism, ideology, imperialism, individual, industry, materialism, pragmatic, psychology, romantic, sociology, theory, unconscious

The word-form *unconscious* is not a German loan, but a central part of its contemporary meaning comes from the popularization of Freud from the 1920s onwards. The *OED* on CD-ROM can also be searched for all quotes from a given author: the software finds half a dozen quotes from Freud. Such examples show that the significance of etymologies can be seen only if sets of words are studied in their discourse contexts.

8.11 A Further Note on Vocabulary and Text

As I emphasize throughout this book, the vocabulary of a language is not just a list of words, but a network held together by different types of relationships. In this chapter, I have given examples of borrowing and meaning change, but investigating the overall system would require quantitative techniques which are well beyond the scope of this work. (Tuldava, 1998, provides an excellent discussion of many points.) However, some points can be made informally as follows.

The vocabulary of English has increased over time, at different speeds at different periods of history, in reaction to different external pressures, such as standardization and the need for technical terms. At some periods, this growth has been very rapid indeed, and an inventory of the vocabulary of English which includes all the technical terms which have been introduced over the past hundred years would be huge.

Some words have been in the language for a long period of time, whereas some are more recent acquisitions (such as many words concerning modern technology), and others are fashionable for a short time and then drop out again (the fate of many slang words). So, dictionaries from different periods can be compared to see how much overlap there is in the vocabulary recorded at different times. It turns out that there is a strong positive correlation between the 'age' of a word (how long it has been in the vocabulary) and its frequency of use. Tuldava (1998: 144) gives data on

English and several other languages, including statistics on words which were already in English in the year 1100: conventionally, linguists talk of Old English up to this date, and of Middle English from 1100 to around 1500. There was obviously no sharp break in language history, though there were large changes in the language due to the Norman invasion of 1066. He finds that 94 of the 100 most frequent words in contemporary English (which are almost all function words) were already in the language in the year 1100. This percentage declines steadily, such that 47 per cent of words in the frequency band 401–500 were in the language in 1100, but only 31 per cent of words in the band 901–1,000.

German is more conservative than English, in so far as the corresponding statistics are: frequency band 1–100, 94 per cent (identical to English); band 401–500, 63 per cent; and band 901–1,000, 53 per cent (a much higher retention rate than English). Of the 1,000 most frequent words in English, about 46 per cent have been in the language for at least 900 years; the corresponding figure for German is 68 per cent.

The decline in older words as the frequency of use declines is to be expected, because if a word is in constant, frequent use, it is less likely to drop out than a word which is only rarely used. Therefore one would expect very frequent function words to remain stable over time, whereas less frequent content words will come and go more easily. This is indeed so, and it is an exceptional case that the pronouns *they* and *them* were borrowed into English from Scandinavian, due to the Viking invasions, and replaced the Old English pronouns. So, there is a close connection between the vocabulary of a language (the system on which speakers can potentially draw) and the frequency with which words are used in text (actual language use).

This close connection is also seen in the relations between etymology (Germanic or Romance), word length (shorter or longer), style (formal or informal), and grammar (Ellis 1997: 74–5). There are many pairs of approximate synonyms which consist of a less formal one-syllable Germanic word and a more formal multi-syllable Romance word:

- give, present; tell, recount; show, demonstrate

The Germanic words allow two different grammatical constructions, whereas the Romance words allow only one, for example:

- I gave the book to Susan. I gave Susan the book.
- I presented the book to Susan. *I presented Susan the book.

8.12 Summary and Implications

In this chapter I have illustrated some ways in which new data on etymology and word meaning can be provided both by raw corpora, and also by relational data-bases and corpus-based dictionaries.

(1) *On data and interpretation.* Data-bases and large corpora allow types of semantic study which were previously impossible. However, as Jucker (1994: 154) warns, the *OED* on CD-ROM can be a 'dangerous research tool'. Large amounts of data can be collected with ease, but one needs to check carefully exactly what data the computer software is providing, and only careful interpretation can turn data into evidence.

(2) *On German.* The impact of German on modern everyday English is small, though larger and more varied than often supposed, and the influence is largest in academic areas. All of this perhaps does something to balance the stereotyped *blitzkrieg–lederhosen–kitsch* view of German influence on English.

(3) *On linguistic and encyclopedic knowledge.* Diachronic examples show again (see chapter 7) that there is no clear boundary between linguistic and encyclopedic knowledge. In some cases, knowledge of the foreign origin of a word is essential to understanding aspects of its meaning. For example, many German borrowings have historical and cultural connotations, and French and Italian borrowings have been added to the English vocabulary for cooking and convey the connotation of fine food.

(4) *On contexts.* The examples also show that the most interesting findings often arise, when words are studied, not individually, but in lexical fields, in text-types, and in the light of their source languages. Indeed, these contexts are not independent, since sets of words borrowed from a given language may be used in particular text-types for particular topics. For example, German is the source of many academic words in English.

(5) *On instance and system.* There is a distinction between words in texts (as instances of language in use) and words in the vocabulary (as part of the language system). For example, German borrowings are quite frequent in the vocabulary of English, but have a low frequency of occurrence in texts.

8.13 Background and Further Reading

The *OED* was designed in the late nineteenth century, and publication of the first edition was completed in 1928. This was followed by: second edition

1989, second edition on CD-ROM 1992, and on-line edition on the worldwide web in 2000. On the history of the *OED*, see Aarsleff (1990), Murray (1979), and Winchester (1998). Winchester gives a quasi-novelistic, but largely factual, account with much linguistic detail. On the later editions, see Algeo (1990), Jucker (1994), Durkin (1999), and Simpson and Weiner (2000).

8.14 Topics for Further Study

Since the *OED*, in its CD-ROM and internet versions, is a relational database, it makes possible many research projects which were not possible with the printed version. In the printed version, it is possible only to look up headwords alphabetically, but in the electronic versions, words can also be accessed in other ways. For example, it is possible to search for: all words first recorded in a given year or a given period; all words borrowed from a given language; all words defined by an intersection of these criteria (such as all German loans between 1900 and 1920); all words ending in the suffix -*ness*; all words which have the word *accidental* in their definitions; all words recorded in quotes from Freud or Marx. It is also possible to do a full text search of the dictionary. For example, the word-form *care* occurs not only in citations under the head-word CARE, but also in quotes under many other head-words. Extracting all these quotes, and sorting them chronologically, provides a large amount of data on historical changes in the use of the word over the centuries (see chapter 7.4.2).

If you have access to these CD-ROM or on-line versions, carry out some simple studies. For example, select one or two languages, and investigate what words English has borrowed from them, and whether these words fall into particular semantic fields. Are the words culturally significant? Are they assimilated into English? Jucker (1994) gives examples of other projects.

Part III

Implications

9

Words, Phrases and Connotations: On Lexico-grammar and Evaluative Language

In earlier chapters, I have discussed aspects of evaluative meanings: connotations (chapter 2), discourse prosodies (chapters 4 and 5), and culturally significant key words and phrases (chapters 7 and 8). In this chapter, I will develop some of these concepts, and relate them to the way in which speakers and writers express their point of view in texts. Work in corpus linguistics (especially Sinclair 1991; Louw 1993; Channell 2000) has shown that many more words and phrases have evaluative functions than is usually recorded in dictionaries. This work has also shown how evidence for evaluative meanings can be collected by quantitative analysis of large corpora (Church et al. 1991; Clear 1993; Stubbs 1995a, 1995b, 1995c).

9.1 Connotations

Evaluative language is usually treated in linguistics under the concept of connotation (chapter 2.6). This term is also used in everyday English. As a character in one of P. D. James's detective stories (*Shroud for a Nightingale*) says:

> Helping the police! Isn't there a sinister connotation about that phrase?

P. D. James's character is correctly pointing to a connotation that would be widely recognized. However, within linguistics, connotations have often been regarded as 'unstable' and 'indeterminate' (Leech 1981: 13), or limited to the 'personal or emotional associations which are suggested by words' (Crystal 1992: 80). The implication is that they are variable across speakers, idiosyncratic, and therefore of limited interest. Connotation therefore receives little discussion even in major textbooks on semantics and pragmatics (it is only briefly mentioned by Lyons 1977 and Levinson 1983). In approaches to semantics which have been heavily influenced by formal logic, it is denotation and truth-conditions which are seen as the central part of meaning, and connotation is ignored as peripheral and incidental (it is not indexed at all in Lappin 1996).

Words do seem to have different personal associations: for example, you might associate *cat* with "aloof and faithless", whereas I might associate it with "small and fluffy". It may be better, however, to say that the associations are attached to the animal itself, and not to the word. Even if we disagree in what we think about cats, we probably understand in a similar way expressions such as *cat burglar* ("very skilled at climbing"), *cat and mouse game* ("skilful, cunning, sadistic"), and *looks like something the cat brought in* ("dirty, bedraggled"). The connotations of the phrases, and the stereotypes which they trigger, are widely shared across a discourse community and appeal to shared cultural values (Moon 1998). In addition, although 'basic' is usually used for aspects of meaning which are undeniable and independent of context of use, the whole point of an utterance may be to express the speaker's attitude, evaluation and point of view. This is what is basic, one might argue, and is what is encoded in a discourse prosody.

Many connotations seem less accessible to intuition than non-evaluative aspects of meaning (involving denotation and truth-conditions), and many connotations for which there is strong corpus evidence are not recorded in dictionaries. It may be that connotations are particularly difficult to retrieve reliably by intuition because they are not directly observable in individual texts, but depend on intertextual norms (see chapter 5). In addition, evaluative meanings are often inexplicit, less clear-cut and, at least sometimes, deniable. Since they are therefore often used in persuasive language, this makes them important to study for practical reasons.

In this chapter, I will assume that the distinction between denotation and connotation is valid, but I will lay most of the emphasis on connotation, by giving examples of lexical and syntactic units which express evaluative meanings, and on the concept of speaker's point of view. The general argument is that evaluative language is open to empirical observation.

9.2   Verbs, Discourse Prosodies and Point of View

In this section I will analyse the discourse prosodies of several lexico-syntactic constructions, and relate this to the point of view – unsympathetic to the events being described – which is conveyed by some verbs. For example, three verbs used to talk about dangers in public places are ACCOST, LURK and LOITER. All three verbs are used in accusations and complaints about other people's behaviour. Speakers are unlikely to describe themselves as doing these activities. ACCOST implies "harassing someone with unwelcome attention", LURK implies "lying in wait for someone with sinister intentions", and LOITER implies "hanging around with no legitimate purpose". The verbs are quite closely related in meaning. Thus one could say of someone:

- he loitered at the street corner, lurking there to accost passers-by [1]

The centre of empathy will be with the person threatened by the accoster, lurker or loiterer. Logically the verbs require the following participants, though they may not all be expressed in the surface structure.

> ACCOST: someone doing the accosting, some reason for the accosting, someone who is accosted (and possibly threatened), the (public) place where this happens
> LURK: someone (or something) doing the lurking, some reason for the lurking, someone who is threatened by the lurking, the place where this happens
> LOITER: someone doing the loitering, the (public) place where this happens

9.2.1 Example 1: I was accosted in the street by a stranger

ACCOST means "to go up to someone, usually a stranger, in a public place, and pay them unwelcome (possibly threatening) attention". The verb alone already predicts that a sequence of events is being recounted, and this contributes to discourse coherence. The typical components in the syntactic structure are

NP1 –	BE *accosted* –	by NP2 –	PP
Patient	Verb	Agent	Location

As noted by Halliday (1992: 74), the verb is frequently passive, usually with *by* plus agent. A reference to a public place is often made explicit in a prepositional phrase (*in the park, at the end of the street*). Characteristic collocates and attested examples are

- abducted, drunk, loiterer, molester, mug, scare, stranger, threatened, unknown
- I was accosted in the street by women I barely know
- he was accosted in his car in London's Kings Road by two men
- it is like being accosted by a hysterical woman on a train

Kuno (1976) proposes some general principles which help to explain the ways in which ACCOST is used. He argues that it is easiest to empathize with the referent of the subject of a clause, and most difficult to empathize with the referent of the agent in a *by*-adjunct of a passive clause. It is also easier to empathize with a referent who has already appeared in the discourse: since one tends to be accosted by strangers, they tend not to have been already mentioned. These principles correctly predict that

    it is uncommon to say   (a)   *I accosted a stranger* [1]
    it is more common to say   (b)   *a stranger accosted me* [1]
    it is most common to say   (c)   *I was accosted by a stranger* [1]

Type-(a) examples are uncommon, because speakers are unlikely to express disapproval of their own actions. *I* seems to occur in subject position only in negative or hypothetical sentences: see (a) below. Type-(b) active sentences do occur: see (b1). But in such cases, the writer's sympathy may be with the subject NP: see (b2), where the object is explicitly marked as disreputable, and the accosting is morally justifiable. However, it is type-(c) passives which are most frequent.

(a)   I can't just walk in and accost an unknown medic
(b1)   a woman accosted me recently and accused me
(b2)   he accosted the thief, who drew a knife
(c1)   we were accosted by armed policemen
(c2)   he was accosted by a youth

There are two discourse motivations for using this type-(c) word-order. First, the passive puts the victim in subject position, and therefore expresses things from their point of view. This person is typically already known and can be referred to briefly, often as a pronoun. Second, such sentences often express explicit disapproval of the agent, and when placed at the end of the clause in the *by*-phrase, the agent can be described in some detail, sometimes in a following relative clause:

- his workers have been accosted by kerb-crawlers
- she was accosted by an old lady, battered and ragged and bent
- he gets accosted in the park by somebody who tries to mug him
- accosted by two men who tried to steal his gold watch
- accosted by staff who thought he was an intruder

(Cobuild, 1990: 403–5, discusses these functions of word-order in passives.)

The lemma is not frequent. Of 74 occurrences in a 50-million-word corpus and in *The Times* in 1995, 34 were active, and 40 were passive, of which 35 had *by* plus agent. ACCOST is one of relatively few verbs to occur mainly with *by* plus agent in the passive: most passives are agentless (Francis et al. 1996: 58).

9.2.2 Example 2: fears lurking just below the surface

LURK means "to lie in wait, half-hidden, in the background, with the intention of causing harm to someone". Again the verb implies a narrative sequence. The typical syntactic structure is

NP – LURK – PP
Agent Verb Location

Although a Patient (someone threatened) is always implied by the meaning of the verb, this cannot be expressed by an object NP in the surface syntax of the clause, since LURK is intransitive.

In well over 90 per cent of cases, the verb LURK occurs with a place adverbial, sometimes a word such as *nearby*, but most frequently a prepositional phrase, such as *in dark corners* or *in the wings*, and most frequently with *beneath* or *behind*. Other characteristic lexis and attested examples are

- background, bushes, corner, danger, dark, death, hidden, mysterious, nameless, predator, prowl, secret, shadows, strange, unseen
- Tom saw a man lurking in the garden
- the stalker was often seen lurking outside her home
- the pessimism lurking beneath the surface
- the menace that lurks below the sea
- danger is always lurking near
- this thought lurked in the dark shadows of his mind
- beware of the sales traps that lurk under those innocent but enticing sales signs
- don't go wandering too far with that creature lurking about

Often the speech act of warning is implicit in the lexis of dangers, problems, and threats, and sometimes the warning is made explicit, as in the last two examples. The following example makes explicit several central features of danger, waiting, something only partly visible:

- Behind her killer, still hardly there, was the Unseen. It lurked just on the edges of vision, shifting, hungering, waiting. [A]

The phraseology around LURK seems to have been stable for hundreds of years. A text search of the *OED* on CD-ROM gave over 100 examples, many similar to those above, including

- the under-earth spirits are such as lurk in dens and little caverns of the earth [citation from 1592]
- those vices that lurk in the secret corners of the soul [citation from 1712]

In nearly 300 occurrences of LURK in a 50-million-word corpus, there were only two cases of first person subject NPs (compare Fillmore 1971: 372), and one of those was hypothetical:

- many of us seem to spend so much of our lives lurking around doctors' waiting rooms
- I feel as if I might in some other form be found lurking under your father's hibiscus

Again, two general principles come into operation. First, a connotation is rarely carried by a single word, but is distributed prosodically across a textual sequence. Second, a connotation is often due to inter-collocations. If we start with LURK as node, then we discover that it often co-occurs with the prepositional phrase *beneath the surface*. In turn, *beneath*, *below* and *under* collocate with *buried* and *hidden*. And most occurrences of *beneath the surface* indicate not a physical location, but refer to an unpleasant state of affairs:

- the bitterness which had been festering *beneath the surface*
- the tensions that had been simmering *beneath the surface*
- the anger that lay just *beneath the surface* had erupted
- fear *lurks beneath the surface*
- just *beneath the surface lurk* prejudices
- the monstrous pit of insecurity which I could sense *lurking* just *under the surface* of the fool's paradise
- hidden fears and aggressions are *lurking* just *below the surface*

9.2.3 Example 3: LOITER *and other verbs*

LOITER has related meanings, co-occurs with similar lexis, and often co-occurs with a prepositional phrase. Typical attested examples are

- a youth was loitering by the door pretending to read a newspaper
- he saw a throng of young men loitering about the entrance
- it's been loitering in some recess of my mind for years

The *Oxford Advanced Learner's Dictionary* (OALD 1995: 893) points to the semantic relations between LURK, PROWL, SIDLE, SLINK, SKULK and SNEAK, and to their shared connotations of "doing something bad, trying not to be noticed, secrecy". But ACCOST and LOITER are not listed in this connection. Dictionaries have no systematic way of relating words which have shared connotations. However, now that dictionaries are prepared from computer-readable data-bases, it would be possible to bring together words which share connotations of "crime", "fear", "hidden danger", and "suspicion", if such labels for connotations can be standardized in the definitions.

9.2.4 Inter-collocations: the example of STREET

Channell (2000) points out that the lemma ROAM has largely positive connotations, whereas the phrase *ROAM the streets* is strongly negative. ROAM denotes "move around without a definite aim or destination". It can have the positive connotation of "freedom" (*free to roam the countryside*), though even such uses may have the disapproving connotation of "directionless and aimless", and some attested uses are very negative (*Thatcherite hordes roaming the buffet cars:* from *The Times*, 23 March 1995). However, the phrase *ROAM the streets* is almost always negative and connotes "dangerous and threatening behaviour", as in

- packs of wild dogs roaming the streets; drunken hooligans roaming the streets; thousands of armed men roaming the streets

The question arises as to where the negative connotations of the phrase come from. One answer (according to Channell's data) is that the subject of the verb is almost always plural, and usually an expression for a large, often threatening, group of people or animals, including

- bands of looters; mobs; packs of wild dogs; sixty teenagers; thousands of armed men

A second answer is that STREET itself is often used non-literally, and that many of these non-literal uses have negative connotations. Not all uses are negative. For example, *the man or woman in the street* has a non-literal meaning ("ordinary people"), but is not disapproving, and the expression *streets ahead* can be positive. In a more recent use, *street* can occur positively as a predicative adjective:

- He cooks from his heart, soul, mind and stomach. What emerges is at once elegant and totally street. [From an article about a Scottish chef, *New Statesman*, 19 June 1998, p. 34.]

Presumably this use has developed from phrases such as *street-wise* and *street cred*, which for some speakers, refer to positively evaluated characteristics, although for other speakers they connote less pleasant aspects of modern life. *Street-wise* means being able to deal with the dangers of big cities. *Street cred* refers mainly to youth culture: see below on the often negative connotation of *youth(s)*. When *street* is used to name roads, it is only used of built-up areas, and usually in the centre of towns and cities, whereas roads in the suburbs are called *road, avenue, crescent* and the like. So, *street* often connotes the inner city and its dangers. Singular *street* occurs frequently in the phrase *street gang(s)*. One can be *accosted in the street* by strangers. If someone has just *walked in off the street*, this implies "someone who lacks experience", or connotes "lack of security". *Street value* is used to refer to the price of illegal drugs. *The stuff bought on street corners* connotes "illegal goods", probably drugs. *Street-walker* is an old-fashioned term for a prostitute. An attested cliché is *hanging about on street corners mugging old ladies*. If someone is put *out on the street(s)* it means they are "unemployed".

The phrase *the streets* most frequently connotes danger. Attested examples include

- a growing menace on the streets; not safe to walk the streets; sleeping rough on the streets; keeps criminals off the streets; put more police on the streets; criminality that breeds gangsterism and death on the streets

I searched 355,000 running words from British and American newspapers published in 1991 for the phrase *the streets*. There were eleven examples, predominantly negative, including:

- terrorist bombs on the streets of Northern Ireland
- vigilante mobs patrol the streets
- on the streets with the community and not stuck behind a desk
- visions of rubbish piled high in the streets
- people can walk the streets without fear of attack
- a generation that once took to the streets
- thousands who took to the streets in the name of democracy

These examples show that both singular and plural are often used non-literally. Some examples connote activities which are illegal or undermine public order in some way. More generally, *the streets(s)* means "out of doors, in public places". It can therefore stand in opposition to "at home or at work", and it can mean "politically active" (*take to the streets*) as opposed to passive. Text analysis often leads to the recognition of antonymic relations which are not evident from words analysed in isolation. In a single newspaper article about social changes in Iran (*New Statesman*, 10 July 1998, pp. 33–4) there were three sentences containing *street(s)*:

- President Khatami, dedicated to reform, is trying to foster a new feeling *on the streets*
- the once dreaded ... thugs who used to beat women *in the street* [for being improperly dressed] have lost their zeal
- football victories [in the World Cup] have brought boys and girls out *onto the streets*

The following points are speculative but techniques are becoming available to develop them. If it is possible to analyse inter-collocations, then we will be able to show how the discourse prosodies of different words and phrases mutually support each other in the expression of a speaker's point of view. We currently have no ways to identify inter-collocations automatically, though manual searches can reveal parts of the networks involved. For example, the following frequent collocations are recorded in the Cobuild (1995b) Collocations on CD-ROM:

- streets <walk, police>
- walk <street>
- corner(s) <street>
- gang(s) <youths, police, street>
- youths <police, gang(s)>

From the analysis above of ACCOST, LURK and LOITER, we also have the beginnings of a network of words and phrases

- accosted – in the street – by a stranger – lurk beneath the surface – hidden beneath the surface – danger – warning

whose inter-collocations begin to show common ways, especially in the mass media, of talking about threats to public safety. This point of view is visible in attested phrases such as

- walk the streets in safety; more police on the streets; anyone can just walk in off the street; hang around street corners; street (corner) gangs; gangs of youths; clashes between youths and police

Such inter-collocations and phrases are most unlikely all to co-occur in a single text, and are therefore not directly observable, but neither are they mysterious. They are indirectly observable in recurrent collocations and intertextual relations. If it is possible to develop more systematic techniques for identifying such lexical fields, then we will have two powerful general techniques of text analysis. First, by identifying networks of inter-collocating words, we will be able to show how prosodies on different words and phrases support each other, and contribute to textual cohesion. Second, by establishing which words and phrases express centres of empathy, we will have a technique for analysing the point of view expressed by texts. (See Pusch 1984: 118; following Kuno 1976.)

9.3 A Lexico-syntactic Example: *MAKE one's way somewhere*

Here is a case of a lexico-syntactic construction with identifiable, but probabilistic, discourse prosodies. This example shows again the abstract nature of extended lexico-semantic units. Corpus data do not generally reveal fixed phrases, but patterns of co-occurring lexis and syntax, which realize much more abstract syntactic frames and/or semantic units. They are characterized by frequent core lexis, but the lexis is typically highly variable, and sometimes highly productive. Consider examples such as

- she *made her way* along the corridor
- the little beetle *found its way* to France in the 1860s
- they have *fought their way* up through the hierarchy
- they *worked their way* up the stream
- he saw Sir Cedric *making his leisurely way* into the hotel bar

The surface syntactic pattern in these cases is

NP – V – NP (= *one's way*) – PP

The pattern is frequent: up to 100 occurrences per million running words.

The core of the construction is a verb followed by a NP whose head is *way* followed by an almost obligatory adjunct. This adjunct is usually a prepositional phrase indicating direction, but can be a single word such as *through* or *back*. Indeed, alone or introducing longer PPs, these are the most frequent words after *way*. These three words inter-collocate, and if we look just at these collocations, we find that *way-through* and *way-back* both often occur in this syntactic construction:

- the road *weaves its way through* a patchwork of farms
- Charles was *working his way through* high school
- the ambulance, *picking its way through* the crowd
- [the firm] has *clawed its way back* into the black
- they had *fought their way back* into the buildings
- we *picked our way back through* the rubble

Way is preceded by a possessive adjective which corresponds to the subject pronoun or noun phrase. I will use *one's way* to indicate the variable phrases such as *my way* and *your way.* This surface structure NP is the direct object of the verb: however, verbs which are normally intransitive can occur in this construction (see below). The most frequent verbs are MAKE, FIND and WORK; also frequent are FIGHT, PUSH, PICK, FEEL, GROPE, THREAD and FORCE. The construction usually has an animate agent in the subject NP: in these cases it expresses the agent's intention to move in a definite direction, and it often (but not always) expresses difficulty where force is used, or where care is necessary:

- I *battled my way* over or through each obstacle
- hordes who had *battered their way* into the Roman provinces
- the young hatch, *chipping their way* out of their shells
- in a futile attempt to *claw his way* back to the surface
- they *forced their way* through the thick vegetation
- he must *grope his way* into the labyrinth
- we *made our way* down the precipitous slope
- he *picked his way* back down the ladder

The construction always implies success in crossing the area or reaching the goal described in the prepositional phrase (Marantz 1992: 184–5). So, a sentence such as

- they chipped their way out of their shells [M]

is interpreted as "they succeeded in getting out of their shells by chipping". Hence the oddity of sentences which specify only the starting point of the movement, but the acceptability of sentences which specify the end point:

- *we battled our way from the bottom of the hill [I]
- we battled our way to the top of the hill [I]

Two semantic features are always conveyed: intention and completion. Intentionality is implied even with verbs which are normally intransitive and non-agentive, or have non-animate subject NPs:

- she was *sleeping her way* to the top
- it is the water *working its way* underground that does this

The sets of semantically related verbs which can occur in the construction are described by Francis et al. (1996: 330–8). Many instances involve twisting or winding movements, difficult or careful movements, or the noise involved in the movement. Often, the construction is used with verbs which denote force and violence (as above), dishonesty, illegal activities or stupidity.

- people who *bluff their way* through music
- politicians who *cheated their way* to government
- we *muddled our way* through

Another recurring use expresses the struggle to reach the top, often in a career

- *fighting his way* to the top of the greasy pole
- he *paid his own way* through law school
- [the firm's] determination to *claw its way* to the top of the publishing industry

However, the construction is very productive, and many other verbs occur. Francis et al. (1996) and Levin and Hovav (1996) document verbs of sound (*we shall sing our way round the world*). Francis et al. (1996: 331) also note just how much productivity the construction allows, and the question arises as to whether there are any constraints on the verbs which could conceivably occur, or whether any verbs (and sometimes even nouns) are interpretable as verbs of motion in the given frame. All these are attested.

- *cooking and eating (and drinking) my way through* this book
- he has *tinkled his way to* fame on an old piano
- I *unpeeled my way through* the sodden address book
- Mrs Thatcher *handbagged her way through* Europe
- they *jackbooted their way through* the crowd
- oozing charm from ev'ry pore, he *oiled his way* around the floor

The last is from a description of dancing in *My Fair Lady* (cited by Wray et al. 1998: 83).

Superficially, the structure is NP–V–NP, where the second NP (*one's way*) looks like the direct object of the verb. It is syntactically obligatory with MAKE, but also with other verbs, perhaps especially with the more innovative verbs (where perhaps more guidance is needed for correct interpretation):

- he has *tinkled his way* to fame on an old piano [A]
- *he has *tinkled* to fame on an old piano [M]

However, it can often be omitted, as in

- the road *weaves its way* through a patchwork of farms [A]
- the road *weaves* through a patchwork of farms [M]

That is, the NP *one's way* is semantically empty: it emphasizes the meaning of directionality which is often expressed in the verb and always expressed in the adjunct.

In summary, the pattern involves: (1) Delexicalization: a single fixed word-form (*way*) is semantically empty; it has a focusing function of repeating part of the meaning of the almost obligatory direction adjunct, and often of the verb. (2) Colligation: an obligatory grammatical item (a possessive adjective corresponding to the subject NP); and a direction adjunct, usually a prepositional phrase. (3) Semantic preferences: sets of verbs which often denote difficulty and/or violence and/or caution; the most frequent verbs can be specified, but the list is open-ended and highly productive. (4) An unpleasant discourse prosody in around half of all cases. There is a pattern of lexical, syntactic and semantic co-occurrence, but it is not possible to list the exponents, and it is not even really possible to list sub-phrases. Even in sub-units such as *MAKE one's way through*, *FIND one's way back* and *WORK one's way along*, both the lemma and *one's* are variables. In some cases even *one's way* can be omitted: the pattern vanishes like the grin on the Cheshire cat.

Hopper and Traugott (1993: 107) point out that lexical (content) words which indicate position are often candidates for becoming place adverbials:

- way, away; back, back home; head, ahead; shore, ashore; side, aside

The delexicalization of *way* in the construction VERB plus *one's way* is an indication of a much more general pattern. (The *way*-construction has also been of interest to scholars working within a post-Chomskyan framework: see Levin and Hovav 1996: 493ff; Marantz 1992; and Israel 1996.)

9.4 A Note on Syntax

In many syntactic descriptions, adverbials are regarded as optional. However, Crystal (1979) points out that adverbials (including prepositional phrases) are much more common than such syntactic descriptions imply. In corpus data, he finds that nearly 60 per cent of clauses contain an adverbial. If clauses which do not show the full range of syntactic variation are ignored (such as those introducing direct speech, e.g. *He said X*, or those composed of semi-fixed phrases. e.g. *and that was that*), then the frequency rises to 66 per cent. He even suggests (p. 164), that an adverbial might be regarded as an obligatory constituent of a clause, and that there has to be a special reason for leaving it out. I have shown that prepositional phrases almost always occur with ACCOST, LURK, LOITER, and the *way*-construction. For some of these cases, there is an obvious communicative reason for including a locative: if you are warning someone, then they need this information.

A general finding of corpus linguistics is that words which share a meaning also share a pattern (Sinclair 1991: 53ff). This hypothesis of a close correlation between meaning and lexico-syntactic form is thoroughly documented by Francis et al. (1996, 1998). In this chapter, I have shown this principle operating on a small class of verbs.

9.5 A Cognitive View

An unsolved problem for all theories of semantics is the inevitable circularity involved in using words to define the meaning of words. Metalinguistic labels for semantic features have to be used, and whether these are plausibly universal features (such as "animate", "inanimate"; "human", "non-human"; "female", "male"), or much more specific features of discourse prosodies, the labels are still words in English (or some other language). The first examples of discourse prosodies (Sinclair 1991; Louw 1993) were given general evaluative labels, such as "unpleasant" and "pleasant". Often the speaker is implying "disapproval" (more rarely approval) of some state of affairs, and this is frequently used as a pragmatic label in the Cobuild Dictionary (1995a). But much more specific discourse prosodies have now been proposed (e.g. *naked eye*, "difficulty and size and/or distance": see chapter 5.6.1; or *budge*, "failed attempt and frustration": Sinclair 1998).

Little is known about how evaluative meanings should be labelled. When many more discourse prosodies have been analysed, generalizations may emerge about the kinds of meanings which speakers often express, as they talk about the world. For example, the *way*-construction expresses a meaning which frequently recurs in human interaction: someone successfully completes a journey, often by struggling through difficulties. The use of UNDERGO (see chapter 4.4.1) expresses a related idea of people being forced to submit to and overcome difficult circumstances. The phraseologies around ACCOST, LURK and LOITER, along with non-literal uses of STREET, are all used to tell stories of the dangers which can lie hidden in people's paths, and to connote dangers in tales of city life. These proposals are speculative at present, but they contain the hint of a systematic way of analysing how speakers typically talk about the world and evaluate it. The notion of a journey in which difficulties are overcome is certainly central to many of the stories which we tell each other (compare Lakoff and Johnson 1980, on the metaphor of life as a journey). It may eventually be possible to show how recurrent meanings are typically encoded in the lexico-grammar. As G. Francis (1993: 146, 155) puts it, we may be able to analyse 'the typical meanings that human communication encodes', and 'recognize the untypical and hence foregrounded meanings when we come across them'.

This approach to meaning fits naturally into a frame semantics, in which phrases trigger 'agglomerates of cultural information' (Moon 1998: 166). Phrases such as

- accosted by a stranger; lurking in the shadows; loitering on street corners; fighting one's way to the top; forced to undergo a serious operation

activate stored scenarios of the things which typically happen to people. We know how the world works, and given such a phrase, we can predict other components of the stories in which they occur. These ideas are also compatible with a theory of social cognition which sees linguistic repertoires (ways of talking) as sustaining certain views of social reality. Condor and Antaki (1997) give an overview.

9.6 A Syntactic Example: *BE*-passives and *GET*-passives

In this book, I am concerned with words and phrases, though I often emphasize that lexis and syntax are inseparable. It is usually assumed that connotations are conveyed by lexical units, but here is a clear example where an evaluative discourse prosody is conveyed by a syntactic structure.

There are two main passive constructions in English, with BE and GET, and there is considerable overlap in their uses, so that some verbs occur in both constructions.

- she thought she was going to *be killed*
- it was mailed just before he *got killed*
- three years later he *was arrested* in Holland
- I didn't *get arrested* for shop-lifting

However, several independent studies have shown that the communicative motivation for using the GET-passive is its negative connotations. Quirk et al. (1985: 161) point out that it 'often reflects an unfavourable attitude towards the action'. For example, *How did that window get opened?* [I?] implies that the speaker thinks it should have been left shut. Francis et al. (1996: 58–9) argue more explicitly that the GET-passive often indicates that 'something unpleasant is happening'. It is therefore frequent with verbs such as

- addicted, caught up in, criticized, distorted, frightened, injured, kicked out, mixed up in, picked on, turned down

In corpus studies of the meanings of different passives (Hübler 1992; Collins 1996; Carter and McCarthy 1999), there is a consensus that the BE-passive is usually more neutral in meaning, whereas the GET-passive more often expresses emotive or interpersonal meanings, and either the speaker's attitude to the events described, or a focus on the subject-referent's situation. The event may occasionally be advantageous to the subject of the passive clause, but is much more often disadvantageous: the event has unfortunate consequences for the subject-referent. A few typical examples are:

- we nearly got chucked out
- customers get embarrassed when talking about money
- one child gets hurt
- they got kicked out
- they got separated from the others
- I got walked on by a rather large and muddy boxer dog

In a spoken corpus, Carter and McCarthy (1999: 49, 50) found "adversative" meanings in nearly 90 per cent of GET-passives, and fewer than 5 per cent "beneficial" meanings. In a mixed spoken and written corpus, Collins (1996: 52) found 67 per cent "adversative" and 23 per cent "beneficial". Absolute figures certainly depend on the data sample and on exactly how the construction is defined, but there is no doubt about the direction of strong regularities which emerge from independent studies of different corpora. I leave readers to examine the sample lines in concordances 9.1 and 9.2, and to check whether these percentages are confirmed in this small illustrative sample.

1. Knowing my luck I'll get crushed by a bloody tractor. MX'll be shouting
2. GY] you're more likely to get hit by a bus walking out this [FOX] Yeah
3. ould walk out of here and get hit by a car [M01] Right [MOX] I mean you
4. ant. [M01] That's where I got hit by a car. See that on my knee there.
5. you're afraid you might get hit by a golf ball. Right? I think it's ti
6. ean the same argument get stopped by a policewoman then Frank you you yo
7. only person I know who got sacked by a psychotherapist [F01] Mm [F03]
8. n Bond Street and I got walked on by a rather large and muddy boxer dog
9. my mate yesterday he got attacked by a terrier what was mooching around
10. Hwere a critique that got coopted by a very different group of people in
11. oman she gets flatly contradicted by Bernard every time she opens her mou
12. M01] Well things like getting hit by cars. Falling off the back of a lor
13. apists get fooled and manipulated by clients who are not coming to thera
14. ay I've seen lambs getting killed by dogs. Erm [F02] Killed by dogs [M02
15. dependency that it gets activated by doing a certain amount of drinking
16. F0X] Mm. [F01] Yeah we get funded by er West Midlands Arts and the City
17. scientists get er get pleased by erm elegant solutions and things of
18. rather do it erm and I get bored by erm [tc text=pause] because I mean
19. chool gates and that she got struck by her mother for just going round the
20. f it. Erm er if you do get struck by Jerusalem recovery is not disastrou
21. [ZGY] [M01] do you get offended by mother-in-law jokes? [F04] No. No
22. and erm but it it got reviewed by music critics on the whole erm
23. t I sometimes get a bit irritated by MX who he feels that er now we've g
24. r reason why you would get teased by other people [F04] Well [ZF1] some
25. ep in his car and he got attacked by people with a baseball bat. And er
26. Mm [F03] So she must get accepted by some people more because of that
27. my Game Boy before it got stolen by some vicious bastard. [M02] Sorry.
28. she is doing and she gets caught by somebody [F01] Mm [M01] [ZGY]
29. ed their tails if they get caught by something [ZGY] [M01] Uh huh. This
30. name of pub] until we got overrun by students. [F0X] Merchant bankers
31. the rain forest getting destroyed by the acid rain. [F01] And what is ac
32. erm I think they got stopped by the army or something for just
33. d up I had to go back and got hit by the bouncers. Now what has happened
34. weren't going to ge get thumped by the er visiting supporters. [M01] M
35. it don't you. And get frustrated by the fact that you can't do things a
36. me of people just getting struck by the Holy Spirit. He told me of peop
37. the fascist army and get captured by the partisans who decide to
38. don't know whether they get paid by the patient or whether he's just
39. when I went to my dad I got dared by the people that the girl that lived
40. nipulated and getting manipulated by the pop charts and stuff like that
41. You were just getting barbecued by the power of the Spirit weren't you
43. FO2] Oh [M01] And No you get done by the teacher [F02] Oh [F01] Well why
44. ool and once again MX got branded by the teachers as lazy and the other
45. e class. [F01] Did you get teased by the teachers in the class? [F02] No
46. jungle. Only we didn't get eaten by the tiger. [M01] That's right. [MO2
47. most they mostly get influenced by their erm parents [F0X] Mm [F05] wh
48. X] Because they're getting backed by their governments to actually do it
49. [F0X] Pervy dirty MX. He got done by t' cops right 'cos [F0X] Yeah. He d
50. ads over there at erm get coached by well ordinary people er do you

Concordance 9.1 Fifty examples of GET-passives

Notes: The data are from the Lund corpus and from the spoken language sub-corpus of the Bank of English (CobuildDirect). [FOX] etc. are speaker identification codes.

1. he Dalkon Shield was manufactured by a company called A H Robbins in the
2. one point it was going to be done by a Japanese company into a into a
3. he and I were both interviewed by a man who wrote a book called The
4. since been strongly corroborated by a number of studies [ZGY] which is
5. ho helped a man who'd been struck by a train near Harrogate and there ar
6. gineering degrees are now awarded by about forty institutions and some to
7. space has been rather compromised by an intrusive clutter of parapets
8. and he said this kit can be made by any eleven-year-old boy. I'll go I'
9. generally I mean I was influenced by certain political peoples in my own
10. range of patterns which are used by doctor and patient to discuss the
11. Is learn effectively being taught by dragons you know. So teaching style
12. of these assets has been claimed by emergent states and individual repu
13. nd how they might be being shaped by er changes in the NHS. I mean and
14. airport and being body searched by er the Revolutionary Guards. [M01]
15. ew of the mall which is dominated by erm high-level walkways to left and
16. t that we're now being surrounded by fumes in the j in this little villa
17. here heat is put in are separated by half ocean bases from those places
18. Yeah [F02] Selby. And I was told by my mother I went with a friend of m
19. hink that was probably stimulated by Nature Conservancy. [M01] Yes I thi
20. e alpha particle which is stopped by only a few tens of microns [ZF1] of
21. articular risks which are managed by particular companies where I think
22. eenagers are now being questioned by police at Gosport in Hampshire abou
23. they were short and I was invited by Professor MX to come down on a
24. Hollingsworth are being comforted by relatives. This is the update. It's
25. of the deans were firmly squashed by Senate for one reason or another
26. ndustries that are being replaced by some new ones not in any vast
27. Relations [M01] This was produced by that public relations company
28. r er when the police were misused by Thatcher's government. Er do you
29. min which were to be administered by the benevolent city. In such an air
30. us mys er myself. One is employed by the community one is employed by
31. r bit [M01] The men were well led by the Company Commander Lieutenant MX
32. what is is actually commissioned by the controller and not for us for
33. sions. We were terribly impressed by the courtesy of most of them. Er th
34. hink that the course was affected by the death of FX's husband
35. nced that decisions that are made by the Development Corporation plannin
36. that that confidence is confirmed by the events of nineteen-ninety-six a
37. ar erm weapons that were supplied by the French governments were being
38. elves and what they were supplied by the government so some authorities
39. h erm you know our hands are tied by the National Curriculum [M02] Yeah.
40. NCAR when INCAR was solely funded by the National Science Foundation in
41. s most of that is now been bought by the parish council and there's car
42.] I dunno whether this is written by the same author but I don't get the
43.] Yeah [M01] And is that affected by the season? Do you do it at differe
44. of us were at time being detained by the security police and spending ma
45. isms they are are finally humbled by the smallest thing on earth [M05]
46. ones that are going to be cleared by the snow ploughs first and obviousl
47. when this was officially approved by the university and thereafter it wa
48.] but not being openly advertised by the water company that the office
49. if you if you are frightened by this person then you have although
50. Friend of Iraq and it is launched by two Kurdish cousins. Their families

Concordance 9.2 Fifty examples of BE-passives

As is often the case, lexis and syntax vary according to text-type. In general the BE-passive is much more frequent, but the BE-passive is least frequent, and the GET-passive most frequent, in spoken data. In table 9.1, I have defined passives simply as BE or GET followed by a past participle. Occurrences in four sub-corpora were as follows:

Table 9.1 BE-passives and GET-passives: occurrences per million words

	BE-passive	GET-passive	GET as percentage of BE
British spoken	2,742	364	13.3
British books	7,611	106	1.4
The Times	8,896	88	1.0
BBC news	11,212	55	0.5

The very low frequency of GET-passives in the up-market *Times* newspaper and in the BBC data reflects the strong prescriptions against the use of GET in general (in sentences such as *The doctor has got this poster in his surgery*).

In summary: There is no clear boundary between the BE- and GET-passives, but they show strong tendencies to occur in different contexts. The main evidence of their different connotations is the co-occurrence of the GET-passive with lexis which has unpleasant connotations. There are strong probabilistic relations between lexico-syntax (BE versus GET), semantics (different preferred collocates), pragmatics (expression of speaker attitude) and distribution across text-types (formal versus informal).

9.7 Summary and Implications

In this chapter, I have argued as follows:

(1) Evaluative meanings are conveyed not only by individual words, but also by longer phrases and syntactic structures, and by co-occurring node and collocates. Repeated instances of collocation across a corpus provide objective, empirical evidence for evaluative meanings.

(2) Repeated patterns show that evaluative meanings are not merely personal and idiosyncratic, but widely shared in a discourse community. A word, phrase or construction may trigger a cultural stereotype.

(3) Since a speaker's evaluative stance is likely to be expressed in a prosody across stretches of text, this is an important mechanism of textual cohesion (see chapter 5).

(4) Evaluative and attitudinal meanings are often thought to be due to conversational inferences (Grice 1975); however, many pragmatic

meanings are conventionally associated with lexico-syntactic structures. (This point is made in discussions of construction grammar: see Kay 1995.)

(5) The over-emphasis on conversational inferences is probably due to a reliance on invented data, which have been stripped of markers of speaker attitude. Almost all the classic work on speech act theory (Austin 1962; Searle 1969), conversational implicatures (Grice 1975) and relevance theory (Sperber and Wilson 1995) relies on invented data.

However, there certainly remain unresolved questions in the approach which I have proposed:

(1) Evaluative connotations are more common than previously suspected, but it is not yet clear how many lexical items and syntactic structures express evaluative meanings.

(2) Semantics is inevitably circular, since some words are used to define the meanings of other words, and it is not yet clear what metalanguage should be used to describe evaluations.

(3) If descriptions of evaluative meanings and cultural stereotypes can be made reasonably precise, it seems plausible that this will tell us about the important meanings expressed in a discourse community, but speculations here are at an early stage.

9.8 Background and Further Reading

At different stages in twentieth-century linguistics, lexis, semantics and pragmatics were variously ignored, or seen as an unsystematic remainder, as opposed to syntax, which was seen as highly structured and rule-governed. However, a discipline progresses by turning chaos into order, and linguists and philosophers have had considerable success in showing that all of these areas are internally highly organized, and related to each other in principled ways.

The view of corpus semantics represented in this book, and the neo-Firthian tradition from which it has developed, has always been sceptical of separating the levels of lexis, syntax, semantics and pragmatics. A central argument is that 'there is a strong tendency for sense and syntax to be associated' (Sinclair 1991: 65). Hunston and Francis (1998), summarizing their experience of writing a major grammar of English verbs (Francis et al. 1996), write that 'verbs sharing a pattern also [share] aspects of meaning' (p. 46), and argue that 'syntax and lexis are completely interdependent' (p. 62). (See also Hunston and Francis 2000.) However, other traditions of language study have proposed different relations between these levels.

Classic distinctions between syntax, semantics and pragmatics were drawn in the 1930s by Morris (1938). Syntax concerns how linguistic signs relate to one another (in collocation and colligation), semantics concerns how linguistic signs relate to the external world (in reference and denotation), and pragmatics concerns how linguistic signs relate to their users (in the expression of speaker attitude).

Lexis was long dismissed by grammarians as 'a collection of isolated facts' (Sweet 1899), or 'an appendix to the grammar, a list of basic irregularities' (Bloomfield 1933: 274). This view was carried over into early models of transformational syntax, where the lexicon plays no significant role. Chomsky (1957) initially argued that form and meaning are independent, and that syntax and semantics must be sharply distinguished:

> The notion grammatical cannot be identified with meaningful or significant in any semantic sense...[W]e are forced to conclude that grammar is autonomous and independent of meaning...[U]ndeniable, though only imperfect correspondences hold between formal and semantic features in language... [M]eaning will be relatively useless as a basis for grammatical description.
> (Chomsky 1957: 15, 17, 101)

It was similarly long thought that semantics itself depended on non-linguistic knowledge and was therefore not amenable to linguistic description: compare Bloomfield's pessimistic views on this topic (see chapter 2.9.1).

Since the mid-1960s, many views have been put forward of the syntax–semantics relation, from an insistence on a sharp distinction, to a complete denial of the division. Discussions became part of broad programmes of work, linking linguistic and philosophical approaches to language. Katz and Fodor (1963) and Katz and Postal (1964) made the first attempts to integrate semantics into a transformational grammar; and in the first major collection of articles on semantics in a Chomskyan tradition, Maclay (1971) gave a useful overview of these early shifts in Chomskyan grammar, and Fillmore (1971) surveyed the generalizations about lexis which a grammar has to contain. Katz (1981: 1–44) describes developments from Zellig Harris to Noam Chomsky. By the 1990s, one standard textbook (Haegemann 1991: 25) argues that 'sentence structure is to a large extent determined by lexical information', thus completely reversing the early Chomskyan view that lexical items are inserted at a late stage into syntactic structures. Seuren (1998) also interprets Chomskyan work from the 1950s to the 1970s, and defends the 'semantic syntax' position which he has long advocated (Seuren 1974). The concept of autonomous syntax, at least modularity-plus-interaction, is still maintained in much work (for example, several papers in Newmeyer 1988): the evidence is not only linguistic, but also psychological and neurological, based on child language acquisition and cases of language pathology. However, what started as arguments for the autonomy of syntax has often developed into arguments for the isomorphism of syntax and semantics.

The most problematic area has often been seen to be pragmatics, and Bar-Hillel's (1971: 405) warning is often quoted:

> Be careful with forcing bits and pieces you find in the pragmatic waste-basket into your favourite syntactico-semantic theory. It would perhaps be preferable to first bring some order into the contents of this waste-basket.

If semantics is seen to concern aspects of sentence meaning which do not vary across contexts of use, then pragmatics concerns those aspects of utterance meaning which differ across contexts. Semantics has often been seen as concerning truth conditions (but see chapters 1.2 and 1.10), whereas pragmatics concerns everything else, because pragmatic meanings depend on local assumptions, beliefs or purposes (Levinson 1983: 5ff; Kempson 1988: 139). Much work therefore investigates whether it is possible to distinguish clearly between semantics (more linguistic aspects of meaning) and pragmatics (including speaker attitude and hearer interpretation). It was argued influentially by Grice (1975) that much interpretation relies on general principles of communicative cooperation and inference. It is often concluded that much relies on real-world knowledge and that pragmatics cannot therefore be a well-defined module which relies on purely linguistic knowledge (Horn 1988: 115). Levinson (2000) provides a radical reinterpretation of Grice, and of the relation between sentence and utterance meaning.

There is no clear consensus, but the current trend, in independent traditions, seems to be towards a model of language in which lexis plays a central role. The relations between lexis, syntax, semantics and pragmatics are receiving concentrated attention, but any work in this area has its theoretical axe to grind. The following are useful brief statements, perhaps all the more valuable because they represent attempts to develop grammatical traditions which are slightly outside the mainstream: Fillmore (1985), Fillmore and Atkins (1994), Hopper (1991), Hudson (1995), Kay (1995).

Fillmore and Atkins (1994) and Hudson (1995) contain detailed examples, and are particularly relevant to questions of lexicography.

9.9 Topics for Further Study

(1) The *OED* on CD-ROM or on-line enables the user to find words which have been used to define other words. For example:

- ACCOST occurs in the definitions of TACKLE and WAYLAY
- AMBUSH occurs in the definitions of LURK and WAIT
- LOITER occurs in the definitions of DAWDLE and SAUNTER
- LURK occurs in the definitions of AMBUSH and SKULK
- SKULK occurs in the definitions of LURKING and MOOCH
- WAYLAY occurs in the definitions of AMBUSH and WAIT

This certainly does not provide an automatic method of identifying sets of words with shared semantic features, since the *OED* does not have a restricted defining vocabulary, and does not have a standardized semantic metalanguage for defining meanings. Nevertheless, by using a bit of intuition and guesswork, it is possible to build up sets of words which are related in meaning. Use a machine-readable dictionary which allows such searches to investigate this set of related words in more detail. Or investigate other such sets and semantic fields.

(2) Investigate whether there are any constraints on the verbs which can occur in the *MAKE one's way* construction. For example, you might design a small experiment as follows. I opened a dictionary at four random pages, took the first verb on each page, and tried to invent plausible sentences. The following all seem interpretable:

- I counted my way up the steps [I]
- they jeered their way through the concert [I]
- she practised her way through the exercises [I]
- he shook his way down the line of outstretched hands [I]

This is, of course, an intuitive judgement on invented sentences. However, some attested examples of the construction do seem highly idiosyncratic, one-off creations.

10

Data and Dualisms: On Corpus Methods and Pluralist Models

In each of the earlier chapters, I have given examples of patterns of language use, often comparing patterns in an individual text with wider intertextual norms of use. Many of the patterns I have illustrated are consistent and found in independent corpora: they are autonomous and independent of speakers. They are reproduced by speakers, though speakers are often unaware of them, and they are observable only across the language use of many speakers in a discourse community. It is this layer of organization between lexis and grammar which is the main finding of corpus linguistics. Computer-assisted methods have demonstrated order where previously only randomness or idiosyncrasy were visible.

Corpus linguistics therefore provides a new point of view for studying language, and the point of view allows new things to be seen. In a famous and influential statement, Saussure (1916) argued that 'far from the object of study preceding the point of view, it is rather the point of view which creates the object'. Due to advances in technology, new observational methods have made it possible to collect new types of data and to study patterns which had previously been invisible, but the point of view does not create the patterns. What we see certainly varies according to our point of view, and it follows that any view is partial, but it does not follow that what we observe has been created by the point of view or by the observational tools.

In this final chapter, I will try to assess some of the principles and problems of corpus linguistics, under three main headings: its central principles, frequent criticisms and possible answers, and some implications of corpus study for classic problems of linguistic dualism.

10.1 Principles

Corpus linguistics is based on two principles of empirical observational study:

(1) The observer must not influence what is observed. Data and analysis must be independent. What is selected for observation admittedly depends on such factors as convenience, personal interests and prior hypotheses. Nevertheless, corpus data were part of natural language use and not produced for purposes of linguistic analysis.
(2) Repeated events are significant. The first task of corpus linguistics is to describe what is usual and typical. Unique events certainly occur, but can be described only against the background of what is normal and expected. The frequent occurrence of lexical or grammatical patterns is good evidence of what is typical and routine in language use.

Certain characteristics of corpus linguistics follow from these principles. First, it is inherently sociolinguistic: the data are attested texts, real acts of communication used in a discourse community (Teubert 1999a, 1999b). Second, it is inherently diachronic: it studies what has frequently occurred in the past. Third, and more obviously, it is inherently quantitative. It is surprising that many approaches to language study in the past have dismissed the idea of observing language use or counting things, yet much linguistic description contains no statements of proportions. It is as if chemists knew about the different structure of iron and gold, but had no idea that iron is pretty common and gold is very rare; or as if geographers knew how to compare countries in all kinds of ways, but had never noticed that Canada is bigger than Luxembourg (Kennedy 1992: 339, 341).

Corpus methods can organize huge masses of data, and make visible patterns which were only, if at all, dimly suspected. In giving access to new data, the technology opens up research topics which were previously inconceivable. We now have facts about language use which no amount of introspection or manual analysis could discover, and it will take some time before this mass of new information can be correctly interpreted. The computer will not do everything, and Firth's (1957: 1) warning is still relevant:

> The passion for the accumulation of so-called facts, the piling-up of trivialities to be treated statistically, perhaps with defective theoretical principles, are all too common symptoms among the scientific technicians multiplying in our midst.

10.2 Problems?

Here are some frequently formulated objections to corpus studies (see also Partington 1998: 144ff).

Objection number 1. It is often objected that corpus data are decontextualized. A concordance is also called a KWIC index (Key Words in Context), but a concordance places words in very small contexts, often just one short concordance line. A KWIC index, it is argued, therefore ignores the context of communication.

In fact, most concordance software allows the user to look at larger contexts, defined as sentences or paragraphs, or to scan up and down a longer stretch of text. However, the main answer here is that it is not possible to look at everything at once, but that a focus on restricted collocational spans has revealed new patterns.

Many studies can be accused of ignoring context because, however much context is studied, it is always possible to demand more. In a study of spoken language, a written transcription can only imperfectly represent intonation. An audio-recording will add intonation, yet ignore features of the visual context, and a video-recording will contain no information about the previous history of interaction of the participants. And so on. In any case, the claim that there is often evidence for the evaluative connotations of a node word within a short span on either side is an empirical finding which is open to test. Often a surprisingly small amount of context (co-text) is required for such studies. In addition, corpus linguistics demands that individual texts be interpreted against the usage of many speakers, and therefore against the intertextual norms of general language use. This is an aspect of context which cannot be studied without computer-assisted methods.

Objection number 2. It is often objected that, due to restrictions imposed by its technology, corpus linguistics over-emphasizes the importance of single word-forms and collocations.

Word-forms and their co-occurrences are certainly simple for the computer to recognize in raw corpora: just strings of letters separated by spaces or punctuation marks. Technology increases our powers of observation, but every observational tool emphasizes something. We do not normally complain that microscopes over-emphasize tiny little things, that telescopes only allow us to study far-away things, or that x-rays give too much prominence to the insides of things (Partington 1998: 144). The simple answer to these objections is, again, that one cannot study everything at once. There are always limits to what we can look for with observational hardware and software. Different tools (computational or otherwise) are good at doing different jobs, and no tool will do all jobs that might be desirable. It is best to look at things the other way round: if you want to study words and phrases, then corpus methods are a good way to do it, because they show that the vocabulary is not an unsystematic remainder. The patterns are made visible by the observational tools, but the evidence that they are not created by these tools is that findings can be replicated across independent corpora. This kind of replication is not possible in work based on introspective data (see chapter 6.1 and 6.7). In addition, it is precisely this level of organization (collocations plus other co-occurrence phenomena) which has previously gone unrecognized.

Objection number 3. It is often objected that corpora are not representative. A corpus, it is argued, cannot represent a whole language, and is therefore merely a collection of what it is convenient to collect.

Corpus designs are often referred to as either opportunistic or balanced. At one extreme, texts are collected, because they are easily available, and for practical reasons, many corpora are biased towards written language, because spoken language is so much more difficult to collect and record, and collections of written text are, in turn, often biased towards journalism. At the other extreme is an approach which tries to be principled by basing text collection on a theoretical model of language variation. A corpus is here judged according to how narrowly or broadly it samples the language. Corpus size is usually cited as its number of running words, but this should be combined with the number of different texts and text-types which are sampled. In practice, most large corpora are a compromise between the two extremes.

Some researchers also talk of a representative corpus, but the concept of a representative sample of the English language makes little sense. The population to be sampled (uses of the English language) is huge, and even corpora which seem very large by today's standards (thousands of millions of words) are hardly a drop in the ocean, when compared with the size of what is being sampled. In fact, the population to be sampled is potentially infinite. Not only are huge quantities of text being added every day, but the language is constantly changing, and new text-types are being created (TV chat shows are a relatively new text-type, but now common). A sample can be representative only if the population to be sampled is homogeneous, and this is possible only in special cases, say with a specialized sub-genre corpus (such as editorials from quality newspapers or research articles on biochemistry). Every time we enlarge a corpus, we increase the heterogeneity of the data, and there will always be text-types which we have not sampled, or which are arguably under-represented. Unfortunately, the same problem arises with the concept of a balanced corpus: who is to say what percentage of the corpus should consist of weather forecasts, lonely hearts ads, business reports, the lyrics of pop songs, or whatever?

Here, the short answer is that we can always design bigger and better corpora – given unlimited time and money. We can wait for the perfect corpus, or we can go ahead, and thereby find out more about what improvement could be made in the design of the next corpus. Corpus work is cumulative, and for many of the more frequent features of language, relatively modest corpora provide adequate evidence. In addition, a general principle should be not to rely on any single corpus, but to check results in independently designed corpora, which each have different biases.

Objection number 4. It is often objected that corpus studies average away variation. Statements which make claims about the whole language are misleading, because language use is inherently variable, but statements based on large corpora, it is argued, over-emphasize features which are frequent at the expense of less frequent features.

This is a problem which has started to attract attention. Frequency counts from large corpora may well mean that the researcher does not notice uses which cluster in particular genres. For example, if a word frequency analysis is based on largely automatic methods which are programmed to ignore low-frequency items, then the words *thou, thee, thy* and *thine* will probably be too infrequent to register. However, these words, which are infrequent in general English, are likely to be frequent and significant in religious texts. This provides another reason to check findings in different independent corpora, and to compare small specialized corpora (which can be designed by individual reserchers) against large general corpora (which it is realistic only for large groups to maintain).

Objection number 5. It is often objected that corpora provide only positive data. A corpus can reveal only what does occur and not what cannot occur. Only native-speaker intuition, it is argued, can tell us what is impossible.

This is correct, but is true of any form of observational research. In any case, intuition might predict that some form never occurs: we can check in a corpus, and observations might either support or refute the intuition. Here is a simple example. The Linguistic Data Consortium makes available corpora for linguistic research and argues for the need for very large quantities of running text, hundreds of millions of words, to solve many problems in text processing. In a discussion of these topics, LDC (1999) argues that *last year* and *lost year* are both possible English sequences, but that *last year* is frequent, whereas *lost year* is 'vanishingly unlikely'. I checked this in a very large text collection. (I used the 200 million or so world-wide web documents indexed by an internet search engine.) Certainly, *last year* was very common: about 1,600 times more frequent than *lost year. Last year* occurred around 2.36 million times. But *lost year* occurred 1,408 times, in phrases such as *making up for a lost year*. The LDC argument seems to have been based on a faulty intuition about what is likely to occur.

In a syntactic case, which has important consequences for linguistic theory, Sampson (1996) discusses multiple central embedding, in sentences such as:

- but don't you find that sentences [that people [you know] produce] are easier to understand

Such sentences are often claimed not to occur, but Sampson cites several attested examples, and comments (p. 25) on the change of intellectual direction which he was led to by such clear counter-examples to a widely held assertion in mainstream neo-Chomskyan linguistics:

> If intuition could get the facts of language as wrong as this, there seemed little purpose in continuing to pursue abstract philosophical arguments.... There had to be some way of engaging with the concrete empirical realities of language.

Objection number 6. It is often objected that corpus linguistics studies only performance. Corpora are evidence only about performance (actual language behaviour), and, so it is argued, give no insight into competence (native speakers' knowledge of the potential of their language).

This objection involves a misunderstanding: corpus linguistics does not study 'mere' performance data. The classic objection to performance data (Chomsky 1965: 3) is that they are affected by 'memory limitations, distractions, shifts of attention and interest, and errors'. However, there is a distinction between language use and performance. Corpus linguistics does not study idiosyncratic details of performance which are, by chance, recorded in a corpus. On the contrary, it reveals units which frequently recur, sometimes hundreds or thousands of times, and which cannot possibly be due to chance. Quantitative work with large corpora automatically excludes single and possibly idiosyncratic instances, in favour of what is central and typical. Aarts (1991) discusses this distinction, and proposes an observation-based grammar in which a criterion is the 'currency' of constructions.

In addition, nothing I have said means that intuition should be ignored. Even if native speakers can often provide, from intuition, only a few accurate examples of collocates, these intuitions can be tested against attested data, and this can reveal a different type of introspective knowledge. It may not be possible to elicit from native speakers (many) collocates for a given node, but once attested collocates are listed, native speakers can recognize, in retrospect, that they are indeed characteristic. Indeed, if native speakers did not have this competence, they could not recognize untypical collocations in literature, advertising or jokes. Fox (1987) reports a small experiment in which she tried to elicit the typical collocates of common words from native speakers. She concludes that, once they are told what the most frequent collocate is, 'it is so obvious that no-one can imagine not guessing it correctly', but 'the important thing is that they had not' (p. 146). The many examples I have given of collocations could be used in experiments of this kind. What requires to be investigated in more depth is the relation between data from corpora, elicitation experiments and introspection.

10.3 Dualisms and Monisms

There is considerable contemporary debate about the appropriate balance between corpus data and intuitive data, but this empiricist–rationalist debate goes back to discussions in ancient Greece. One view was that grammar should be the empirical and observational study of the actual usage of the poets and prose writers. Another view held that the study would have higher esteem if it was based on logical and psychological principles (Robins 1988: 464–5). This argument is still unresolved, and much twentieth-century linguistics has been based on two related dualisms: *langue–parole* and competence–performance, which have precursors in seventeenth-century French philosophy.

10.3.1 Cartesian dualism

A common view is that human beings are both body and mind, and can be understood only with reference to both their physical aspects (we have bodies and perform actions in the real physical world), and also to their mental aspects (we have minds, we think and feel). This body–mind dualism, derives from a philosophical tradition developed by René Descartes in the seventeenth century. Some version of this distinction now probably seems common-sense to many people, although we do not have to propose, as Descartes did, a radical distinction between physical and mental substance.

In his *Discourse on Method*, Descartes (1637) discusses a question which is nowadays much more urgent than when he asked it: is it possible to teach machines to use a human language? Descartes answers 'no', and argues that the linguistic ability of machines is in principle severely limited. Imagine, he says (in Part 5 of the *Discourse*), machines whose outward appearance exactly resembles human beings:

> [T]here would still be two absolutely reliable tests which prove that they are not really human beings. The first is that they could never use words or other signs which are organized in the ways that we express our thoughts to each other. We can easily imagine a machine which has been constructed so that it emits sounds... for example, if we touched it in one place, it might ask

what we want it to say; if we touched it somewhere else, it might exclaim that it is hurt, and so on. But we cannot imagine it arranging the sounds differently, in order to reply appropriately to what is said in its presence, although even human beings of the lowest level of intelligence can do that.

(my translation)

Descartes distinguishes sharply between external, observable behaviour (the machines look like humans), and internal, unobservable mental acts. External aspects of language, such as sounds, ignore an essential point about human language, which is that the sounds convey thoughts between minds. He concedes that mechanical, routine aspects of behaviour might be carried out by machines, but this would be mere simulation (surface appearance), since machines could not react appropriately to unpredictable behaviour from other people.

Thus, Descartes distinguishes between different aspects of language: external–internal, observable–unobservable, physical–mental and routine–creative. He is arguing that mental activities cannot be reduced to physical activities, and rejecting what is usually called (in twentieth-century discussions) 'behaviourism'. This extreme rejection of reductionism leads to the problem of explaining how these two phenomena, which are so profoundly different, could ever interact. This is the general problem with dualisms: creating the two contrasting concepts seems to leave them always in opposition to each other.

There is a continuing line of thought in much of the twentieth-century debate about the essential nature of language, which runs from Descartes on body–mind, via Saussure on *parole–langue*, to Chomsky on behaviour–mind, performance–competence, and E-language and I-language. (See chapter 3.2. Chomsky is the author of a 1966 book entitled *Cartesian Linguistics*.) Since Saussure, many linguists have used such oppositions when attempting to define the nature of language: its essential, as opposed to its merely accidental, properties. For example, all human languages display essential kinds of structural (syntactic) organization. However, the fact that a given language is in world-wide use, whereas another language is geographically restricted, is due to historical and social factors, and has nothing to do with its structural organization.

Language can be conceived of in many different ways, depending on point of view. A standard view has been that language has two essential aspects. First, it is behaviour, individual and unpredictable in its details: this is *parole* or performance. Second, it is knowledge: it has an underlying organization, which is known unconsciously by individual native speakers, and shared to a large extent by members of a speech community. This is usually known as competence (if we are thinking of the individual speaker), or as *langue* (if we are thinking of the shared system). These dualisms have been extremely influential and productive, but have been increasingly drawn into question, especially in sociolinguistics, discourse analysis, and corpus linguistics, which have all shown that behaviour is much more highly patterned than previously suspected.

Hodge and Kress (1988: 16) show that, in Saussure's conception, different dualisms are logically related to each other. Saussure's most famous pairs of categories are often discussed in isolation, but they are part of a rigorous scheme of successive stages of idealization. In his attempt to define the essential core of language, he distinguished first between what is internal, and what is external (for example, political and social history, and geography). From this division, he retains only one half: the internal. He then divides this aspect of language again into two: *langue* and *parole*. He argues that *parole* is too idiosyncratic for systematic study and discards it. He retains *langue*, and divides this again into two: the synchronic and the diachronic. He discards diachronic change (again as being piecemeal and irrational). He retains synchronic language phenomena, and divides these again into two axes: which were later renamed syntagmatic and paradigmatic. The schema then looks like this (Hodge and Kress 1988: 17):

⎡ internal   ⎡ *langue*   ⎡ synchrony   ⎡ paradigmatic
⎣ (external)   ⎣ (*parole*)   ⎣ (diachrony)   ⎣ (syntagmatic)

The bracketed topics in this schema indicate the contents of 'Saussure's rubbish bin'.

These dualisms receive repeated discussion in much twentieth-century linguistics, albeit in different forms. For Saussure, *langue* is social, and *parole* is individual. For Chomsky, competence is individual, and performance is the category to which the social is relegated, then to be ignored. These dualisms have also been resisted: by Hymes (1972), who opposes communicative competence to both performance and competence (see chapter 3.2); by Labov (1972: 185ff) who discusses the Saussurian paradox; and by Halliday (1978) and Sinclair (1991) who reject the competence–performance distinction outright.

For those who see insoluble problems with dualism, there are only two ways out. A model of language must be based on either fewer or more contrasting elements. Fewer than two clearly means one, and monist positions have been proposed by Bloomfield and Firth. More than two includes three, and pluralistic positions (not exclusively concerning language) have been proposed by Popper and Searle.

10.3.2 Monism: version 1

A monist position must abandon one term of the dualism, either the physical or the mental. If we abandon the physical, then we have to adopt a position known as solipsism: all we can be sure of is that minds exist, and we may just be imagining the existence of the external physical world. I will not discuss this position, since I am not aware of any serious linguistic theory which proposes solipsism.

In the uneasiness over dualisms, linguists have, however, abandoned the mental. Related views, more or less extreme, are known as physicalism, materialism, and (often within linguistics) behaviourism. An extreme view radically denies the existence of the mind. A less extreme view concentrates on behaviour, and assumes, for theoretical purposes, that the mind does not exist. For example, Bloomfield (1933: vii) adopts a monist position in his famous abandonment of psychology in favour of mechanism: 'Mechanism is the necessary form of scientific discourse.' Whether Bloomfield really believed that 'we don't have minds' is not important. He was proposing the principle that a scientist 'must proceed as if he held the materialistic view' (p. 38, see also p. 142). Another famous statement along these lines is: 'The scientific method is quite simply the convention that the mind does not exist' (Twaddell 1935: 57).

Bloomfield argued that language involves observable behaviour, that science has to be based on observable facts, that the mind is unobservable and therefore inaccessible, and that the admission of mental facts would therefore be an unnecessary complication. Quine takes a similar view: 'The bodily states exist anyway: why add the others?' (quoted by Popper 1994: 8). Thus Bloomfield appears to have been driven to making monist statements because of his assumptions about how science must operate. (See chapter 2.9.1 on problems which therefore arose in his approach to semantics.)

People have strong intuitions that they have mental states (including thoughts, feelings and wishes), and that language involves essential mental processes of understanding. (These intuitions are themselves mental states.) So, strictly behaviourist views are often felt to be strongly counter-intuitive, even if many people would accept a partly reductionist view that the mind is what the brain does. A major Chomskyan contribution has been to show the richness of mental knowledge.

10.3.3 Monism: version 2

The Firth–Halliday–Sinclair approach has also been explicitly monist. Firth (1957: 2n) denounces dualisms as 'a quite unnecessary nuisance', and explicitly describes (1935: 53; 1957: 2) his position as monist, and both Halliday (1978: 38, 51) and Sinclair (1991: 103) reject the competence–performance distinction. However, here the rejection of dualism argues that apparent dualisms are the result of an error in our thinking, namely looking at the same phenomenon from different points of view. This variant of reductionism is a favourite Hallidayan rhetorical move, though the view that behaviour and knowledge run in parallel, and are aspects of the same thing, also has a long history. Popper (1994: 109) points out Spinoza's argument in the seventeenth century: if we look at reality from the inside, then it is mind; if we look at it from the outside, then it is matter.

Halliday (1991, 1992) argues that the weather and the climate are the same phenomenon, regarded from different time depths. If we are thinking of the next few hours, then we are thinking of the weather, and this perspective determines what kinds of actions we might take (for example, going to the beach, packing an umbrella). If we are thinking of the next century, then we are thinking of the climate, and this perspective determines different kinds of actions (such as legislating against industrial processes which destroy the ozone layer). If the climate changes, then obviously this affects the weather. Conversely, each day's weather affects the climate, however minimally, either maintaining the status quo, or helping to tip the balance towards climatic change. Instance and system, micro and macro, are two sides of the same coin, relative to the observer's position. Similarly, every instance in a text perturbs the overall probabilities of the system, if only to an infinitesimal extent: the system is inherently probabilistic (Halliday 1992, 1993a).

Halliday here builds in a time dimension. The term weather refers to short-term events (the sun is shining, it is windy), whereas the climate refers to long-term states (a maritime or continental climate). With reference to language, a further distinction seems necessary. An utterance (a behavioural event) is an event in time, but a sentence (a unit of *langue*) is timeless: it is an object which stands, not in temporal, but in logical relations (such as paraphrase and contradiction) to other sentences. Furthermore, a text is never just an instance: it has to be interpreted against the history of the discourse. Any stretch of language has meaning only as a sample of an enormously large body of text, and represents the results of a process, where each selection has meaning by virtue of all the other selections which might have been made, but have been rejected (Sinclair 1965: 76–7). A crucial distinction here is between the potential of the system and the actual choice which is made.

So, text and discourse (in Foucault's sense: see chapter 7.2 and 7.7) are names for different segments between instance and system. The data from large corpora put linguistics in an increasingly good position to address the dualisms of individual and social, small-scale and large-scale, micro and macro.

10.3.4 The Saussurian paradox

There are many aspects to the Saussurian paradox (Labov 1972: 185ff). Several of the dualisms which trouble linguistics are present in Saussure's distinction between *langue* and *parole*. *Langue* is the abstract language system that is shared by members of a speech community. *Parole* is the concrete language behaviour of individual speakers and writers. Saussure observes that language is a social institution, and not a creation of the individual speaker. *Langue* is 'la partie sociale du langage, extérieure à l'individu'. Society consists of individuals, but is external to individuals. As Firth (1957: 29) puts it: 'We are in the world, and the world is in us.' As Bernstein (1990: 94) puts it: 'How does the outside become the inside, and how does the inside reveal itself and shape the outside?'

One of the most famous formulations of this problematic is by Marx (1852):

> Die Menschen machen ihre eigene Geschichte, aber sie machen sie nicht aus freien Stücken, sondern unter unmittelbar vorgefundenen, gegebenen und überlieferten Umständen. Die Tradition aller toten Geschlechter lastet wie ein Alp auf dem Gehirne der Lebenden.

> [Human beings make their own history, yet they do not make it of their own free will, but under directly encountered, given circumstances, which have been handed down to them. The tradition of all the dead generations weighs like a nightmare on the minds of the living.]

As Giddens (1984: xxi) points out, attempts to work out what this statement implies about individual and society, freedom and constraint, creativity and tradition, have shaped the social sciences. Linguistics (and other disciplines) have been constantly beset by the dualisms of subject and object, internal and external, agency and structure, process and product, *parole* and *langue*, language use and language system, creativity and rules, intended action and unintended consequences.

In the tradition of autonomous linguistics from Saussure to Chomsky, *langue* or competence are conceived as systematic and as the only true object of study, although they are both unobservable. *Parole* or performance are considered unsystematic and idiosyncratic, and therefore, at best, of only peripheral interest. In addition, *parole* is by definition observable only in passing fragments: as a whole, it is also unobservable. Mainstream twentieth-century linguistics has therefore defined itself with reference to a dualism, both halves of which are unobservable. Much of the significance of corpus linguistics lies in possibilities for breaking out of this impasse, since concordancers and other software allow millions of words of data to be searched for patterns which otherwise remain invisible.

10.4 Pluralist Positions

A theory of language use must account for both linguistic behaviour and linguistic knowledge, but we need more than this two-way distinction. At least a three-way distinction is needed, as follows.

(1) We can observe the actual choice of vocabulary which a speaker/writer has made in particular texts.
(2) But suppose we say that the speaker has a large vocabulary. Here we are referring to something quite different: not behaviour, but the knowledge of an individual. Linguists refer to the 'mental lexicon' (Aitchison 1987) as something psychological and private. It is not directly observable, though we can carry out experiments and make inferences about its contents and organization.
(3) And suppose we say that English has a large vocabulary. Here we are referring to something different again: something public, that is recorded in dictionaries. This does not correspond to the mental lexicon of any individual, since no-one knows all the words in a large dictionary. In addition, the meaning of the words is not something individual: I cannot decide to use words just to mean what I wish. Although vocabulary in this sense is also not directly observable, word meaning is 'a public state of affairs' (Carr 1990: 42).

In summary, we use the term 'vocabulary' to talk about three rather different things: something that is

chosen and actually used in texts (observable);
stored in the mind (private and unobservable);
recorded in dictionaries (public but also not directly observable).

10.5 Brute and Institutional Facts

We therefore require distinctions between actual behaviour, individual mental phenomena and conventional social facts, and attempts to relate facts of these different kinds place language within a broader theory of social behaviour.

Anscombe (1958) distinguishes between 'brute facts' and facts which exist only 'in the context of our institutions'. Suppose, he says, someone orders some groceries. If a grocer brings a bag of potatoes to my house, then this is a brute fact. But if we talk of my *ordering* the potatoes, the grocer *supplying* me with them, his sending me *a bill* which I *pay*, so that I then *own* the potatoes, then these events are only interpretable in the context of a set of institutions. These include conventions involving trust between people (such as money) and social relations (such as ownership). Although giving someone a bill consists partly in an observable brute fact, namely handing over a piece of paper, this hardly explains the point of the event, which is unobservable, and depends on shared beliefs about money, commitments to pay, and property. Along with many features of the world, ownership is not observable, but we talk about it, and perceive the social world in terms of it. The unobservable facts include speech acts: it is a brute fact that I produce an utterance such as *Could you send me ten kilos of potatoes*, but again this hardly expresses the point of the utterance, and the reciprocal obligations which it sets in train. Rawls (1955) argues that there are rules of practices which are logically prior to particular cases. With reference to Anscombe's bag of potatoes: we can only talk of someone ordering and paying a bill for goods, if we presuppose the institutions of money, buying and selling, and property. Buying potatoes is a move in an elaborate game (set within a legal framework).

These ideas are best known to linguists in a form developed by Searle (1969: 50ff), who disposes of dualism as follows. There are brute (physical) facts and psychological (individual, mental) facts, but there also are 'many kinds of facts' which are not matters of individual opinion, and which do not fit this two-way picture. They include getting married, being convicted of a crime, and winning a game of baseball. (Baseball is also one of Rawls's examples.) Searle calls them institutional facts, because they 'presuppose the existence of certain human institutions'. These institutions depend, in turn, on the distinction between regulative and constitutive rules (Searle 1969: 33ff). Regulative rules regulate behaviour which already exists independently of the rules (e.g. 'Officers must wear ties at dinner'). Constitutive rules themselves create or define the forms of behaviour (e.g. the rules of chess). Thus it is only within the social institution of marriage, which is defined by a set of constitutive rules, that uttering a certain sentence counts as a particular kind of promise, and counts as getting married. The fact that two people have got married cannot be reduced either to a piece of behaviour (they both uttered some words), or to individual mental feelings or opinions: there is a social reality which is irreducible to either of these other sets of facts. Searle (1995) develops these ideas in a more recent book, in which his work on speech acts becomes the basis of a theory of the construction of social reality.

10.6 Physical, Psychological and Social

A view of language can be based around a three-way distinction. Depending on how we look at it, language is (1) utterances (unique events, realized by actual physical behaviour), (2) individual knowledge (personal competence), or (3) social knowledge, shared across a community, and possibly recorded in dictionaries and grammars. We can make inferences about the third aspect from the patterns observable across the usage of many speakers, when their behaviour is recorded and made publicly accessible in corpora.

It is often pointed out that Saussurian *parole* is equivalent to Chomskyan performance: both are actual, personal behaviour. However, whereas Chomskyan competence is individual and psychological, Saussurian *langue* is interpersonal and social: a social fact. (Though Saussure is notoriously vague on the ontological status of this social knowledge.) If we put Saussure, Chomsky and Searle together, we have a three-part model. The first approximation would be

(1) brute facts: *parole*/performance/behaviour;
(2) psychological facts: individual competence;
(3) social (institutional) facts: *langue*.

In slightly different terms, Popper (1972, 1994) proposes a pluralist and interactionist theory of knowledge and the body–mind problem. He proposes three spheres of experience.

(1) World 1 is the external world of physical bodies with their physical states and processes. It contains objects such as stones, trees and chairs.
(2) World 2 is subjective knowledge: that is, the private, mental states and processes (thoughts, beliefs, feelings, intentions, etc.) of individual human minds.
(3) World 3 is objective knowledge. He uses the term *objective*, not to mean "objectively true", but to refer to the public products of human minds, including the contents of books, arguments, theories, problems, and critical discussions. World 3 is closely dependent on written language, since it is when arguments are written down and formulated clearly that they can most easily be discussed and criticized.

Searle's view of 'an objective world' (Searle 1995: 1) seems close to Popper's view of 'objective knowledge'. His distinction (p. 7) between 'physical particles in fields of force', 'consciousness' and 'social facts' also seems to parallel Popper's World 1 of physical facts, World 2 of mental phenomena, and World 3 of autonomous public knowledge. Further, Searle's view (e.g. p. 37) that many institutional facts depend on prior linguistic forms seems related to Popper's views on the role of (especially written) language in creating World 3.

Popper (1994: 3) points out that private psychological verbs can indicate subjective knowledge, but that when they are used in projecting clauses, they can mark objective knowledge. When we say *He knew he was exceeding the speed limit*, then we are talking of subjective World 2 knowledge. But when we say *It is well known that water consists of hydrogen and oxygen*, then we are talking of objective World 3 knowledge. One of Popper's favourite examples involves numbers. Arithmetic, geometry and statistics originated in practical needs, such as commerce and taxation, measuring land and navigation, and computing actuarial tables. Once these ideas exist (for example, the idea that there is a series of natural numbers, which starts *one*, *two*, *three* and continues without end), then, within this system, problems and patterns are discovered.

However, there are different kinds of objects in World 3. Searle (1995) gives an account of how social facts arise, which is much more detailed than Popper's account of World 3. Popper is specifically concerned with forms of scientific knowledge, such as prime numbers, which were discovered as an unintended consequence of the number system. Searle discusses a range of everyday social phenomena, and how they arise due to collective intentionality. There is a further logical difference. Popper's prime numbers continue to exist even if everyone forgets about them: since they were unintended, they do not depend on collective intentionality. Whereas, as Searle points out with reference to the ex-German Democratic Republic, if people just cease to believe in a state, then it vanishes in a puff of smoke. Nevertheless, the two positions seem, in broad outline, compatible or complementary, in so far as they are both proposing a pluralist alternative to mind–body dualisms.

Leech (1983: 48–56) gives a sympathetic account of a Popperian position, and relates Popper and Searle. He argues that a missing link in Popper's view of Worlds 1 to 3 is a world of societal facts, which is precisely what Searle discusses. This, argues Leech, intervenes between Worlds 2 and 3, to give this pluralist model:

(1) a language as physical facts
(2) a language as mental states
(3) a language as social (institutional) facts
(4) a language as an autonomous system

10.7 Worlds 1, 2 and 3

Perhaps in the following section, I am pursuing the obvious, but I would like to try and make as clear as possible the concept of public, inter-subjective facts, which are distinct from the knowledge of any individual. The word *book* is ambiguous, as between *book* [+ concrete] and *book* [− concrete], and I can make two different statements about a book on my desk:

[1] This book belongs to me.
[2] This book was written by Henry Sweet.

In [1], I am referring to an individual physical object, which sat in a bookshop, before I bought it, and brought it home. This is a World 1 object, and I could use it as a paperweight or for propping open a window. In [2], I am not referring to the physical object. Presumably Henry Sweet never saw this particular physical object, much less has he written it. What he wrote is something with an abstract status, which is embodied in the World 1 object on my desk, but also in many other objects, which can be stored in other forms, including microfiche and computer files. If any one of these World 1 objects is destroyed, this does not mean that we have lost Henry Sweet's ideas: we can go and read them in some other instantiation of the book. In [2], the book is a World 3 object, and [2] is a shorthand way of saying something like.

[3] The *content of* this book was written by Henry Sweet.

We can also phrase things the other way round. If I say [1], then I do not mean that the ideas in the book belong to me. I can own the World 1 object, but not the World 3 object. Also, I can have a version of its content in my mind, as a World 2 object, but this will not be the same as the World 3 object. Even the author, Henry Sweet himself, did not have the whole content of the book in his mind. This may sound paradoxical. However, first, he probably wrote many details in the book, which he later forgot. Second, the arguments in the book doubtless have many consequences (perhaps they contain logical entailments or contradictions) of which he was not aware. Once ideas are written down, they take on a life of their own.

Popper (1996: 101–2) phrases it in this way. Books belong to World 1, but their content belongs to World 3. Two copies of a book belong to World 1, in so far as they are different physical objects, but they belong to World 3, in so far as they have the same content. Similarly, libraries and manuscripts of lectures belong simultaneously to World 1 and World 3. If someone picks up a book or hears a lecture in a language they do not understand, then they can see or hear only its World 1 aspect: marks on a page or noises passing between people. If they understand the language, and make an attempt to follow the arguments, then it is the World 3 aspect which is important.

Searle (1995) makes a related point. The book on my desk is, in one sense, a physical object. I could use it as a paperweight, but it was not intended to be used in this way. It was produced with the intention that it be read, and it is not just my personal, individual opinion that this is the intended function of books. It is 'matter of objectively ascertainable fact' (p. 10) that it is a book (and not a paperweight). Actually, Searle (1995: 9–10) makes the point with reference to an object with particular physical properties: it is composed of wood and metal, but in addition it *is* a screwdriver. This is despite the fact that a screwdriver could be used for other purposes (such as a weapon), and that other objects (such as a coin) could be used as a screwdriver. Both the intentionality and the consensus about this intentionality are essential.

One of my university colleagues has in her office a copy of Searle's (1995) book which has been badly chewed by her dog. The dog had treated the book as a physical World 1 object, and not appreciated it as a World 3 object. She has kept the book, because, although the World 1 object is badly chewed and in a pretty sorry state, it is nevertheless readable and still has value as a World 3 object. The book (World 1 object) used to belong to the university library, so she had to pay for another World 1 copy of the book for the library. (This is a true story. The dog's name is Willie.)

World 3 objects such as books come into existence only because an author has thoughts and ideas (which are states or events in World 2), which are then recorded, by writing them in longhand or typing them into a word processor. The recording, in some World 1 form, is crucial, and written language has a crucial role to play in the creation of World 3 objects. Once the ideas are written down, they can be duplicated, and read by other people, and therefore criticized and improved. They have gained a life of their own, independent of World 2 and of their creator. In this sense, Popper argues that World 3 is autonomous.

There are certainly limitations to Popper's work in this area. He has only a rudimentary conception of language (Botha 1992: 188). He proposes a view of the biological bases of human language, but makes no reference to discussions of mind/brain relations in Chomskyan linguistics. Neither does he make any reference to work on language functions since Bühler (1934), and he discusses to only a limited extent the necessary interaction between Worlds 1, 2 and 3.

However, we now have a series of distinctions on which an alternative to dualism could be based. On this account, utterances are physical World 1 phenomena, competence is a mental World 2 phenomenon, and languages are World 3 objects (Popper 1972: 157; Carr 1990: 3 *et passim*). As I will argue below, corpora are also a different kind of World 3 object.

10.8 A Pluralist Model

An alternative to both monism and dualism is an explicitly pluralist position. In chapter 3.2, I discussed Hymes's (1972) pluralist revision of the two-way Chomskyan competence–performance opposition. A comparable model is proposed by Tuldava (1998: 13ff), from which figure 10.1 is adapted. First, Tuldava distinguishes between the potential of the system (what is formally possible) and the realization of the system (what actually occurs). Second, he distinguishes between dynamic and static aspects of language and language in use: process and product. These aspects can vary independently, giving us four ways of looking at language.

A text is the only aspect of language which is directly observable. It is the product of linguistic behaviour: a small set of choices out of what is possible, and a realization of the language system. A spoken text is a piece of behaviour; so also is a handwritten letter. We can look at a text as a static product (what has been chosen), and count the frequency of items in it. Or, as I did in chapter 6.6, we can look at it, from a different point of view, as the outcome of a process of linguistic behaviour in time, which involves a constantly changing choice of new and old vocabulary. Without computational help, we can look only at a small fragment of text. With computational assistance we can observe patterns which recur across many individual texts.

A text consists of a sequence, in time or space, of word-forms. These are word-tokens, which are repeated with different frequencies. A vocabulary consists of a timeless list of word-types, which can be word-forms, lemmas or other lexical items. A vocabulary is one part of the language system. This is a

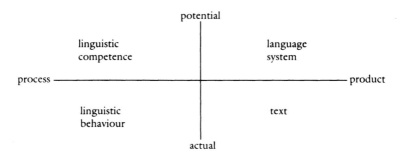

Figure 10.1 Process and product, potential and actual (based on discussion in Tuldava 1998: 13ff)

static inventory of what is possible: essentially a vocabulary plus a list of larger units and rules of combination. The system is social and inter-subjective, and not known in its entirety by any individual. No single person's linguistic competence includes the whole vocabulary of the language, but speakers can learn new words, and draw on this vocabulary if required. The system cannot be observed directly, but norms of use can be inferred from observations of texts. Speakers intend to communicate with each other, but they do not intend to produce and maintain a language. This is the unintended product of their linguistic behaviour and knowledge.

Sentences are types. They are timeless units of the language system, but they are not events: they do not occur. Utterances are tokens. They are units of language behaviour, which occur in time and space, and which are both caused (by mental intentions, about which we know very little), and have causal effects. Linguistic competence is knowledge of types (such as lemmas and sentences). Language behaviour produces utterance tokens. The language system is inter-subjective, social and public. Linguistic competence is individual, mental and private.

Linguistic behaviour belongs to World 1 events. The linguistic competence of an individual exists in World 2. The language system is a World 3 object. An individual text, such as specific spoken utterances or an individual written text, is also a World 1 object. However, behaviour and texts can only be interpreted against norms, so, as soon as we start to discuss the meaning of a text, we are considering it as a World 3 object, and as soon as we record utterances, and collect them in a corpus, then we are creating a different kind of World 3 object. What is still not entirely integrated into this account (as pointed out by Leech 1983: 54–5) is language as a social phenomenon. This is where a large corpus can help us to observe the patterns of repetition of micro-events (individual utterances) across the behaviour of many speakers, and therefore to glimpse the macro-patterns, which we perceive as a language.

10.9 Performance Data, Corpora and Routine Behaviour

A corpus is a collection of texts, designed for some purpose, usually teaching or research. It does not fit directly into the four-way schema above, because it is neither linguistic behaviour, nor linguistic knowledge, nor a linguistic system. A corpus is not something that a speaker does or knows, but something constructed by a researcher. It is a record of performance, usually of many different users, and designed to be studied, so that we can make inferences about typical language use. Because it provides methods of observing patterns of a type which have long been sensed by literary critics, but which have not been identified empirically, the computer-assisted study of large corpora can perhaps suggest a way out of the paradoxes of dualism.

It is often objected (see section 10.2 above) that a corpus is (mere) performance data, but this is a shorthand formulation which disguises important points. Utterances are actual behaviour, spoken or written: they are acts performed by individuals, and ultimately they are physical events, noises made in the world or marks made on a page. A corpus is a collection of utterances and therefore a sample of behaviour. However, a corpus is not itself the behaviour, but a record of this behaviour. Or if you like: an utterance is an event in time, but a corpus is not an event. This distinction has crucial consequences. Popper (1994: 7) gives this example. Meteorologists make records of changes in temperature. The temperatures are physical states (in World 1), but the measurements have been selected, and the record has been designed, for some purpose, by human beings. The sequence of temperatures cannot be directly studied for the patterns it displays: but the record can be. Through the intermediary of the intentions and design of human beings (in World 2), the physical states in the world (in World 1) can be converted into a form of public knowledge (in World 3). Developing Halliday's analogy, temperature records can be used to study not only local variations in the weather, which might be directly observable and remembered in a rough and ready way, but also to study longer-term variations in the climate, which are not directly observable, and need a record to replace individual human memory.

A large general corpus is one stage further away again from a record of performance. First, it is a sample of the language use of many speakers, not of one individual's performance. Second, it is constructed according to a theory of language variation, which is open to discussion and criticism. Third, the corpus can exist in many copies, on paper and in computer-readable form. This makes the data of linguistics publicly accessible, and offers an alternative to the ultimately private data of intuitions.

What is observed is always partly determined by the observational methods used and by the available data: essentially by what it is possible and/or convenient to do. Thus, different aspects of reality are foregrounded by different methods. Concordances make repetitions visible, and corpus linguists tend to emphasize the repetitive and routine nature óf language use. However, these repetitions are really there, and can now be studied. So, what is it that corpora make visible? Saussure (1916: 171) distinguished syntagmatic and paradigmatic (associative) relations. A syntagmatic relation holds between items *in praesentia*, which co-occur in a linear string. A concordance line is a fragment of *parole*, where a single instance of syntagmatic relations can be observed. We are interested in more, however, than what happens to have occurred once in such a fragment. A paradigmatic relation is a potential relation between items *in absentia*, which have a psychological reality ('des termes *in absentia* dans une série mnémonique virtuelle', p. 171). Since paradigmatic relations are a virtual mental phenomenon, they are unobservable.

In an individual text, neither repeated syntagmatic relations, nor any paradigmatic relations at all, are observable. However, a concordance makes it possible to observe repeated events: it makes visible, at the same time, what frequently co-occurs syntagmatically, and how much constraint there is on the paradigmatic choices. The co-occurrences are visible on the horizontal (syntagmatic) axis of the individual concordance lines. The repeated paradigmatic choices – what frequently recurs – are equally visible on the vertical axis: especially if the concordance lines are re-ordered alphabetically to left or right (Tognini-Bonelli 1996).

Chomskyan linguistics has emphasized creativity at the expense of routine, which is seen as habit and as the unacceptable face of behaviourism. Other linguists (such as Firth and Halliday) and sociologists (such as Bourdieu and Giddens) have emphasized the importance of routine in everyday life. For example, Bourdieu (1991) develops a concept of *habitus*, as a set of dispositions to act in certain ways, a myriad of ingrained mundane processes which become second nature: they are a product of history, but they also reproduce history (pp. 12–13) in the routine flow of day-to-day life. Giddens (1984) proposes a substantial theory of routine, which he sees as the predominant form of everyday activity (p. 282). The routines of social life are apparently minor and trivial, but have a compelling force, such that daily life is inconceivable without tradition and custom. Since daily life is reconstituted in repetition, there is an inherent relation between routine, trust and confidence. Giddens (1984: 68–73) draws on work on discourse analysis for his discussions of how humans are constantly watchful of their own and others' behaviour. The routine character of everyday encounters has to be worked at in situations of co-presence.

Corpus linguistics offers new ways of studying linguistic routines: what is expected, predictable, usual, normal and typical in the utterance-by-utterance flow of spoken and written language in use. It has as yet only the outlines of a theory which can relate individual texts to text corpora, which can use what is frequent in corpora to identify what is typical in the language, and which can use findings about frequently recurring patterns to construct a theory of the relation between routine and creative language use. However, we now have methods for studying patterns which are not visible directly to a human observer, but which are nevertheless stable across the language performance of many speakers. These methods make it possible to study patterns which are not limited to what an individual can perceive or remember, and offer new ways of studying the material base of many of society's activities. One of the most elegant defences of such study is by Burrows (1987: 2–3, see chapter 6.9 above), who talks of 'evidence to which the unassisted human mind could never gain consistent, conscious access'.

When Chomskyan linguistics took a decisive step away from studying behaviour and its products, to studying the cognitive system which underlies behaviour, this led to the discovery of many new facts about language. Equally, when corpus linguistics took a decisive step towards the study of patterns across large text collections, this also led to the discovery of many new facts. The approaches are currently often seen as being in opposition, and the dualisms are perpetuated, but the long-term aim must be to integrate the insights from different approaches.

10.10 Summary and Implications

The kind of probabilistic model of language use, especially of collocations, which I have discussed throughout the book, has implications for several central areas of language study.

(1) *A theory of language competence.* Language use is a balance between routine and creativity. Concepts such as 'current' or 'natural' language (Sinclair 1991: 174) have intuitive plausibility, but are not well understood. Corpora can provide evidence about why some ways of saying things sound idiomatic, natural and native-like, whilst others do not: words are not learned individually, but in association with other words.

(2) *A theory of parole.* Corpus study shows that language use is much more highly organized than previously suspected. It is governed, not by the kinds of categorical rules that linguistics has often dealt with, but by tendencies and probabilities. Only with large corpora and appropriate software is it possible to observe repeated patterns across the language use of many speakers and writers.

(3) *A theory of lexis–grammar relations.* Such an approach gives lexis a much more central place in language use and a greatly expanded syntagmatic dimension (Hunston and Francis 2000). This is a very different orientation from much linguistic theory since the 1950s (see chapter 9.8 above), and it will take a long time before an appropriately revised division of labour between an expanded lexis and a reduced syntax has been worked out.

(4) *A theory of connotation.* If all words have predictable collocates, then lexical meaning is distributed over several words, the meaning of an individual word is influenced by these collocates, and the balance between propositional and connotational meaning shifts towards the latter. Many

more words have evaluative connotations and discourse prosodies than previously recognized. (This has implications, which I have not discussed here, for the practice and theory of stylistics and of translating.)

(5) *A theory of textual cohesion.* The findings presented about semantic feature sharing (especially in chapters 2.5 and 5.6 above) have implications for the frequent semantic redundancy of language in use. A theory of lexical collocation is a theory of the extent to which lexis is predictable, and can therefore serve as one mechanism of textual cohesion.

It is often thought that corpus analyses show that much of language use is made up of fixed phrases or prefabricated chunks, but this is a misleading way of looking at things. There are certainly such fixed phrases, but it turns out to be surprisingly difficult to find phrases which are absolutely fixed. The finding is rather that there are very many recurring semantic patterns which have expected lexical realizations, but which can be highly variable in their lexis. These patterns are often very simple in their structure but, due to contextual variables, very complex in their consequences. This is a finding which recurs across the whole of the natural sciences. Consider the parallels between corpus linguistics and geology. Both disciplines are based on an assumed relation between process and product. By and large, the processes are not observable: they must be inferred from the products.

Geologists are interested in processes which are not directly observable, because they take place across vast periods of time. What is observable is the products of these processes: individual rocks and geographical formations. These products are the observable traces of processes which have often taken place a long time in the past. They are highly variable, because any specific instance is due to local environmental conditions. Nevertheless, these variable products are due to highly general processes of destruction (such as erosion) and construction (such as sedimentation; see Love 1991).

Corpus linguists are interested in processes which are not directly observable because they are instantiated across the language use of many different speakers and writers. What is directly observable is the individual products, such as utterances and word combinations. (In addition, repetitions of such patterns, across time, can be made observable if different occurrences are displayed by concordancers and other software.) These individual word combinations are the observable traces of general patterns of collocation and colligation. They are highly variable due to local sociolinguistic contexts. Nevertheless, these variable products are due to highly general processes of probability and expectation.

There are several general tests of an approach to language study. Perhaps the most important is whether taking a particular point of view can help us to learn things: there is no doubt that corpus studies have provided many new and surprising facts about language use. Another test is whether looking at things from a given perspective can suggest ways out of paradoxes which have plagued linguistics. Corpus study may eventually provide a way of avoiding unfortunate dualisms and of integrating different kinds of cognitive and behavioural data.

10.11 Background and Further Reading

On the relevance of Popper to linguistics, see Leech (1983: 54–5), Carr (1990) and Botha (1992: 183ff). Swales's (1990) view of the documentary world of science is an institutional variant of this World 3 view of knowledge (though Swales does not refer to Popper).

Ideas similar to Popper's on World 3 are put forward by Ziman (1978: 106–8), who distinguishes between (1) the material domain of the external physical world, (2) the mental domain of perceptions and thoughts, and (3) what he calls the 'noetic' domain, which depends on language in order to create and maintain knowledge as a social institution. Ziman refers to Popper, and to similar ideas in Polanyi (1958). Searle (1969, 1995) distinguishes between physical, psychological and institutional facts. And Giddens's (1984: 8–12) views on the importance of the unintended consequences of intentional actions for a theory of the social world also come close to Popper's views. Unfortunately, the major theorists, Popper, Searle and Giddens, do not refer to one another's work, and, as far as I know, no systematic comparison of their ideas has appeared.

References

Aarsleff, H. (1990) The original plan for the *OED* and its background. *Transactions of the Philological Society*, 88, 2: 151–61.

Aarts, J. (1991) Intuition-based and observation-based grammars. In K. Aijmer and B. Altenberg (eds), *English Corpus Linguistics*. London: Longman, pp. 44–62.

Aijmer, K. and Altenberg, B. (eds) (1991) *English Corpus Linguistics*. London: Longman.

Aitchison, J. (1987) *Words in the Mind: An Introduction to the Mental Lexicon*. Oxford: Blackwell.

Algeo, J. (1990) The emperor's new clothes: the second edition of the society's dictionary. *Transactions of the Philological Society*, 88, 2: 131–50.

Algeo, J. (1991) *Fifty Years Among the New Words: A Dictionary of Neologisms, 1941–1991*. Cambridge: Cambridge University Press.

Allerton, D. J. (1984) Three (or four) levels of word co-occurrence restriction. *Lingua*, 63: 17–40.

Anscombe, G. E. M. (1958) On brute facts. *Analysis*, 18, 4: 69–72.

Armstrong, S. (ed.) (1994) *Using Large Corpora*. Cambridge, MA: MIT Press.

Aston, G. and Burnard, L. (1998) *The BNC Handbook*. Edinburgh: Edinburgh University Press.

Atkinson, D. (1999) *Scientific Discourse in Sociohistorical Context*. Mahwah, NJ: Erlbaum.

Austin, J. L. (1962) *How to Do Things with Words*, ed. J. O. Urmson. Oxford: Clarendon Press.

Ayto, J. (1989) *The Longman Register of New Words*. London: Longman.

Baker, C. and Freebody, P. (1989) *Children's First School Books*. Oxford: Blackwell.

Baker, M., Francis, G. and Tognini-Bonelli, E. (eds) (1993) *Text and Technology*. Amsterdam: Benjamins.

Baldwin, M. (1951) *I Leap over the Wall*. London: Hamish Hamilton.

Ball, C. N. (1994) Automated text analysis: cautionary tales. *Literary and Linguistic Computing*, 9, 4: 295–302.

Bar-Hillel, Y. (1971) Out of the pragmatic waste-basket. *Linguistic Inquiry*, 2: 401–7.

Barnbrook, G. (1996) *Language and Computers*. Edinburgh: Edinburgh University Press.

Bayley, P. (1997) Language and the law: arguments about ethnicity. In G. E. Bussi, M. Bondi and F. Gatta (eds), *Understanding Argument*. Forlì: Biblioteca della Scuola Superiore di Lingue Moderne per Interpreti e Traddutori, pp. 89–103.
Benson, M. (1990) Collocations and general purpose dictionaries. *International Journal of Lexicography*, **3**, 1: 23–35.
Benson, M., Benson, E. and Ilson, R. (1997) *The BBI Dictionary of Word Combinations*, rev. edn. Amsterdam: Benjamins.
Benveniste, E. (1954) Civilisation: contributions à l'histoire du mot. In E. Benveniste, *Problèmes de linguistique générale*. Paris: Gallimard (1966), pp. 336–45.
Berger, P. and Luckmann, T. (1966) *The Social Construction of Reality*. London: Allen Lane.
Bernstein, B. B. (1990) *Class, Codes and Control*, vol. 4. London: Routledge.
Biber, D. (1988) *Variation across Speech and Writing*. Cambridge: Cambridge University Press.
Biber, D. (1993a) Using register-differentiated corpora for general language studies. *Computational Linguistics*, **19**: 219–41. Also in Armstrong 1994: 179–201.
Biber, D. (1993b) Co-occurrence patterns among collocations. *Computational Linguistics*, **19**: 531–8.
Biber, D., Conrad, C. and Reppen, R. (1998) *Corpus Linguistics*. Cambridge: Cambridge University Press.
Biber, D., Johansson, S., Leech, G., Conrad, S. and Finegan, E. (1999) *Longman Grammar of Spoken and Written English*. London: Longman.
Bloomfield, L. (1933) *Language*. New York: Holt, Rinehart and Winston. (Page references to British edn, London: Allen and Unwin, 1935.)
Bolinger, D. (1976) Meaning and memory. *Forum Linguisticum*, **1**, 1: 1–14.
Botha, R. P. (1992) *Twentieth-Century Conceptions of Language*. Oxford: Blackwell.
Bourdieu, P. (1991) *Language and Symbolic Power*. Oxford: Polity.
Brazil, D. (1995) *A Grammar of Speech*. Oxford: Oxford University Press.
Brown, G. (1994) Modes of understanding. In G. Brown, K. Malmkjaer, A. Pollitt and J. Williams (eds), *Language and Understanding*. Oxford: Oxford University Press, pp. 9–20.
Brown, G. and Yule, G. (1983) *Discourse Analysis*. Cambridge: Cambridge University Press.
Brumfit, C. (ed.) (1995) *Language Education in the National Curriculum*. Oxford: Blackwell.
Bublitz, W. (1996) Semantic prosody and cohesive company: 'somewhat predictable'. *Leuvense Bijdragen: Tijdschrift voor Germaanse Filologie*, **85**, 1–2: 1–32.
Bublitz, W. (1998). 'I entirely dot dot dot': copying semantic features in collocations with up-scaling intensifiers. In R. Schulze (ed.), *Making Meaningful Choices in English*. Tübingen: Narr, pp. 11–32.
Bühler, K. (1934) *Sprachtheorie: Die Darstellungsfunktion der Sprache*. Jena: Fischer.
Burrows, J. F. (1987) *Computation into Criticism*. Oxford: Clarendon Press.
Buyssens, E. (1959) Negative contexts. *English Studies*, **40**: 163–9.

Caldas-Coulthard, R. and Coulthard, M. (eds) (1996) *Texts and Practices: Readings in Critical Discourse Analysis*. London: Routledge.
Cameron, D. (1995) *Verbal Hygiene*. London: Routledge.
Cameron, D. (1997) Performing gender identity. In S. Johnson and U. H. Meinhof (eds), *Language and Masculinity*. Oxford: Blackwell, pp. 47–64. (Also in A. Jaworski and N. Coupland (eds), *The Discourse Reader*. London: Routledge, 1999, pp. 442–8).
Carr, P. (1990) *Linguistic Realities*. Cambridge: Cambridge University Press.
Carter, R. and McCarthy, M. (1999) The English *get*-passive in spoken discourse: description and implications for an interpersonal grammar. *English Language and Linguistics*, 3, 1: 41–58.
Channell, J. (1994) *Vague Language*. Oxford: Oxford University Press.
Channell, J. (2000) Corpus-based analysis of evaluative lexis. In S. Hunston and G. Thompson (eds), *Evaluation in Text: Authorial Stance and the Construction of Discourse*. Oxford: Oxford University Press, pp. 38–55.
Chatman, S. (1969) New ways of analysing narrative structure, with an example from Joyce's *Dubliners. Language and Style*, 2, 1: 3–36.
Chomsky, N. (1957) *Syntactic Structures*. The Hague: Mouton.
Chomsky, N. (1965) *Aspects of the Theory of Syntax*. Cambridge, MA: MIT Press.
Chomsky, N. (1966) *Cartesian Linguistics*. New York: Harper and Row.
Chomsky, N. (1986) *Knowledge of Language: Its Nature, Origin and Use*. New York: Praeger.
Choueka, Y., Klein, S. T. and Neuwitz, E: (1983) Automatic retrieval of frequent idiomatic and collocational expressions in a large corpus. *ALLC Journal*, 4, 1: 34–8.
Church, K., Gale, W., Hanks, P. and Hindle, D. (1991) Using statistics in lexical analysis. In U. Zernik (ed.), *Lexical Acquisition*. Englewood Cliffs, NJ: Erlbaum, pp. 115–64.
Church, K., Gale, W., Hanks, P., Hindle, D. and Moon, R. (1994) Lexical substitutability. In B. Atkins and A. Zampolli (eds), *Computational Approaches to the Lexicon*. Oxford: Oxford University Press, pp. 153–77.
Church, K. and Hanks, P. (1990) Word association norms, mutual information and lexicography. *Computational Linguistics*, 16, 1: 22–9.
Church, K. and Mercer, R. L. (1994) Introduction to the special issue on computational linguistics using large corpora. In S. Armstrong (ed.), *Using Large Corpora*. Cambridge, MA: MIT Press, 1–24.
CIDE (1995) *Cambridge International Dictionary of English*, ed. P. Procter. Cambridge: Cambridge University Press.
Clear, J. (1993) From Firth principles: computational tools for the study of collocation. In M. Baker, G. Francis and E. Tognini-Bonelli (eds), *Text and Technology*. Amsterdam: Benjamins, pp. 271–92.
Clear, J. (1996) 'Grammar and nonsense': or syntax and word senses. In J. Svartvik (ed.), *Words: Proceedings of an International Symposium*. KVHAA Konferenser 36. Stockholm: Almquist and Wiksell, pp. 213–41.

Cobuild (1987) *Collins COBUILD English Language Dictionary*, ed. J. Sinclair. London: HarperCollins.
Cobuild (1990) *Collins COBUILD English Grammar*, ed. J. Sinclair. London: HarperCollins.
Cobuild (1995a) *Collins COBUILD English Dictionary*, ed. J. Sinclair. London: HarperCollins.
Cobuild (1995b) *Collins COBUILD English Collocations on CD-ROM*. London: HarperCollins.
Cole, P. and Morgan, J. L. (eds) (1975) *Speech Acts: Syntax and Semantics*, vol. 3. New York: Academic Press.
Collins, P. C. (1996) *Get*-passives in English. *English World-Wide*, 15, 1: 43–56.
Condor, S. and Antaki, C. (1997) Social cognition and discourse. In T. A. van Dijk (ed.), *Discourse as Structure and Process*. London: Sage, pp. 320–47.
Coulthard, M. (ed.) (1992) *Advances in Spoken Discourse Analysis*. London: Routledge.
Coulthard, M. (ed.) (1994) *Advances in Written Text Analysis*. London: Routledge.
Cowie, A. P. (1994) Phraseology. In R. E. Asher (ed.), *The Encyclopedia of Language and Linguistics*. Oxford: Pergamon, pp. 3168–71.
Cox, B. (1991) *Cox on Cox: An English Curriculum for the 1990s*. London: Hodder and Stoughton.
Crowley, T. (ed.) (1991) *Proper English? Readings in Language, History and Cultural Identity*. London: Routledge.
Cruse, D. A. (1986) *Lexical Semantics*. Cambridge: Cambridge University Press.
Crystal, D. (1979) Neglected grammatical factors in conversational English. In S. Greenbaum and G. Leech (eds), *Studies in English Linguistics*. London: Longman, pp. 153–66.
Crystal, D. (1991) Stylistic profiling. In K. Aijmer and B. Altenberg (eds), *English Corpus Linguistics*. London: Longman, pp. 221–38.
Crystal, D. (1992) *An Encyclopedic Dictionary of Language and Languages*. Oxford: Blackwell.
Crystal, D. (1995) *The Cambridge Encyclopedia of the English Language*. Cambridge: Cambridge University Press.
De Beaugrande, R. (1996) The 'pragmatics' of doing language science: the 'warrant' for large-corpus linguistics. *Journal of Pragmatics*, 25: 503–35.
Descartes, R. (1637) *Discours de la méthode* [English translation by J. Vietch, *A Discourse on Method*. London: Dent, 1912].
Du Gay, P., Hall, S., Janes, L., Mackay, H. and Negus, K. (1997) *Doing Cultural Studies*. London: Sage.
Dunning, T. (1993) Accurate methods for the statistics of surprise and coincidence. *Computational Linguistics*, 19, 1: 61–74. [Also in Armstrong 1994: 61–74.]
Durkin, P. N. R. (1999) Root and branch: revising the etymological component of the *Oxford English Dictionary*. *Transactions of the Philological Society*, 97, 1: 1–49.
Ellis, R. (1997) *SLA Research and Language Teaching*. Oxford: Oxford University Press.

Erman, B. and Warren, B. (2000) The idiom principle and the open choice principle. *Text*, **20**, 1: 29–62.
Fairclough, N. (1992) *Discourse and Social Change*. Oxford: Polity.
Fillmore, C. J. (1971) Types of lexical information. In D. D. Steinberg and L. A. Jakobovitz (eds), *Semantics*. Cambridge: Cambridge University Press, pp. 370–92.
Fillmore, C. J. (1985) Frames and the semantics of understanding. *Quaderni di Semantica*, **6**, 2: 222–54.
Fillmore, C. J. and Atkins, B. T. S. (1994) Starting where the dictionaries stop: the challenge of corpus lexicography. In B. T. S. Atkins and A. Zampoli (eds), *Computational Approaches to the Lexicon*. Oxford: Clarendon, pp. 349–93.
Fillmore, C. J., Kay, P. and O'Connor, M. C. (1988) Regularity and idiomaticity in grammatical constructions: the case of *let alone*. *Language*, **64**, 3: 501–38.
Firth, J. R. (1935) The technique of semantics. *Transactions of the Philological Society*, 36–72.
Firth, J. R. (1957) A synopsis of linguistic theory, 1930–1955. *Studies in Linguistic Analysis*, special volume, Philological Society. Oxford: Blackwell, pp. 1–32.
Foucault, M. (1980) *Power/Knowledge*, ed. C. Gordon. London: Harvester.
Fox, G. (1987) The case for examples. In J. Sinclair (ed.), *Looking Up*. London: Collins, pp. 137–49.
Francis, G. (1993) A corpus-driven approach to grammar: principles, methods and examples. In M. Baker, G. Francis and E. Tognini-Bonelli (eds), *Text and Technology*. Amsterdam: Benjamins, pp. 137–56.
Francis, G. (1994) Labelling discourse: an aspect of nominal-group lexical cohesion. In M. Coulthard (ed.), *Advances in Written Text Analysis*. London: Routledge, pp. 83–101.
Francis, G., Hunston, S. and Manning, E. (1996) *Grammar Patterns 1: Verbs*. London: HarperCollins.
Francis, G., Hunston, S. and Manning, E. (1998) *Grammar Patterns 2: Nouns and Adjectives*. London: HarperCollins.
Francis, W. N. (1979) Problems of assembling and computerizing large corpora. In H. Bergenholtz and B. Schaeder (eds), *Empirische Textwissenschaft*. Berlin: Scriptor, pp. 110–23.
Füger, W. (1980) *Concordance to James Joyce's 'Dubliners'*. Hildesheim and New York: Georg Olms.
Gerbig, A. (1996) *Lexical and Grammatical Variation in a Corpus*. Frankfurt: Peter Lang.
Giddens, A. (1984) *The Constitution of Society*. Oxford: Polity.
Glück, H. and Sauer, W. (1990) *Gegenwartsdeutsch*. Stuttgart: Metzlersche Verlagsbuchhandlung.
Gordon, D. and Lakoff, G. (1975) Conversational postulates. In P. Cole and J. L. Morgan (eds), *Speech Acts. Syntax and Semantics*, vol. 3. New York: Academic Press, pp. 83–106.
Graddol, D. and Swann, J. (1988) Trapping linguists: an analysis of linguists' responses to John Honey's pamphlet 'The Language Trap'. *Language and Education*, **2**, 2: 95–111.

Granger, S. (1996) Romance words in English: from history to pedagogy. In J. Svartvik (ed.), *Words: Proceedings of an International Symposium*. KVHAA Konferenser 36. Stockholm: Almqvist and Wiksell, pp. 105–21.
Grice, H. P. (1975) Logic and conversation. In P. Cole and J. L. Morgan (eds), *Speech Acts. Syntax and Semantics*, vol. 3. New York: Academic Press, pp. 41–58.
Haegemann, L. (1991) *Introduction to Government and Binding Theory.* Oxford: Blackwell.
Halliday, M. A. K. (1978) *Language as Social Semiotic.* London: Edward Arnold.
Halliday, M. A. K. (1991) Corpus studies and probabilistic grammar. In K. Aijmer and B. Altenberg (eds), *English Corpus Linguistics*. London: Longman, pp. 30–43.
Halliday, M. A. K. (1992) Language as system and language as instance: the corpus as a theoretical construct. In J. Svartvik (ed.), *Directions in Corpus Linguistics.* Berlin: Mouton, pp. 61–77.
Halliday, M. A. K. (1993a) Quantitative studies and probabilities in grammar. In M. Hoey (ed.), *Data, Description, Discourse*. London: HarperCollins, pp. 1–25.
Halliday, M. A. K. (1993b) On the language of physical science. In M. A. K. Halliday and J. R. Martin, *Writing Science*. London: Falmer.
Halliday, M. A. K. and Hasan, R. (1976) *Cohesion in English.* London: Longman.
Hanks, P. (1987) Definitions and explanations. In J. Sinclair (ed.), *Looking Up*. London: Collins, pp. 116–36.
Hart, C. (1969) Eveline. In C. Hart, *James Joyce's 'Dubliners'*. London: Faber and Faber.
Hayes, D. P. (1988) Speaking and writing: distinct patterns of word choice. *Journal of Memory and Language*, 27: 527–85.
Hodge, R. and Kress, G. (1988) *Social Semiotics*. Oxford: Polity.
Hoey, M. (1991) *Patterns of Lexis in Text*. Oxford: Oxford University Press.
Hopper, P. J. (1991) On some principles of grammaticization. In E. C. Traugott and B. Heine (eds), *Approaches to Grammaticalization*. Amsterdam: Benjamins, pp. 17–35.
Hopper, P. J. and Traugott, E. J. (1993) *Grammaticalization*. Cambridge: Cambridge University Press.
Horn, L. R. (1988) Pragmatic theory. In F. J. Newmeyer (ed.), *Linguistics: The Cambridge Survey*, vol. 1. Cambridge: Cambridge University Press, pp. 113–45.
Horn, L. R. (1996) Presupposition and implicature. In S. Lappin (ed.), *The Handbook of Contemporary Semantic Theory.* Oxford: Blackwell, pp. 299–319.
Howarth, P. (1998) Phraseology and second language proficiency. *Applied Linguistics*, 19, 1: 24–44.
Hübler, A. (1992) On the get-passive. In W. G. Busse (ed.), *Anglistentag 1991 Proceedings*. Tübingen: Niemeyer, pp. 89–101.
Hudson, R. A. (1995) Identifying the linguistic foundations for lexical research and dictionary design. In D. E. Walker, A. Zampolli and M. Calzolari (eds), *Automating the Dictionary.* Oxford: Oxford University Press, pp. 21–51.
Hudson, R. A. (1996) *Sociolinguistics*, 2nd edn. Cambridge: Cambridge University Press.

Hunston, S. and Francis, G. (1998) Verbs observed: a corpus-driven pedagogic grammar. *Applied Linguistics*, **19**, 1: 45–72.
Hunston, S. and Francis, G. (2000) *Pattern Grammar: A Corpus-driven Approach to the Lexical Grammar of English*. Amsterdam: Benjamins.
Hunston, S. and Thompson, G. (eds) (2000) *Evaluation in Text: Authorial Stance and the Construction of Discourse*. Oxford: Oxford University Press.
Hymes, D. (1972) On communicative competence. In J. Pride and J. Holmes (eds), *Sociolinguistics*. Harmondsworth: Penguin, pp. 269–93.
Hymes, D. (1992) The concept of communicative competence revisited. In M. Pütz (ed.), *Thirty Years of Linguistic Evolution*. Amsterdam: Benjamins, pp. 31–58.
Israel, M. (1996) The *way* constructions grow. In A. Goldberg (ed.), *Conceptual Structure, Discourse and Language*. Stanford: CSLI (Center for the Study of Language and Information), pp. 217–30.
Jakobson, R. (1971) *Selected Writings*, vol. 2. The Hague: Mouton.
Johansson, S. and Oksefjell, S. (1996) Towards a unified account of the syntax and semantcs of GET. In J. Thomas and M. Short (eds), *Using Corpora for Language Research*. London: Longman, pp. 57–75.
Johnson, A. (1993) The use of informal interviews in the study of 'care' in family life. Unpublished PhD thesis, University of Nottingham.
Johnson-Laird, P. N. (1983) *Mental Models*. Cambridge: Cambridge University Press.
Johnson-Laird, P. N. (1988) *The Computer and the Mind*. London: Fontana.
Jones, S. and Sinclair, J. (1974) English lexical collocations. *Cahiers de Lexicologie*, **24**: 15–61.
Joyce, J. (1914) *Dubliners*. Harmondsworth: Penguin (1956).
Jucker, A. H. (1994) New dimensions in vocabulary studies: Review article of *The Oxford English Dictionary* (2nd edition) on CD-ROM. *Literary and Linguistic Computing*, **9**, 2: 149–54.
Jucker, A. H. (1996) Das Fremde in der eigenen Sprache: Fremdwörter im Deutschen und im Englischen. In L. Bredella and H. Christ (eds), *Begegnungen mit dem Fremden*. Giessen: Verlag der Ferber'schen Universitätsbuchhandlung, pp. 233–47.
Justeson, J. S. and Katz, S. M. (1991) Redefining antonymy: the textual structure of a semantic relation. In *Using Corpora*. Proceedings of 7th Annual Conference of the UW Centre for the New OED and Text Research, Oxford.
Justeson, J. S. and Katz, S. M. (1995) Technical terminology. *Natural Language Engineering*, **1**, 1: 9–27.
Katz, J. J. (1981) *Language and Other Abstract Objects*. Oxford: Blackwell.
Katz, J. J. and Fodor, J. (1963) The structure of a semantic theory. *Language*, **39**, 2: 170–210.
Katz, J. J. and Postal, P. (1964) *An Integrated Theory of Linguistic Description*. Cambridge, MA: MIT Press.
Kay, P. (1995) Construction grammar. In J.-O. Östmann and J. Blommaert (eds), *Handbook of Pragmatics*. Amsterdam: Benjamins, pp. 171–7.
Kempson, R. (1988) Grammar and conversational principles. In F. J. Newmeyer, *Linguistics: The Cambridge Survey*, vol. 2. Cambridge: Cambridge University Press, pp. 139–63.

Kennedy, G. (1992) Preferred ways of putting things with implications for language teaching. In J. Svartvik (ed.), *Directions in Corpus Linguistics*. Berlin: Mouton, pp. 335–73.

Kjellmer, G. (1991) A mint of phrases. In K. Aijmer and B. Altenberg (eds), *English Corpus Linguistics*. London: Longman, pp. 111–27.

Klotz, M. (1997) Ein Valenzwörterbuch englischer Verben, Adjektive und Substantive. *Zeitschrift für Angewandte Linguistik*, 27: 93–111.

Krishnamurthy, R. (1996) Ethnic, racial and tribal: the language of racism? In R. Caldas-Coulthard and M. Coulthard (eds), *Texts and Practices: Readings in Critical Discourse Analysis*. London: Routledge, pp. 129–49.

Kuno, S. (1976) Subject, theme and the speaker's empathy. In C. N. Li (ed.), *Subject and Topic*. New York: Academic Press, pp. 417–44.

Labov, W. (1972) The study of language in its social context. In *Sociolinguistic Patterns*. Philadelphia: University of Pennsylvania Press, pp. 183–259.

Laduslaw, W. A. (1996) Negation and polarity items. In S. Lappin (ed.), *The Handbook of Contemporary Semantic Theory*. Oxford: Blackwell, pp. 321–41.

Lakoff, G. and Johnson, M. (1980) *Metaphors We Live By*. Chicago: University of Chicago Press.

Lappin, S. (ed.) (1996) *The Handbook of Contemporary Semantic Theory*. Oxford: Blackwell.

LDC (1999) Introduction to the Linguistic Data Consortium. http://www.ldc.upenn.edu/ldc/about/ldc_intro.html. (Accessed 24.11.1999.)

LDOCE (1995) *Longman Dictionary of Contemporary English*, 3rd edn, ed. D. Summers. London: Longman.

Leech, G. N. (1981) *Semantics*, 2nd edn. Harmondsworth: Penguin.

Leech, G. N. (1983) *Principles of Pragmatics*. London: Longman.

Levin, B. and Hovav, M. R. (1996) Lexical semantics and syntactic structure. In S. Lappin (ed.), *The Handbook of Contemporary Semantic Theory*. Oxford: Blackwell, pp. 487–507.

Levinson, S. C. (1983) *Pragmatics*. Cambridge: Cambridge University Press.

Levinson, S. C. (2000) *Presumptive Meanings: The Theory of Generalized Conversational Implicature*. Cambridge, MA: MIT Press.

Loftus, E. F. and Palmer, J. C. (1974) Reconstruction of automobile destruction: an example of the interaction between language and memory. *Journal of Verbal Learning and Verbal Behavior*, 13, 585–9.

Lorenz, G. (1999) *Adjective Intensification: Learners versus Native Speakers. A Corpus Study of Argumentative Writing*. Amsterdam: Rodopi.

Louw, B. (1993) Irony in the text or insincerity in the writer? The diagnostic potential of semantic prosodies. In M. Baker, G. Francis and E. Tognini-Bonelli (eds), *Text and Technology*. Amsterdam: Benjamins, pp. 157–76.

Love, A. M. (1991) Process and product in geology. *English for Specific Purposes*, 10: 89–109.

Lyons, J. (1968) *Introduction to Theoretical Linguistics*. Cambridge: Cambridge University Press.

Lyons, J. (1977) *Semantics*. Cambridge: Cambridge University Press.

Lyons, J. (1987) Semantics. In J. Lyons, R. Coates, M. Deuchar and G. Gazdar (eds), *New Horizons in Linguistics 2*. Harmondsworth: Penguin, pp. 152–78.
McCrone, D., Morris, A. and Kiely, R. (1995) *Scotland – the Brand*. Edinburgh: Edinburgh University Press.
Maclay, H. (1971) Linguistics: overview. In D. D. Steinberg and L. A. Jakobovitz (eds), *Semantics*. Cambridge: Cambridge University Press, pp. 157–82.
Makkai, A. (1972) *Idiom Structure in English*. The Hague: Mouton.
Malinowski, B. (1923) The problem of meaning in primitive languages. In C. Ogden and I. A. Richards, *The Meaning of Meaning*. London: Trench and Trubner, pp. 296–336.
Marantz, A. (1992) The *way*-construction and the semantics of direct arguments in English: a reply to Jackendoff. In T. Stowell and E. Wehrli (eds), *Syntax and the Lexicon*. New York: Academic Press, pp. 179–88.
Marx, K. (1852) Der 18te Brumaire des Louis Napoleon. *Die Revolution*. In K. Marx and F. Engels, *Werke*, vol. 8. Berlin: Dietz (1960).
Mason, O. (1999) Parameters of collocation: the word in the centre of gravity. In J. Kirk (ed.), *Corpora Galore*. Amsterdam: Rodopi, pp. 267–80.
Mey, J. L. (1993) *Pragmatics: An Introduction*. Oxford: Blackwell.
Miller, J. (1993) Spoken and written language. In R. J. Scholes (ed.), *Literacy and Language Analysis*. Hillsdale, NJ: Erlbaum, pp. 99–141.
Mills, S. (1995) *Feminist Stylistics*. London: Routledge.
Moon, R. (1994) The analysis of fixed expressions in text. In M. Coulthard (ed.), *Advances in Written Text Analysis*. London: Routledge, pp. 117–35.
Moon, R. (1997) Paper read to Annual Meeting, BAAL (British Association for Applied Linguistics), September.
Moon, R. (1998) *Fixed Expressions and Idioms in English*. Oxford: Clarendon Press.
Morgan, J. L. and Sellner, M. B. (1980) Discourse and linguistic theory. In R. J. Spiro et al. (eds), *Theoretical Issues in Reading Comprehension*. Hillsdale, NJ: Lawrence Erlbaum, pp. 165–200.
Morris, C. W. (1938) Foundations of the theory of signs. In O. Neurath, R. Carnap and C. W. Morris (eds), *International Encyclopedia of Unified Science*. Chicago: Chicago University Press, pp. 77–138.
Murray, K. M. E. (1979) *Caught in the Web of Words: James Murray and the Oxford English Dictionary*. Oxford: Oxford University Press.
Myers, G. (1994) Narratives of science and nature in popularizing molecular genetics. In M. Coulthard (ed.), *Advances in Written Text Analysis*. London: Routledge, pp. 179–90.
Nair, R. B. (1992) Gender, genre and generative grammar: deconstructing the matrimonial column. In M. Toolan (ed.), *Language, Text and Context*. London: Routledge, pp. 227–54.
Nattinger, J. R. and De Carrico, J. S. (1992) *Lexical Phrases and Language Teaching*. Oxford: Oxford University Press.
Newmeyer, F. J. (ed.) (1988) *Linguistics: The Cambridge Survey*, 4 vols. Cambridge: Cambridge University Press.

Nunberg, G., Sag, I. A. and Wasow, T. (1994) Idioms. *Language*, 71, 3: 491–538.
OALD (1995) *Oxford Advanced Learner's Dictionary*, 5th edn, ed. A. S. Hornby and J. Crowther. Oxford: Oxford University Press.
OED (1989) *The Oxford English Dictionary*, 2nd edn, 20 vols, ed. J. A. Simpson and E. S. C. Weiner. Oxford: Clarendon.
Pagano, A. (1994) Negatives in written text. In M. Coulthard (ed.), *Advances in Written Text Analysis*. London: Routledge, pp. 250–65.
Palmer, F. (1971) *Grammar*. Harmondsworth: Penguin.
Paltridge, B. (1994) Genre analysis and the identification of textual boundaries. *Applied Linguistics*, 15, 3: 288–99.
Partington, A. (1998) *Patterns and Meanings*. Amsterdam: Benjamins.
Paterson, L. (1987) Review of Burrows, *Computation into Criticism*. *Times Higher Education Supplement*, 2 October.
Pawley, A. (2000) Developments in the study of formulaic language 1970–2000. Paper read to the Annual Conference of the AAAL (American Association for Applied Linguistics), Vancouver, March.
Pawley, A. and Syder, F. H. (1983) Two puzzles for linguistic theory. In J. C. Richards and R. W. Schmidt (eds), *Language and Communication*. London: Longman, pp. 191–226.
Pennycook, A. (1994) *The Cultural Politics of English as an International Language*. London: Longman.
Pfeffer, J. A. (1987) *Deutsches Sprachgut im Wortschatz der Amerikaner und Engländer*. Tübingen: Niemeyer.
Pfeffer, J. A. and Cannon, G. (1994) *German Loanwords in English: An Historical Dictionary*. New York: Cambridge University Press.
Phillips, M. K. (1985) *Aspects of Text Structure*. Amsterdam: North Holland.
Phillips, M. K. (1989) *Lexical Structure of Text*. Discourse Analysis Monograph 12. Birmingham: English Language Research.
Phillipson, R. (1992) *Linguistic Imperialism*. Oxford: Oxford University Press.
Piper, A. (2000) Lifelong learning, human capital, and the soundbite. *Text*, 20, 1: 109–46.
Polanyi, M. (1958) *Personal Knowledge*. London: Routledge and Kegan Paul.
Popper, K. R. (1972) *Objective Knowledge*. Oxford: Clarendon.
Popper, K. R. (1994) *Knowledge and the Body–Mind Problem*. London: Routledge.
Popper, K. R. (1996) *Alles Leben ist Problemlösen*. München: Piper.
Porzig, W. (1934) Wesenhafte Bedeutungsbeziehungen. *Beiträge zur Geschichte der deutschen Sprache und Literatur*, 58: 70–97.
Pusch, L. F. (1984) *Das Deutsche als Männersprache*. Frankfurt: Suhrkamp.
Quirk, R. and Stein, G. (1991) On having a look in a corpus. In K. Aijmer and B. Altenberg (eds), *English Corpus Linguistics*. London: Longman, pp. 197–203.
Quirk, R., Greenbaum, S., Leech, G. and Svartvik, J. (1985) *A Comprehensive Grammar of the English Language*. London: Longman.
Raban, J. (1989) *God, Man and Mrs Thatcher*. London: Chatto.
Rawls, J. (1955) Two concepts of rules. *The Philosophical Review*, 64: 3–32.

Renouf, A. (1987) Corpus development. In J. Sinclair (ed.), *Looking Up*. London: Collins, pp. 1–40.
Robins, R. H. (1988) Appendix: History of linguistics. In F. J. Newmeyer (ed.), *Linguistics: The Cambridge Survey*, vol. 1. Cambridge: Cambridge University Press, pp. 462–84.
Rosten, L. (1971) *The Joys of Yiddish*. Harmondsworth: Penguin.
Ruthven, K. K. (1989) Unlocking ideologies: 'key-word' as a trope. *Southern Review*, 22: 112–18.
Sadock, J. M. (1988) Speech act distinctions in grammar. In F. J. Newmeyer (ed.), *Linguistics: The Cambridge Survey*, vol. 2. Cambridge: Cambridge University Press, pp. 183–97.
Said, E. (1978) *Orientalism*. London: Routledge and Kegan Paul.
Sampson, G. (1996) From central embedding to corpus linguistics. In J. Thomas and M. Short (eds), *Using Corpora for Language Research*. London: Longman, pp. 14–26.
Sandig, B. and Selting, M. (1997) Discourse styles. In T. A. Van Dijk (ed.), *Discourse as Structure and Process*. Discourse Studies volume 1. London: Sage, pp. 138–56.
Saussure, F. de (1916) *Cours de Linguistique Générale*. Paris: Payot.
Saville-Troike, M. (1989) *The Ethnography of Communication*, 2nd edn. Oxford: Blackwell.
Schiffrin, D. (1994) *Approaches to Discourse*. Oxford: Blackwell.
Scott, M. (1997a) *WordSmith Tools*, version 2.0. [Computer software.] Oxford: Oxford University Press.
Scott, M. (1997b) *WordSmith Tools Manual*. Oxford: Oxford University Press.
Scott, M. (1997c) PC analysis of key words: and key key words. *System*, 25, 2: 233–45.
Scott, M. (1997d) The right word in the right place: key word associates in two languages. *AAA: Arbeiten aus Anglistik und Amerikanistik*, 22, 2: 235–48.
Searle, J. R. (1969) *Speech Acts*. Cambridge: Cambridge University Press.
Searle, J. R. (ed.) (1971) *The Philosophy of Language*. London: Oxford University Press.
Searle, J. R. (1975) Indirect speech acts. In P. Cole and J. L. Morgan (eds), *Speech Acts. Syntax and Semantics*, vol. 3. New York: Academic Press, pp. 59–82.
Searle, J. R. (1976) The classification of illocutionary acts. *Language in Society*, 5: 1–24.
Searle, J. R. (1995) *The Construction of Social Reality*. London: Allen Lane.
Seuren, P. A. M. (ed.) (1974) *Semantic Syntax*. Oxford: Oxford University Press.
Seuren, P. A. M. (1998) *Western Linguistics: An Historical Introduction*. Oxford: Blackwell.
Simpson, J. and Weiner, E. (2000) An on-line OED. *English Today*, 16, 3: 12–19.
Sinclair, J. (1965) When is a poem like a sunset? *A Review of English Literature*, 6, 2: 76–91.
Sinclair, J. (ed.) (1987) *Looking Up*. London: Collins.

Sinclair, J. (1991) *Corpus, Concordance, Collocation*. Oxford: Oxford University Press.
Sinclair, J. (1992) Trust the text. In M. Davies and L. Ravelli (eds), *Advances in Systemic Linguistics*. London: Pinter, pp. 5–19. [Also in Coulthard 1994, pp. 12–25.]
Sinclair, J. (1996) The search for units of meaning. *Textus* 9: 75–106.
Sinclair, J. (1998) The lexical item. In E. Weigand (ed.), *Contrastive Lexical Semantics*. Amsterdam: Benjamins, pp. 1–24.
Sinclair, J., Mason, O., Ball, J. and Barnbrook, G. (1998) Language independent statistical software for corpus exploration. *Computers and the Humanities*, 31, 3: 229–55.
Skehan, P. (1998) *A Cognitive Approach to Language Learning*. Oxford: Oxford University Press.
Smadja, F. (1993) Retrieving collocations from text. Xtract. *Computational Linguistics*, 19, 1: 143–77. [Also in Armstrong 1994, pp. 143–77.]
Sperber, D. (1996) *Explaining Culture: A Naturalistic Approach*. Oxford: Blackwell.
Sperber, D. and Wilson, D. (1995) *Relevance: Communication and Cognition*, 2nd edn. Oxford: Blackwell.
Stanzel, F. K. (1984) *A Theory of Narrative*. Cambridge: Cambridge University Press.
Steinberg, D. D. and Jakobovitz, L. A. (eds) (1971) *Semantics*. Cambridge: Cambridge University Press.
Strauss, G., Hass, U. and Harras, G. (1989) *Brisante Wörter von Agitation bis Zeitgeist: Ein Lexikon zum öffentlichen Sprachgebrauch*. Berlin: de Gruyter.
Stubbs, M. (1986) Language development, lexical competence and nuclear vocabulary. In K. Durkin (ed.), *Language Development in the School Years*. London: Croom Helm, pp. 57–76.
Stubbs, M. (1989) The state of English in the English state: reflections on the Cox Report. *Language and Education*, 3, 4: 235–50.
Stubbs, M. (1995a) Collocations and semantic profiles: on the cause of the trouble with quantitative studies. *Functions of Language*, 2, 1: 23–55.
Stubbs, M. (1995b) Corpus evidence for norms of lexical collocation. In G. Cook and B. Seidlhofer (eds), *Principle and Practice in Applied Linguistics*. Oxford: Oxford University Press, pp. 245–56.
Stubbs, M. (1995c) Collocations and cultural connotations of common words. *Linguistics and Education*, 7, 4: 379–90.
Stubbs, M. (1996) *Text and Corpus Analysis: Computer-assisted Studies of Language and Culture*. Oxford: Blackwell.
Stubbs, M. (1997) 'Eine Sprache idiomatisch sprechen': Computer, Korpora, Kommunikative Kompetenz und Kultur. In K. J. Matheier (ed.), *Norm und Variation*. Frankfurt: Lang, pp. 151–67.
Stubbs, M. (2001) Texts, corpora and problems of interpretation. *Applied Linguistics*, 22, 2: 149–72.
Summers, D. (1993) Longman/Lancaster English language corpus: criteria and design. *International Journal of Lexicography*, 6, 3: 181–95.

Svartvik, J. (ed.) (1992) *Directions in Corpus Linguistics*. Berlin: Mouton.
Svartvik, J. (ed.) (1996) *Words: Proceedings of an International Symposium*. KVHAA Konferenser 36. Stockholm: Almqvist and Wiksell.
Svartvik, J., Eeg-Olofsson, M., Forsheden, O., Oreström, B. and Thavenius, C. (1982) *Survey of Spoken English*. Lund: Lund University Press.
Svartvik, J. and Quirk, R. (eds) (1980) *A Corpus of English Conversation*. Lund: Gleerup.
Swales, J. M. (1990) *Genre Analysis*. Cambridge: Cambridge University Press.
Sweet, H. (1891) *A New English Grammar: Logical and Historical*. Oxford: Clarendon.
Sweet, H. (1899) *The Practical Study of Language*. Oxford: Oxford University Press (1964).
Tadros, A. (1994) Predictive categories in expository text. In M. Coulthard (ed.), *Advances in Written Text Analysis*. London: Routledge, pp. 69–82.
Teubert, W. (1999a) Corpus linguistics: a partisan view. http://solaris3.ids-mannheim.de/ijcl/teubert_cl.html. (Accessed 24 November 1999.)
Teubert, W. (1999b) Korpuslinguistik and Lexikographie. *Deutsche Sprache*, 27, 4: 292–313.
Thatcher, M. (1993) *The Downing Street Years*. London: HarperCollins.
Thomas, J. and Short, M. (eds) (1996) *Using Corpora for Language Research*. London: Longman.
Thompson, G. and Hunston, S. (2000) Evaluation: an introduction. In S. Hunston and G. Thompson (eds), *Evaluation in Text: Authorical Stance and the Construction of Discourse*. Oxford: Oxford University Press.
Thompson, K. (ed.) (1997) *Media and Cultural Regulation*. London: Sage.
Tognini-Bonelli, E. (1996) Corpus theory and practice. Unpublished PhD thesis, University of Birmingham.
Toolan, M. (ed.) (1992) *Language, Text and Context*. London: Routledge.
Trask, R. L. (1993) *A Dictionary of Grammatical Terms in Linguistics*. London: Routledge.
Trench, Richard Chevenix (1851) *On the Study of Words*. London: Parker. [Extract in Crowley 1991.]
Trench, Richard Chevenix (1858) Proposal for the publication of a New English Dictionary by the Philological Society. *Transactions of the Philological Society*. [Extract in Crowley 1991.]
Trier, J. (1931) *Der deutsche Wortschatz im Sinnbezirk des Verstandes*. Heidelberg: Winter.
Tuldava, J. (1998) *Probleme und Methoden der quantitativ-systemischen Lexikologie*. [Translated from Russian original (1987).] Trier: Wissenschaftlicher Verlag.
Turner, G. (1990) *British Cultural Studies*. London: Routledge.
Twaddell, W. F. (1935) On defining the phoneme. Reprinted in M. Joos (ed.), *Readings in Linguistics*. Washington: American Council of Learned Societies (1957), pp. 55–80.
Ullmann, S. (1957) *The Principles of Semantics*. Oxford: Blackwell.

Ure, J. (1971) Lexical density and register differentiation. In G. Perren and J. L. M. Trim (eds), *Applications of Linguistics*. London: Cambridge University Press, pp. 443–52.
Van Dijk, T. A. (ed.) (1997a) *Discourse as Structure and Process*. Discourse Studies volume 1. London: Sage.
Van Dijk, T. A. (ed.) (1997b) *Discourse as Social Interaction*. Discourse Studies volume 2. London: Sage.
Weinert, R. (1995) The role of formulaic language in second language acquisition: a review. *Applied Linguistics*, 16, 2: 180–205.
Weisgerber, L. (1950) *Vom Weltbild der deutschen Sprache*. Düsseldorf: Schwann.
Widdowson, H. G. (1978) *Teaching Language as Communication*. Oxford: Oxford University Press.
Widdowson, H. G. (1983) *Learning Purpose and Language Use*. Oxford: Oxford University Press.
Widdowson, H. G. (1991) The description and prescription of language. In J. Atlatis (ed.), *Linguistics and Language Pedagogy: The State of the Art*. Georgetown University Roundtable on Languages and Linguistics 1991, pp. 11–24.
Widdowson, H. G. (1995) Discourse analysis: a critical view. *Language and Literature*, 4, 3: 157–72.
Wierzbicka, A. (1999) *Emotions across Languages and Cultures: Diversity and Universals*. Cambridge: Cambridge University Press.
Williams, R. (1976, 2nd edn 1983) *Keywords*. London: Fontana.
Willis, J. D. (1990) *The Lexical Syllabus*. London: Collins.
Winchester, S. (1998) *The Surgeon of Crowthorne: A Tale of Murder, Madness and the Oxford English Dictionary*. London: Viking. [Also Harmondsworth: Penguin, 1999.]
Winter, E. (1977) A clause-relational approach to English texts: a study of some predictive lexical items in written discourse. *Instructional Science*, 6: 1–92.
Wittgenstein, L. (1953) *Philosophical Investigations*. Oxford: Blackwell.
Wray, A. and Perkins, M. R. (2000) The functions of formulaic language: an integrated model. *Language and Communication*, 20: 1–28.
Wray, A., Trott, K. and Bloomer, A. (1998) *Projects in Linguistics*. London: Arnold.
Yang, H. (1986) A new technique for identifying scientific/technical terms and describing science texts. *Literary and Linguistic Computing*, 1, 2: 93–103.
Youmans, G. (1991) A new tool for discourse analysis: the vocabulary management profile. *Language*, 67, 4: 763–89.
Youmans, G. (1994) The vocabulary management-profile, two stories by William Faulkner. *Empirical Studies of the Arts*, 12, 2: 113–30.
Yule, G. (1996) *The Study of Language*, 2nd edn. Cambridge: Cambridge University Press.
Ziman, J. (1978) *Reliable Knowledge*. Cambridge: Cambridge University Press.
Zipes, J. (ed.) (1993) *The Trials and Tribulations of Little Red Riding Hood*, 2nd edn. London: Routledge.

Name Index

Aarsleff, H., 193
Aarts, J., 225
Aitchison, J., 50, 232
Algeo, J., 165, 169, 174, 175, 181, 184, 193
Allerton, D. J., 120
Anscombe, G. E. M., 233
Antaki, C., 211
Aston, G., xvii
Atkins, B. T. S., 218
Atkinson, D., 121
Austin, J. L., 6, 21, 146, 216
Ayto, J., 151, 153, 165, 169

Baker, C., 169
Baker, M., xvii
Baldwin, M., 173–4
Ball, C. N., 70
Barnbrook, G., 74, 78, 123, 130, 133, 144
Bar-Hillel, Y., 218
Bayley, P., 146
Benson, M., 95, 165
Benveniste, E., 145
Berger, P., 118, 162
Bernstein, B. B., 231
Biber, D., xvi, xvii, 67–8, 77, 98, 122
Bloomfield, L., 31, 43–5, 88, 180, 217, 228–9
Boas, F., 180
Bolinger, D., 78, 120
Botha, R. P., 237, 244
Bourdieu, P., 162, 241

Brazil, D., 103
Brown, G., 10, 117, 166
Brumfit, C., 168
Bublitz, W., 63, 121
Bühler, K., 180, 237
Burnard, L., xvii
Burrows, J. F., 142, 242
Buyssens, E., 51

Cameron, D., 7, 168
Cannon, G., 180–2, 184
Carr, P., 232, 238, 244
Carter, R., 212
Caxton, W., 157
Channell, J., 9, 89, 105, 197, 203
Chatman, S., 125, 141
Chomsky, N., 60, 71–2, 217, 225, 227–8, 231, 234
Choueka, Y., 97
Church, K., 61, 78, 101, 105, 197
Clear, J., 70, 78, 89, 197
Cobuild *see* Subject Index
Cole, P., 21
Collins, P. C., 212
Condor, S., 211
Cowie, A. P., 78
Cox, B., 168
Crowley, T., 159
Cruse, D. A., 50
Crystal, D., 84, 172, 197, 210

De Beaugrande, R., 71, 89
De Carrico, J. S., 78

Name Index

Descartes, R., 226–7
Du Gay, P., 177
Dunning, T., 102, 129
Durkin, P. N. R., 193

Ellis, R., 191
Erman, B., 122

Fairclough, N., 153
Fillmore, C. J., 59, 60, 202, 217–18
Firth, J. R., 21, 22, 67, 221, 228, 229–31, 241
Fodor, J., 217
Foucault, M., 161, 165, 230
Fox, G., 225
Francis, G., xvii, 22, 65, 78, 87, 109, 113–14, 121–2, 158, 208, 210–12, 216, 242
Francis, W. N., xvi, 68
Freebody, P., 169
Freud, S., 186, 190
Füger, W., 142

Gerbig, A., 48
Giddens, A., 162, 231, 241, 244
Glück, H., 6
Gordon, D., 21
Graddol, D., 156, 161
Granger, S., 178
Grice, H. P., 11, 12, 21–2, 215–16, 218
Grimm Brothers, 161, 169, 180

Haegemann, L., 217
Hall, S., 168
Halliday, M. A. K., 21, 117, 121, 199, 228, 230, 240–1
Hanks, P., 58, 78
Harris, Z., 217
Hart, C., 125, 128, 139
Hasan, R., 121
Hayes, D. P., 69
Hegel, G. W. F., 190
Heidegger, M., 186
Herder, J. G. von, 180, 190
Hodge, R., 228

Hoggart, R., 168
Hopper, P. J., 209, 218
Horn, L. R., 11, 218
Hovav, M. R., 208–9
Howarth, P., 78
Hübler, A., 212
Hudson, R. A., 167, 218
Humboldt, W. von, 180
Hunston, S., 22, 109, 114, 122, 166, 216, 242
Hymes, D., 60–1, 228, 238

Israel, M., 209

Jakobson, R., 11
James, P. D., 197
Johnson, A., 153
Johnson-Laird, P. N., 117
Jones, S., 29
Joyce, J., 123, 125–40
Jucker, A. H., 171, 177, 179, 192–3
Justeson, J. S., 97, 103

Katz, J. J., 71, 217
Katz, S. M., 97, 103
Kay, P., 216, 218
Kempson, R., 218
Kennedy, G., 221
Kjellmer, G., 95, 102, 109, 121
Klotz, M., 66
Kress, G., 228
Krishnamurthy, R., 147–9, 168
Kuno, S., 200, 206

Labov, W., 228
Laduslaw, W. A., 51
Lakoff, G., 21
Lappin, S., 198
Leech, G. N., 57, 197, 235, 239, 244
Levin, B., 208–9
Levinson, S. C., 21, 22, 197, 218
Loftus, E. F., 118
Lorenz, G., 33
Louw, B., 51, 66, 78, 197, 210
Love, A. M., 243

Luckmann, T., 118, 162
Lyons, J., 22, 50, 72, 103, 121, 197

Maclay, H., 217
Makkai, A., 59
Malinowski, B., 21
Marantz, A., 207, 209
Marx, K., 190, 231
Mason, O., 29, 78
McCarthy, M., 212
McCrone, D., 150
Mercer, R. L., 61, 101
Mey, J. L., 22
Miller, J., 120
Mills, S., 23
Moon, R., 75, 78, 119, 121, 164, 198, 211
Morgan, J. L., 21, 109
Morris, C. W., 89, 217
Müller, M., 180
Murray, K. M. E., 193
Myers, G., 121

Nair, R. B., 23
Nattinger, J. R., 78
Newmeyer, F. J., 217

Pagano, A., 119
Palmer, F., 31
Palmer, J. C., 118
Paltridge, B., 124–5
Partington, A., 22, 61, 77–8, 98, 121, 149, 221–2
Paterson, L., 142
Paul, H., 180
Pawley, A., 20, 59, 61, 78, 120
Pennycook, A., 150
Perkins, M. R., 78
Pfeffer, J. A., 174, 180–2, 184
Phillips, M. K., 121
Phillipson, R., 149
Piper, A., 168
Polanyi, M., 244
Popper, K. R., 228–9, 230, 234–8, 240, 244

Porzig, W., 121
Postal, P., 217
Pusch, L. F., 206

Quine, W. van O., 229
Quirk, R., xvii, 32, 212

Raban, J., 150, 157
Rawls, J., 233
Renouf, A., xvii
Robins R. H., 226
Rosten, L., 183
Ruthven, K. K., 167

Sadock, J. M., 22
Said, E., 148
Sampson, G., 224–5
Sandig, B., 23
Sauer, W., 6
Saussure, F. de, 146, 221, 227–8, 231, 234, 240–1
Saville-Troike, M., 22
Schiffrin, D., 22
Schuchardt, H., 180
Scott, M., xix, 123, 129–30, 133, 167, 168
Searle, J. R., 21, 22, 59, 216, 228, 233–5, 237, 244
Sellner, M. B., 109
Selting, M., 23
Seuren, P. A. M., 9, 21, 71, 217
Simpson, J., 171, 193
Sinclair, J. McH., xvii, 16, 22, 29, 33, 51, 60, 63–6, 74, 77–8, 87–9, 92, 99, 100, 102, 105, 108, 120, 130, 144, 197, 210, 216, 228, 230, 242
Skehan, P., 78
Smadja, F., 68, 95, 97
Sperber, D., 149, 162, 216
Spinoza, B., 230
Stanzel, F. K., 132
Stein, G., 32
Strauss, G., 145
Strawson, P. F., 21

Summers, D., xvii
Svartvik, J., xvii
Swales, J. M., 125, 244
Swann, J., 156, 161
Sweet, H., 40, 180, 217
Syder, F. H., 59, 61, 78, 120

Tadros, A., 121
Tebbit, N., 156
Teubert, W., xii, 4, 20, 221
Thatcher, M., 150, 154–5, 157
Thompson, G., 166
Thompson, K., 149, 150
Tognini-Bonelli, E., 66, 241
Trask, R. L., 58
Traugott, E. J., 209
Trench, R. C., 170, 188
Trier, J., 121
Tuldava, J., 28, 133–4, 144, 190–1, 238
Turner, G., 168
Twaddell, W. F., 229

Ullmann, S., 121
Ure, J., 41

Van Dijk, T. A., 22

Warren, B., 122
Weber, M., 190
Weiner, E., 171, 193
Weinert, R., 78
Weisgerber, L., 121
Widdowson, H. G., 5, 10, 61, 121
Wierzbicka, A., 145, 186
Williams, R., 145, 148, 150, 154–5, 161, 167–8, 172–3, 181, 188, 190
Willis, J. D., 78
Wilson, D., 216
Winchester, S., 193
Winter, E., 121
Wittgenstein, L., 21, 146
Wray, A., 78, 208
Wundt, W., 180

Yang, H., 97, 121
Youmans, G., 124–5, 133–40, 143–4
Yule, G., 23, 117, 166

Ziman, J., 143, 244
Zipes, J., 161–2, 164, 168–9

Subject Index

actual *see* possible and actual
antonymy, 38–9, 103–4
  see also hyponymy; synonymy
attested data, xiv, 24–5, 221, 225
  see also corpus; data; methods, empirical and observational

behaviourism, 44, 229, 241
brute and institutional facts, 232–5

Cobuild, xvii, 18, 28, 30–1, 47–8, 52, 57, 62, 72, 80, 95–6, 98, 151, 155, 162, 181, 185, 200, 205, 210
  Cobuild data-base, 58, 66–70, 75–7, 102
  Cobuild dictionary, 171, 176–7, 179, 182–3, 187
coherence, 10–11, 117–19
  see also cohesion
cohesion, 10–11, 100, 108–15, 243
  see also coherence
colligation, 65, 87–8
  see also lexico-grammar
collocation, 24, 29–30, 44–9, 58, 64, 87, 148–9, 151, 155–6, 162–4, 199–206
  collocate, xv, 29–30
  phrase, 24
  restricted, 57–8
  span, 29, 62
  strength of attraction, 81–4, 88
  see also extended lexical unit; words and phrases analysed

common-sense knowledge *see* cultural knowledge
communicative competence, 60–1, 228
competence and performance, 60–1, 225–7, 234, 237–9, 242
  see also communicative competence; dualisms, *langue* and *parole*
concordance, 61–2, 222, 240–1
  of *angst*, 189
  of BE-passives, 214
  of CAUSE, 46
  of GET-passives, 213
  of *undergo*, 93
connotation, 34–5, 167, 197–8, 242–3
  see also cultural keyword; denotation; discourse prosody; evaluative meaning
content word, 39–41, 127–8, 134
  see also function word; lexical density
convention, 11, 20
  see also expectation; idiomaticity
core vocabulary, 41–3, 52–3
  see also frequency
corpus, 25, 66–7, 239–42
  corpora, examples of, xvi
  possible bias in, 67–8, 82, 223–4
  representativity, 223–4
  world-wide web as text collection, xix, 224
  see also data; methods, empirical and observational
corpus semantics, 4, 19–20, 50

co-selection *see* collocation; lexico-grammar
co-text, 100
creativity and routine, 58, 101–2, 111–12, 227, 231, 239, 241–2
cultural keyword, 146–64, 168–9, 171, 175–7, 181–2, 188
see also keyword (statistical)
cultural knowledge, 3–4, 9–12, 20, 166–7, 192
see also cultural keyword; schema

data
attested, modified, invented, xi, 24–5
first-, second-, third-order, 66–7
observable, 4, 16
see also corpus; intuitive data; methods
data-base, 69–70
see also Cobuild, data-base
delexicalization, 32–4, 209
denotation, 34–5, 58
see also connotation; reference
dictionaries, 4, 30, 62, 170–1, 232, 234
see also Cobuild dictionary; *Oxford English Dictionary*
disapproval, 33–4
see also discourse prosody
discourse, 147–8, 150, 166
see also discursive formation; text and discourse
discourse prosody, 65–6, 88, 90–1, 105–8, 188, 198–206, 243
see also connotation; evaluative meaning
discursive formation, 164–5
distribution of lexis, 43, 101–2, 121, 125, 130–2, 141
see also frequency
dualism, 220, 226–8
see also competence and performance; *langue* and *parole*; paradigmatic and syntagmatic; pluralism

encyclopedic knowledge *see* cultural knowledge

etymology, 191
etymological fallacy, 171–3
see also loan words
evaluative meaning, 6, 146, 167, 187–8, 197, 215, 222, 243
see also cultural keywords; discourse prosody
evidence *see* corpus; data; methods
expectation, 7, 10, 20, 241
see also creativity and routine; typicality
extended lexical unit, 31–2, 49, 59–60, 63–5, 87–9, 96, 109–10, 122
see also collocation; delexicalization; lexico-grammar; meaning, units of; semantic-feature sharing

false friends, 185–8
see also loan words
fixed phrase *see* extended lexical unit
frame *see* schema
frequency of words and phrases, 39–42, 61–3, 69–70, 80–1, 126–32, 160, 162–3, 184–5, 206, 224
see also core vocabulary; statistical methods; typicality
function word, 39–41, 126–7, 134
see also content word; lexical density

genre *see* text type
grammatical word *see* function word

head-word *see* lemma
hyponymy, 39
see also antonymy; synonymy

idiomaticity, 57–9, 95, 120, 147, 242
see also typicality
I-language and E-language, 60–1
instance and norm, 166, 192, 221, 230, 239
see also expectation
institutional facts *see* brute and institutional facts; World 3
intertext, 101, 220, 222
introspective data *see* intuitive data

SUBJECT INDEX

intuitive data, limitations of, xiv, 71–2, 142, 166, 216, 221, 224–6, 240, 242

keywords (statistical), 129–30
   see also cultural keywords
KWIC see concordance

langue and *parole*, 101, 104, 119–20, 227–8, 230–1, 234
   see also competence and performance
lemma, xiv, 25–8, 69, 99
lemmatization, 83, 125, 128
lexeme see lemma
lexical density, 39–41
lexical field see lexical set
lexical item, 31
   see also collocation; extended lexical unit
lexical profile, 84–7, 89–96
lexical set, 27–8, 35–6, 81, 102, 118–19, 121, 158
lexical variation, 47, 92, 102, 119, 243
lexical word see content word
   see also function word; lexical density
lexico-grammar, 18–19, 153, 156, 197, 199–210, 211–15, 220, 242
Little Red Riding Hood, 161–4, 168–9
loan words, 170, 174–84
   Arabic, 176
   Chinese, 176–7
   French, 175–6, 178
   German, 174–88
   Japanese, 177
   Russian, 179
   Yiddish, 183
   see also false friends

meaning as use, 4, 13–16, 19–20, 50
meaning, units of, 30–4, 58–60, 62–6
   see also antonymy; denotation and connotation; evaluative meaning; extended lexical units; hyponymy; lexical set; reference; synonymy

methods
   comprehensive coverage of data, 84, 89–95
   empirical and observational, 43–5, 50, 61–2, 143–4, 152, 166, 220–6, 229, 232, 241–3
   see also corpus; data; replication; statistical methods
monism, 229–31
   see also dualism
multi-word unit see extended lexical unit

node see collocation

observation see methods
Oxford English Dictionary, 152, 155, 157, 170–1, 173–7, 179–85, 188, 192–3, 218–19

paradigmatic and syntagmatic, 228, 240–1
patterns, 61–2
performance see competence and performance
phrase, 3, 24, 63
   see also collocation
phraseology, 59, 78, 80
   see also extended lexical units
pluralism, 232–9
   see also dualism; monism
positional frequency table, 95
   of *proper*, 159
   of *undergo*, 94
possible and actual, 13–19, 230, 238
pragmatics see semantics and pragmatics
precision and recall, 70–1
predictability see expectation
probability, 29, 63–4, 230, 242–3
   see also expectation; frequency; typicality
process and product, 230–1, 238, 243
propositional meaning, 33
   see also denotation; reference
prosody see discourse prosody

real world knowledge *see* cultural knowledge
recall *see* precision and recall
reference, 34
  see also denotation
replication, 16, 123–4, 140–1, 143, 167, 212, 223
  see also methods, empirical and observational
routine *see* creativity and routine
  see also convention; expectation

Saussurian paradox, 228, 231–2
schema, 10–11, 96
semantic-feature sharing, 63, 243
  see also delexicalization
semantic field, 35–6
  see also lexical set
semantic preference, 65, 88
semantic prosody *see* discourse prosody
semantics and pragmatics, 217–18
span *see* collocation
speech act, 6, 8, 21
statistical methods, 70–1, 73–5, 126–32, 133–40, 221
  see also frequency; probability
synonymy, 36–9, 71, 102–5
  see also antonymy; hyponymy
syntagmatic *see* paradigmatic and syntagmatic

text and discourse, 5–6, 230
text structure, 124–5, 135–40
text-type, 20, 23, 97–8, 120–1, 177–8, 223
  lonely hearts ads, 17–19, 22
  new text types, 5–6, 223
  recipe, 95–6
  technical English, 91
token *see* type and token
truth conditions, 8–9
type and token, 133–4, 238–9
type–token ratio, 134–5
typicality, 58–9, 61, 221, 239
  see also expectation; frequency

vague language, 9
vocabulary management profile, 133–40

word *see* content and function words; frequency; lemma; type and token; word-form
word-form, 25–8, 222
  see also lemma
words and phrases analysed, main examples:
  ACCOST, 199–201, 211
  AMID, 98–9
  AMUSEMENT, 48–9
  ANGST, 186–9
  APPLAUSE, 64
  ARGUE–HEAT, 30, 74
  BACHELOR, 72
  BACKDROP, 86
  BANK, 14–16
  BE-passive, 211–15
  BLITZ, 185–6
  BODILY, 77
  BODY, CORPSE, etc., 37–8
  BRIDE and GROOM, 76
  CARE, 19, 151–4
  CASE, 77
  CAUSE, 45–9, 65–6, 112, 114–15
  CHOP, 95–6
  COMMIT, 64
  COMMUNITY, 154
  CONFORM, 63
  CONFUSE, 25
  CONSUME, 27
  DEADLOCK, 84
  DISTINCTLY, 75, 106–7
  DOSE, 84, 86–7
  DRY, WET, 38
  EDUCATE, 69
  ETHNIC, RACIAL and TRIBAL, 147–9, 166
  FLAK, 185–6
  GET-passive, 211–15
  GOSSIP, 7, 22
  GROUP etc., 148–9
  GROW, RISE, SOAR, etc., 98, 107

HERITAGE, 149–51, 166
HIT, SMASH, etc., 118–19
HITHERTO, 76
HORSE, 35–6
LARGE, 65
LAVISH, 106
LITTLE, SMALL, etc., 12, 162–4, 166
LOITER, 202–3, 211
LURK, 201–2, 211
MAKE ONE'S WAY etc., 206–9, 219
NAKED EYE, 108–11, 120
PROPER, 154, 156–60, 166
PROVIDE, 24, 65
RECKLESS, 85–6

RESEMBLANCE, 85
ROUND, 3–4
SALT, 43–5
SEEK, 18–19, 27–8, 63
SMALL, 11
SOMEWHAT, 70–1
STANDARD, 154–6
STREET, 203–5, 211
SUNDAY, MONDAY, etc., 16–17
SURGERY, 13–14
TAKE, 32
TALK, CHAT, etc., 7–8
TRENDY, 160–1
UNDERGO, 89–95, 97, 115–16
UNTOLD, 112, 114
World 3, 234–8, 240, 244

Printed in the United States
154278LV00009B/1/P